"Those studying discourse analysis will love this book which is richly illustrated with examples from diverse languages and cultures. Using a delightfully reader-friendly style, Bernadette Vine adroitly introduces students to the major approaches and the most important figures in discourse analysis."

Janet Holmes, *Victoria University of Wellington, New Zealand*

"For anyone wanting to know how discourse analysis is done, and why it is done in different but related ways, *Understanding Discourse Analysis* will provide an excellent, practical guide. It is accessible, features authentic data from different contexts and languages, and is highly interactive."

Michael Handford, *Cardiff University, UK*

Understanding Discourse Analysis

Understanding Discourse Analysis provides students with an accessible and well-illustrated introduction to discourse analysis. Explaining the main terminology and frameworks and presenting key findings of discourse studies, this book:

- Explores the development of discourse analysis
- Covers four key approaches to analysing discourse
- Uses authentic spoken or written texts in all examples
- Features data from the Wellington Language in the Workplace Project database
- Includes examples from a wide range of languages from around the world, such as Chilean Spanish, Korean and Serbo-Croatian

Written by an active researcher, this textbook is a fascinating and engaging introduction to discourse analysis and is ideal for students studying this topic for the first time.

Bernadette Vine is Senior Researcher and Corpus Manager for the Wellington Language in the Workplace Project, based at the School of Linguistics and Applied Language Studies, Victoria University of Wellington, New Zealand (www.wgtn.ac.nz/lwp). Bernadette's research interests include workplace communication, leadership and New Zealand English.

Understanding Language Series

Series Editors:

Patience Epps, The University of Texas at Austin, USA

Oliver Bond, University of Surrey, UK

Consultant Editors: Bernard Comrie, University of California, Santa Barbara, USA & Greville Corbett, University of Surrey, UK

The Understanding Language series provides approachable, yet authoritative, introductions to major topics in linguistics. Ideal for students with little or no prior knowledge of linguistics, each book carefully explains the basics, emphasising understanding of the essential notions rather than arguing for a particular theoretical position.

Other titles in the series

Understanding Second Language Acquisition
Lourdes Ortega

Understanding Pragmatics
Gunter Senft

Understanding Child Language Acquisition
Caroline Rowland

Understanding Semantics, Second Edition
Sebastian Löbner

Study Skills for Linguistics
Jeanette Sakel

Understanding Language Change
Kate Burridge and Alexander Bergs

Understanding Phonology, Fourth Edition
Carlos Gussenhoven and Haike Jacobs

Understanding Linguistic Fieldwork
Felicity Meakins, Jennifer Green and Myfany Turpin

Understanding Syntax, Fifth Edition
Maggie Tallerman

Understanding Corpus Linguistics
Danielle Barth and Stefan Schnell

Understanding Discourse Analysis
Bernadette Vine

For more information on any of these titles, or to order, go to www.routledge.com/series/ULAN

Understanding
Discourse Analysis

Bernadette Vine

LONDON AND NEW YORK

Designed cover image: © Getty Images | LazingBee

First published 2023
by Routledge
4 Park Square, Milton Park, Abingdon, Oxon OX14 4RN

and by Routledge
605 Third Avenue, New York, NY 10158

Routledge is an imprint of the Taylor & Francis Group, an informa business

© 2023 Bernadette Vine

The right of Bernadette Vine to be identified as author of this work has been asserted in accordance with sections 77 and 78 of the Copyright, Designs and Patents Act 1988.

All rights reserved. No part of this book may be reprinted or reproduced or utilised in any form or by any electronic, mechanical, or other means, now known or hereafter invented, including photocopying and recording, or in any information storage or retrieval system, without permission in writing from the publishers.

Trademark notice: Product or corporate names may be trademarks or registered trademarks, and are used only for identification and explanation without intent to infringe.

British Library Cataloguing-in-Publication Data
A catalogue record for this book is available from the British Library

Library of Congress Cataloging-in-Publication Data
Names: Vine, Bernadette, author.
Title: Understanding discourse analysis / Bernadette Vine.
Description: Abingdon, Oxon ; New York, NY : Routledge, 2023. | Series: Understanding language | Includes bibliographical references and index. | Summary: "Understanding Discourse Analysis provides students with an accessible and well-illustrated introduction to discourse analysis, explaining the main terminology and frameworks and presenting key findings of discourse studies"— Provided by publisher.
Identifiers: LCCN 2022040134 (print) | LCCN 2022040135 (ebook) | ISBN 9781032025896 (hardback) | ISBN 9781032025889 (paperback) | ISBN 9781003184058 (ebook)
Subjects: LCSH: Discourse analysis.
Classification: LCC P302 .V498 2023 (print) | LCC P302 (ebook) | DDC 401/.41—dc23/eng/20220917
LC record available at https://lccn.loc.gov/2022040134
LC ebook record available at https://lccn.loc.gov/2022040135

ISBN: 978-1-032-02589-6 (hbk)
ISBN: 978-1-032-02588-9 (pbk)
ISBN: 978-1-003-18405-8 (ebk)

DOI: 10.4324/9781003184058

Typeset in Minion
by Apex CoVantage, LLC

To my family

Contents

Acknowledgements	xiii
Transcription conventions	xiv

PART I
Introducing discourse analysis — 1

1 Introduction to discourse analysis — 3
Introduction — 3
1.1 Definitions — 4
    1.1.1 What is discourse? — 4
    1.1.2 What is discourse analysis? — 5
1.2 What are some of the dimensions of discourse that may be explored? — 6
    1.2.1 Vocabulary — 6
    1.2.2 Syntax — 7
    1.2.3 Turn-taking — 8
    1.2.4 Summary — 10
1.3 What are some of the things we do when we communicate? — 11
    1.3.1 What are some transactional or practical goals? — 11
    1.3.2 What about relational goals? — 12
1.4 Language and identity — 14
1.5 Outline of the rest of the book — 17
Chapter summary — 18
Further reading — 18
Exercises — 19
Notes on exercises — 20

2 The foundations of discourse analysis — 22
Introduction — 22
2.1 The birth of discourse analysis — 22
2.2 Speech Act Theory — 22
    2.2.1 What is Speech Act Theory? — 22
    2.2.2 Searle's taxonomy of speech acts — 23
    2.2.3 Why is Speech Act Theory useful? — 26
2.3 Grice's cooperative principle, implicature and conversational maxims — 26
    2.3.1 Grice's cooperative principle and implicature — 26
    2.3.2 Grice's maxims of conversation — 27
    2.3.3 Why was Grice's work important? — 31

2.4	Hymes' Ethnography of Communication, SPEAKING model	31
	2.4.1 Hymes and the *Ethnography of Communication*	31
	2.4.2 The SPEAKING model	33
	2.4.3 The importance of Hymes' work	34
2.5	Leech's politeness theory	35
	2.5.1 Leech's approach to politeness	35
	2.5.2 Leech's maxims	35
	2.5.3 The importance of Leech's work	39
2.6	Brown and Levinson's politeness theory	39
	2.6.1 Brown and Levinson's approach to politeness	39
	2.6.2 Key concept: face	39
	2.6.3 Threats to face	40
	2.6.4 Politeness strategies	41
	2.6.5 The importance of Brown and Levinson's theory	43
Chapter summary		44
Further reading		44
Exercises		45
Notes on exercises		47

PART II
Some key approaches to analysing discourse — 49

3 Corpus approaches to discourse analysis — 51

Introduction		51
3.1	The origins and development of corpus approaches to discourse analysis	51
3.2	Introducing corpus approaches to discourse analysis	52
	3.2.1 Some basic terms and concepts	52
	3.2.2 Utilising corpora in discourse analysis research	53
3.3	Exploring words and phrases	54
	3.3.1 Basic searches and exploring frequencies	54
	3.3.2 Keywords and exploring distinctiveness	58
	3.3.3 The use of phrases and formulaic language	61
	3.3.4 Collocations and exploring words that frequently occur close to each other	62
	3.3.5 Concordance lines and exploring the immediate discourse context further	65
	3.3.6 Summary	67
3.4	Beyond words and phrases	67
3.5	Why take a Corpus Approach to Discourse Analysis?	68
	3.5.1 Reducing researcher bias	69
	3.5.2 Understanding the incremental effect of discourse	69
	3.5.3 Understanding resistant and changing discourses	69
	3.5.4 Triangulation	69
	3.5.5 Unexpected patterns emerge	70

		Chapter summary	70
		Further reading	71
		Exercises	71
		Notes on exercises	73
4		**Conversation analysis**	**74**
		Introduction	74
	4.1	The origins and development of Conversation Analysis	75
	4.2	What are some key concepts in Conversation Analysis?	75
		4.2.1 Action and sequence	76
		4.2.2 Turn-taking	76
		4.2.3 Adjacency pairs	80
		4.2.4 Sequence organisation	81
		4.2.5 Preference	82
		4.2.6 Repair	84
		4.2.7 Summary	86
	4.3	Beyond "conversation": institutional settings	86
		4.3.1 Medical settings	87
		4.3.2 Legal settings	88
		4.3.3 Media settings	91
		4.3.4 Summary	92
	4.4	New mediums of communication	92
		Chapter summary	94
		Further reading	95
		Exercises	95
		Notes on exercises	97
5		**Interactional sociolinguistics**	**98**
		Introduction	98
	5.1	The origins and development of Interactional Sociolinguistics	98
	5.2	What are some key concepts in Interactional Sociolinguistics?	99
		5.2.1 Contextualisation cues	100
		5.2.2 Conversational inference	102
		5.2.3 Framing	105
		5.2.4 Norms and conversational style	106
		5.2.5 Indexicality and stance	108
		5.2.6 Summary	110
	5.3	Some key topics in Interactional Sociolinguistics	110
		5.3.1 The use of discourse strategies	110
		5.3.2 The construction of routine encounters	112
		5.3.3 The discursive creation of relationships	114
		5.3.4 Identity	115
		5.3.5 Summary	118
		Chapter summary	118
		Further reading	119

	Exercises	119
	Notes on exercises	121
6	**Critical Discourse Studies**	**123**
	Introduction	123
	6.1 The origins and development of Critical Discourse Studies	123
	6.2 What are some key concepts in Critical Discourse Studies?	124
	6.2.1 Power	124
	6.2.2 Ideologies	126
	6.2.3 What about the *critical* aspect of Critical Discourse Studies?	131
	6.2.4 History	133
	6.2.5 Summary	134
	6.3 Key domains in Critical Discourse Studies	134
	6.3.1 Political discourse	134
	6.3.2 Media discourse	136
	6.3.3 Summary	139
	6.4 Types of analysis and methodologies in Critical Discourse Studies	139
	6.4.1 Corpus linguistics and Critical Discourse Studies	140
	6.4.2 Multi-modal analysis in Critical Discourse Studies	141
	Chapter summary	142
	Further reading	143
	Exercises	143
	Notes on exercises	146

PART III
Conclusions and applications   **149**

7	**Key approaches and applications**	**151**
	Introduction	151
	7.1 Comparison of approaches	151
	7.1.1 Types of data explored	151
	7.1.2 Analytic approaches and methods	152
	7.1.3 Issues explored	155
	7.1.4 Summary	157
	7.2 Applications of discourse analysis	157
	7.2.1 Applied Conversation Analysis	157
	7.2.2 Applications within Interactional Sociolinguistics	160
	7.2.3 Applications and Critical Discourse Studies	162
	7.2.4 Applying Discourse Analysis	163
	Chapter summary	163
	Further reading	164

References   **165**
Index   **178**

Acknowledgements

Thank you to Janet Holmes, who gave me invaluable advice and encouragement throughout the process of writing this book. Janet, along with the editors, Oliver Bond and Patience Epps, provided insightful and much appreciated feedback on a draft. Thanks also to the team at Routledge for their support.

The examples in this book come from research from around the world, and I wish to express my appreciation to all the people who undertook and shared their research, and to those who allowed their discourse to be the focus of analysis. I am very grateful to the publishers and authors who gave me permission to use all the data samples featured.

Last, but of course not least, I thank my family, and I dedicate this book to them.

Transcription conventions

These transcription conventions are used for the spoken discourse samples throughout this book. In some discourse analysis research complex conventions are used, making it difficult for non-experts to read transcripts. Examples in this textbook use simplified orthographic transcription conventions and are also described in accessible language so that students can easily read the data examples and thus understand how people achieve goals through their discourse choices. Speech often has false starts, repetition and speech errors. These are normal features of speech and have not been edited out.

All names are pseudonyms, except for public figures.

[laughs]	editorial comments and paralinguistic features such as laughter
[laughs]: yes:	colons show scope of the feature marked
[tut]	bilabial/alveolar/dental clicks
(yeah)	unclear word, transcriber's best guess
( )	unclear speech
//okay\	simultaneous speech – first speaker's utterance
/okay\\	simultaneous speech – second speaker's utterance
	[overlap marking has been shifted to word boundaries]
=	latching, that is, no discernable pause between utterances
ke-	incomplete word
#	showing utterance boundaries when ambiguous
...	section of transcript omitted
+	pause of up to one second
(4)	pauses of four seconds or more noted in brackets
<u>yes</u>	<u>underlining</u> indicates stress, emphasis
yes	**bold** highlights important features being discussed
yes	*italics* denote English translations from another language
	If only the English translation was provided in the source text, then the example will be in italics (with the original language noted)
{you}	word added in English translation to clarify meaning

Sources of examples are noted below each transcript. (Source: LWP) denotes data from the Wellington Language in the Workplace Project database (wgtn.ac.nz/lwp). The majority of the examples are drawn from published research from around the world and in these cases the transcription conventions have generally been changed to the ones outlined here. My apologies for any misinterpretation/misrepresentation in adapting the transcripts.

Part I
Introducing discourse analysis

1

Introduction to discourse analysis

INTRODUCTION

A fundamental characteristic of being human is communication with others. We talk and interact, we exchange information, build relationships, learn about our world, entertain ourselves and others, and negotiate many aspects of our lives when we communicate. Discourse analysis can help us understand how we do these things. It can answer questions such as:

- how do we use language to achieve different types of goals?
- why do we communicate the way we do?
- why and how does this vary from one context to another?

This chapter introduces **discourse analysis** and considers why discourse analysis is a useful tool for understanding communication across a range of genres and settings, and across a range of disciplines.

The chapter begins with some definitions and key concepts that underlie approaches to discourse analysis. In Section 1.1, a definition of **discourse** is provided, along with an explanation of what is meant by **discourse analysis**. Some aspects of discourse that can be examined are highlighted in Section 1.2. Understanding discourse begins with understanding some of the goals that we have when we speak or write – that is, what we *do* with language – and some of these goals are explored in Section 1.3. Practical goals are an aspect of this, but also how people use language to foster or challenge relationships.

Identity has become a major focus of discourse research more recently with exploration of how facets of a person's identity are evident when they communicate. We may consciously signal our identity, but we may also do so quite unconsciously, and so a brief consideration of identity is presented in Section 1.4 of this chapter. Section 1.5 summarises the range of issues, topics and approaches which are covered in the rest of this book.

DOI: 10.4324/9781003184058-2

1.1 DEFINITIONS

1.1.1 What is discourse?

Consider the following examples:

(1) Service encounter

Context: A customer is ordering a cup of coffee in a café. Recorded in New Zealand.

MICHELLE:	hello
KIM:	hi um can I have a regular cappuccino take away please? with cinnamon
MICHELLE:	three eighty thank you
KIM:	thank you
MICHELLE:	thanks
KIM:	awesome thanks

> Adapted from Marra, Meredith, Janet Holmes and Bernadette Vine, "What we share: The impact of norms on successful interaction"; in: Janus Mortensen and Kamilla Kraft (eds.) Norms and the Study of Language in Social Life, Berlin: De Gruyter, 2022 p. 193, ex. 3. Used with permission of De Gruyter. (Source: LWP)

(2) Email

Context: Unsolicited promotional email.

> Wholesale Prescription Medications!
> Our doctors will write you any prescriptions for free !!!
> Lowest Prices – No Prior Prescription Required
> Upon approval, our US licensed doctors will prescribe your medication for free
> And have the medication shipped overnight to your door.

> Adapted from Journal of Pragmatics 38, Barron, Anne, Understanding spam: A macro-textual analysis, p. 901, © 2006, with permission from Elsevier.

In (1) we see a brief exchange between a customer and a service assistant in a café. Example (2) is an excerpt from an unsolicited promotional email. The first is a spoken exchange, while the second involves writing. In the first a customer wants to purchase something, while in the second a seller is trying to solicit business. These examples illustrate language use in two different contexts and with different goals, but both are samples of **discourse**. Each involves language used in a particular setting for a specific purpose. A basic definition that provides a useful starting point for exploring discourse analysis is therefore that **discourse** is *language use in context*.

1.1.2 What is discourse analysis?

Discourse analysis refers to the study of how people communicate. There are a large number of ways this can be done, and different factors are considered as more or less important in different approaches to discourse analysis. All the approaches have a number of common features, however. They all:

- generally consider naturally occurring data as the essential object for analysis, and
- highlight the context in which communication occurs; factors such as who is speaking or writing and to whom, where the people involved are situated and what their goals are

Discourse analysis helps us understand how language is used in real life situations. The way language is used in a situation can give us information about the social, cultural or political context. Discourse analysis has therefore become a common qualitative research method in many humanities and social science disciplines, including linguistics, sociology, anthropology, psychology and cultural studies.

There are many different approaches to the analysis of discourse. Some approaches focus on the immediate text (discourse sample) and reference other factors, such as one person's expert knowledge on a topic, only when speakers or writers explicitly orient to these. Others begin with consideration of wider factors, such as knowledge of the participants' roles in an interaction, or the writer's goals and intended audience. This may also involve consideration of how societal norms and other influences are evident in someone's speech, writing or other forms of communication.

The language examined may come from a whole range of potential sources. Spoken texts include, for example:

- interviews
- private face-to-face conversations or telephone calls
- medical consultations
- meetings
- service encounters, as in (1)

Discourse analysis of written texts may involve examining, for example:

- books and newspapers
- marketing material such as brochures
- business and government documents
- websites, social media posts and comments
- emails, as in (2)

1.2 WHAT ARE SOME OF THE DIMENSIONS OF DISCOURSE THAT MAY BE EXPLORED?

Instead of focusing on isolated units of language, discourse analysts study larger sequences, such as entire conversations, texts or collections of texts. The selected sources can be analysed on multiple levels. In the following examples, small sections of speech or writing are shown which highlight different levels or dimensions of discourse that can be explored. Most of the examples presented are from naturally occurring interaction or writing. Occasionally, data from a simulation or role play is presented. This can be an important source of data when researchers want to focus on a particular infrequently occurring type of language, or where they want to compare language use across languages or between, for instance, native and non-native speakers of a language.

1.2.1 Vocabulary

At the level of vocabulary, texts can be analysed for aspects such as how formal or colloquial the vocabulary is, ideological associations of different words or phrases, the use of intensifiers, (3), or the use of metaphor, (4).

Example (3) is drawn from research exploring **indirect complaints**, that is, where a person complains to someone about something they are frustrated about, but the addressee does not have the power to fix the problem. This type of complaint has also been referred to as a **whinge** (Clyne 1994).

(3)   Family conversation   (Estonian)

Context: Conversation between family members. The daughter, T, is talking about university and complains that she has long breaks between lectures.

T: iga päev on präegu nii et on mingit august
     aga se on vä- õudselt vastik

Translation

T: *there are some kind of breaks {between lectures} every day now*
     but this is ve- awfully nasty

> Adapted from Journal of Pragmatics 153, Rääbis, Andriela, Hennoste, Tiit, Rumm, Andra and Laanesoo, Kirsi, "They are so stupid, so stupid". Emotional affect in Estonian school-related complaints, p. 23, © 2019, with permission from Elsevier.

A feature of complaints is the use of extreme formulations and intensifiers (Pomerantz 1986). In (3), the complaint begins with a fairly neutral description of the situation, that there are breaks between lectures, but this is modified as being extreme because it occurs *iga paev* "every day". As the speaker continues, she explicitly expresses her negative attitude to the situation. She seems to start the word *vaga* "very", then replaces it with a stronger adverb *oudselt* "awfully". She then finishes with the adjective *vastik* "nasty". The use of these words has the effect of legitimising the complaint, highlighting the undesirable nature of the problem for the speaker (Rääbis et al. 2019).

(4) Political discourse

Context: Question and answer session with the media after a briefing from New Zealand Prime Minister Jacinda Ardern on the imminent lockdown and restrictions in March 2020 in response to the Covid-19 crisis. Ardern is describing self-isolation and physical distancing rules.

JACINDA ARDERN: whatever your **bubble** is for the month is the **bubble** that you must maintain that has to be it a group a group of- a small group of individuals who is part of your **bubble** . . . so we're just asking people apply common sense keep your distance from anyone outside of your **bubble** and that's how we'll get through this

Adapted from Vine (2021a)

The New Zealand Prime Minister here uses a metaphor that is designed to help people conceptualise the idea of self-isolation as like being in a *bubble*. Self-isolation was an important part of the New Zealand government's strategy in containing the transmission of Covid-19 at the point that it was just beginning to spread in the community. Being ordered to lockdown and restrict contacts can make people feel that they are being imprisoned so it was felt that there was a need for a positive way of framing the experience. Conceptualising this time as being in a *bubble* was intended to "conjure up images of (fragile) protection, responsibility and mutual support" (Norrie 2020).

1.2.2 Syntax

At the level of syntax, we can explore the way that sentences or utterances are constructed and what this reveals about the intended meaning. For example, what verb tense is used, is it in the active or passive voice, is an interrogative (question), imperative or declarative (statement) form used and why? We do not just want to know what verb someone used but what function this particular verb has in a specific context. What is indexed through the use of one particular form of a verb as opposed to another? Consider (5) and (6):

(5) Government workplace interaction

Context: A finance clerk, Clare, is asking a manager, Sonia, to come and approve a payment. Recorded in New Zealand.

CLARE: do you think you'll have time to come and approve the [payment]?
one payment that Yvette's bonus payment it has been paid it hasn't been paid yet
SONIA: okay

Reprinted under an STM licence from Vine, Bernadette. 2020. Introducing Language in the Workplace, Cambridge University Press, p. 65. (Source: LWP)

Clare is asking someone of higher status here to complete an action and uses an interrogative form to do this. The action involves a reasonably high level of imposition, since Sonia must go to the finance office to complete the approval, although it is a requirement of her job to approve payments. The interrogative form Clare uses is less direct than an imperative such as *come and approve the payment*. It also embeds the request within a question about whether Sonia will have time. The action Clare requires from Sonia is clearly stated but the embedding further softens the request, which can be seen as an acknowledgment of the role relationship between the two women.

In (6), an imperative form of a verb is used.

(6)   Rally slogan   (Korean)

Context: Protest against the Police Commissioner General in South Korea, 16 November 2015.

살인적 폭력 진앞 강신명 경찰청장 즉각 파면하라

Translation

Immediately fire PCG Kang Shinmyung responsible for murderous violent putdown of protesters!

Adapted from Journal of Pragmatics 120, Rhee, Seongha and Koo, Hyun Jung, Audience-blind sentence-enders in Korean: A discourse-pragmatic perspective, p. 111, © 2017, with permission from Elsevier.

Why is the slogan in (6) written using the imperative form of the verb and what effect does this have? This example from Rhee and Koo (2017) shows one of the slogans hoisted in a rally against the incumbent Police Commissioner General in South Korea. The commissioner had allegedly forcibly ended a previous rally against the government and this had resulted in the death of a protester. The call to "fire" the Police Commissioner General in the slogan is expressed with an imperative, and in particular one which does not have the usual modifiers in Korean which soften it and respectfully indicate the intended audience. Rhee and Koo (2017: 111) note that this form brings "the nuance of the absolute necessity, just as, for instance, a command from the absolute being".

1.2.3   Turn-taking

Turn-taking refers to the way people take turns to talk when they interact. Sometimes this may mean that they speak one at a time in an orderly fashion, with only one person having the floor and it then passing to another. At other times there may be overlapping speech. These overlaps may be cooperative or they may signal someone's attempt to take over the floor. Example (7) presents an excerpt from a police interview where there is brief overlapping, but this is not disruptive.

(7) Police interview

Context: The suspect has smashed her neighbour's window. Some of the incident was witnessed by the police officer when he arrived on the scene. He is summing up the information the suspect has provided in the interview and beginning to bring the interview to a close. Recorded in the UK.

POLICE OFFICER: okay alright +++ well basically that's about it um
SUSPECT: okay
POLICE OFFICER: I've not got anything else to ask you obviously you + you've you've admitted smashing it you know it's not yours
SUSPECT: couldn't really deny it //anyway [laugh]: could: I?\
POLICE OFFICER: /n- + no\\

> Adapted and reprinted under STM guidelines from Discourse Studies 10, Stokoe, Elizabeth and Edwards, Derek, 2008. "Did you have permission to smash your neighbour's door?": Silly questions and their answers in police-suspect interrogations, p. 95.

In the first three turns in (7), the police officer begins to wind up the interview, the suspect responds to this with *okay*, and then the police officer sums up the situation. There is no overlapping speech here as the two speakers speak one at a time. In the fourth turn, the suspect agrees with the police officer's summation and there is a brief section of non-disruptive overlapping speech as the police officer responds to the suspect's comment. This suggests that the police officer is satisfied with the responses from the suspect and that the suspect has been cooperating.

Example (8) presents a small excerpt of interaction which includes three points where there is overlapping speech.

(8) Interaction recorded in a car   (Finnish)

Context: A father is driving his friend Niklas and his two children, Iiron and Aaro.

NIKLAS: Alicehan on kans ollu s- aina vaihteleva
          vähä aaltoina hi hyvin
          tyyty//mätön omiin hommiinsa tai\
IIRON: /millon me mennään hotelliin?\\
NIKLAS: //väsy\ny
FATHER: /joo\\
NIKLAS: ja sillai
FATHER: joo
IIRON: i//si\
NIKLAS: /että\\ se niinkön + ei se nyt
          tällä hetkellä mitenkään + pahastikkaa oo mutta + . . .

Translation

NIKLAS: *Alice has also always been fickle in waves quite*
          //unhappy with her own work or\ //tir\ed

IIRON:	/when will we go to a hotel?\\
FATHER:	/yeah\\
NIKLAS:	and like that
FATHER:	yeah
IIRON:	dad//dy\
NIKLAS:	/so that\\ she like + now she is not at the moment in any way + that bad but + . . .

Adapted from Journal of Pragmatics 178, Eilittä, Tiina, Haddington, Pentti and Vatanen, Anna, Children seeking the driver's attention in cars: Position and composition of children's summons turns and children's rights to engage, p. 181, © 2021, with permission from Elsevier.

The father's friend Niklas is talking here about someone called Alice and the father orients to this conversation. He verbally responds with brief tokens, *joo* "yeah" and does not respond to his son's question about when they will go to the hotel which has overlapped Niklas' speech. Iiron's first overlap here could have been disruptive, but in this case the two adults have just continued their conversation and ignored him. Because his father has not responded, Iiron then tries to get his father's attention again, this time at a point in the conversation where the floor might naturally pass to someone else. Niklas however overlaps Iiron and continues his story. The adults evidently feel it is acceptable to ignore the child even when he strategically selects an appropriate point to ask for attention. Turn-taking is explored in more detail in Chapter 4.

1.2.4 Summary

Discourse analysts examine different levels or dimensions of discourse. As illustrated, this could relate to:

- vocabulary
- syntax
- turn-taking

Other aspects that could be examined include:

- sounds (e.g., intonation)
- gestures (e.g., pointing)
- visual components (e.g., the use of pictures in a text)
- style (e.g., formal or informal)
- strategies (e.g., the use of humour)

Exploring different dimensions allows discourse analysts to build up a picture of the way language is being used in a particular context. The interaction between people in a conversation, or the way that someone presents a piece of writing, can reveal cultural conventions and social roles, as well as the particular goals that they may be wanting to achieve. Crucial to analysing discourse is understanding what people want to accomplish through language and other forms of communication and how they do this.

1.3 WHAT ARE SOME OF THE THINGS WE DO WHEN WE COMMUNICATE?

1.3.1 What are some transactional or practical goals?

There are many practical goals that people have when they communicate. Examples include:

- obtaining information or goods
- giving directives and making requests
- complaining
- persuading
- negotiating
- problem-solving

In (1), Kim had a transactional goal – she wanted to buy a cup of coffee. The writers of the email in (2) want readers to purchase medication. Examples (9) and (10) show people with different practical goals. In (9), a builder gives a work experience student a directive.

> (9) Interaction on a construction site
>
> Context: A builder is working with a work experience student on a residential building site. The builder asks the student to complete a task. Recorded in New Zealand.
>
> TOM: just grab a handsaw
> RICK: yep
> TOM: and er chop them off on that line please
>
> From Vine (2014) (Source: LWP).

The builder, Tom, tells Rick to grab a handsaw and then to chop some wood to a required length. He has a practical goal here: he needs this task to be completed so that they can continue with the building of the house.

(10) Telephone call role play (German)

Context: The scenario involves a caller ringing someone because the person called has failed to complete part of a company presentation; designed to elicit an apology. The speakers are both native speakers of German. Recorded in Germany.

MARTINA: [answers phone]: Martina Karens:
CALLER: ja guten Tag Frau Karens
hier Lehmann [sighs]
MARTINA: oh er hallo Herr Lehmann
um ja er
//es tut mir leid also ich ich um\
CALLER: /sie wessen warum ich angerufen habe\\
MARTINA: ich war gerade noch ganz
beschäftigt mit mit um
der Präsentation die

Translation

MARTINA: [answers phone]: Martina Karens:
CALLER: yeah good afternoon Frau Karens
this is Lehmann [sighs]
MARTINA: oh er hello Mr Lehmann
um yes er
//I'm sorry now I I um\
CALLER: /you know why I'm calling\\
MARTINA: I'm currently working really hard
on on um on the presentation that

> Adapted from Journal of Pragmatics 42, Grieve, Averil, "Aber ganz ehrlich": Differences in episodic structure, apologies and truth-orientation in German and Australian workplace telephone discourse, p. 201, © 2010, with permission from Elsevier.

In the telephone call role play in (10), the caller has rung to find out if the person called has finished a presentation, although he does not need to state this, as Martina orients to this as soon as they begin. His goal in ringing was to check on the progress of the task and this is achieved. At another level we could assess the effectiveness of the role play, which had a practical goal of eliciting an apology from the person pretending they have not finished a task. This goal was also achieved.

1.3.2 What about relational goals?

The relationship between people is also always a consideration when people communicate, whether a speaker or writer wants to maintain or foster a relationship with someone, or whether they wish to challenge or damage rapport. The way that the directive was expressed in (9) shows an orientation to relational goals as well as transactional goals. Tom softens his first directive with *just* and the second with *please*. The use of these words helps him foster his relationship with the student, while also directly and explicitly directing him to complete the required task.

The roleplay scenario in (10) was designed to elicit strategies that people use to apologise, a strategy which addresses relational goals. One aspect of maintaining a good relationship with someone is apologising when things go wrong and being able to acknowledge when a problem arises, such as, in this case, the failure to meet a deadline and complete a task on time.

There are many ways that people can attend to their relationships with others. Relational goals may therefore be evident when someone, for example:

- hedges (softens) a directive, as in (9)
- expresses disagreement indirectly
- apologises, as in (10)
- gives a compliment
- tells someone a story with the purpose of entertaining them
- insults someone

Other strategies that people use to directly foster (and at times to challenge) relationships include humour and social talk. Extracts (11) and (12) provide examples of humour from workplace interactions.

(11) Informal workplace meeting (Japanese)

Context: Three men are having an informal work meeting over dinner. This includes a business consultant, Tanimoto, and the sales director of another company, Ashizawa. The men regularly work together. Recorded in Japan.

ASHIZAWA: クライアントはもうほとんど
東京のほうが多いですか今は?
TANIMOTO: 関東多いですね
増えてきましたね５社ぐらいですか
ASHIZAWA: はいはいはい...
TANIMOTO: [ホテル名]はうちの仮事務所
なんです //[笑]\
ASHIZAWA: /[笑]\\

Translation

ASHIZAWA: *do you have far more clients in Tokyo now?*
TANIMOTO: *there are many in the Kanto area probably five companies*
ASHIZAWA: *yeah yeah yeah . . .*
TANIMOTO: *[name of hotel] is our temporary office {in Tokyo}*
//[laughs]
ASHIZAWA: */[laughs]*

Adapted from Murata (2011: 187–188).
Used with permission from the author.

In (11), Tanimoto and Ashizawa are talking about Tanimoto's recent work. Tanimoto says he has five companies he works with in the Kanto area, which includes Tokyo. Tanimoto then jokes that the hotel he stays in when he comes to Tokyo is his temporary office. The humour here helps him build and maintain his good working relationship with Ashizawa.

(12) Formal workplace meeting

Context: Regular weekly meeting of project team in a white collar commercial organisation. Recorded in New Zealand.

SMITHY: um ++
and there's a new issue here which is ongoing training needs
is being examined in the career development project ++
so we'll put that against + Ms Banks shall we?
who is running the ++
train- er the career development project
and is not here to defend herself (4)
jolly good
I've taken up heaps of time

Adapted and reprinted under STM guidelines from Marra, Meredith, Workplace meeting discourse, In: Karen Tracy (ed.), International Encyclopedia of Language and Social Interaction, 2015, pp. 7–8, John Wiley & Sons. (Source: LWP)

Here Smithy assigns a task to someone who is absent. He does this in a humorous way. *Ms Banks* is actually his boss, and in this team is not referred to in such a formal way; she is *Clara* not *Ms Banks*. The tag *shall we?* also marks this as being humorous as he jokingly involves the team in his decision. He holds the floor throughout this small decision-making excerpt, and makes the decision without input from the team, who all remain silent. Nonetheless, the decision does seem straightforward since Clara has responsibility for this area. His comment that Clara *is not here to defend herself* furthers the humour and draws on assumptions about how meetings work and how people respond to being assigned tasks. Smithy's use of humour could be interpreted as softening his display of power.

1.4 LANGUAGE AND IDENTITY

Identity has become a major focus of discourse research more recently with social constructionist perspectives prominent in this area. Social constructionism highlights the vital role of language in the construction of identity, rather than accepting aspects of identity such as gender and age as static categories. Within a social constructionist framework, identity is understood as being enacted through interaction, and people may orient to different aspects of their identity at different times. This challenges notions of objective realities; social phenomena are not inevitable, uncontested or never-changing. Language is considered a fundamental tool for people to both represent and construct the social world.

Consider (13):

(13) Online comment

Context: Comment on a CNN 2009 discussion forum in response to a question about what people thought of a documentary called "Latino in America". Recorded in the US.

I'm a fan of CNN. I'm a 26 yr old Salvadoran-Honduran female born and raised in East L.A. I graduated with a Bachelors of Science from the #11 ranked college in the country, am now a combat veteran working towards further education while serving my Country and always maintaining my Latino culture.

Adapted from Journal of Pragmatics 134, Garcés-Conejos Blitvich,
Pilar, Globalization, transnational identities, and conflict talk:
The superdiversity and complexity of the Latino identity, p. 124,
© 2018, with permission from Elsevier.

The person writing this post explicitly identifies herself as Latina. She also explicitly asserts a number of other aspects of her identity: referring to her age, ethnicity, gender, education and work experience. In responding to the question, she positions herself in relation to the expectations and stereotypes about Latinos in America which were presented in the documentary, which mainly focused on illegal immigrants who were struggling. In doing this, she constructs herself as a part of the group but as someone who is different from the people depicted. She highlights a number of aspects of her identity which she is proud of and reminds people that being Latino is not one thing. The way that people construct the social world draws on social expectations and norms and there is a risk of stereotyping people. A number of stereotypes that had been presented in the documentary are disputed here by the woman's simple but effective statements about who she is.

In (14) we see another aspect of identity involving the construction of someone as an expert on an issue.

(14) Personal telephone call (Mandarin)

Context: Chang has rung an acquaintance, Wang, to ask for her help in finding him a native English language tutor. Recorded in China.

WANG: suoyi bu da jianyi
 [inhales] jiu shi nimende xiangfa you dian tai tianzhen le
 jiu shi laowai tamen ye you hangqing [laughs]
CHANG: o wo zhidao me # na ta yaoshi chaoguo peixun jigou
 wo hai buru qu peixun jigou le shi wa?

Translation

WANG: {I would} not advise that
 [inhales] your ideas are somewhat too naïve
 the foreigners also have their regular teaching prices [laughs]

CHANG: yes I know # if that costs more than training organisations then it would be better for me to go to training organisations is that so?

Adapted from Journal of Pragmatics 178, Yu, Guodong and Wu, Yaxin, Managing expert/novice identity with actions in conversation: Identity construction & negotiation, p. 281, © 2021, with permission from Elsevier.

In (14) we can see Wang constructing herself as an expert in the area (Yu and Wu 2021). Chang has rung her because she works at a university and Chang is hoping she might have a foreign student who can help him with his English. Wang is quite dismissive of Chang here, setting herself up as having more knowledge in this area than he has. Chang has already placed himself in the lower position by seeking her advice and has constructed her as the expert when he does this. We can see further evidence of him doing this at the end of this excerpt when he explicitly orients to her as an expert, asking her if he is better to go to a training organisation.

Taking on a certain role requires talking and interacting in a certain way. In (12) we saw Smithy using humour to soften a decision which he has made without input from others. He is the most senior person at the meeting and has the right to make this decision. As he asserts, it makes sense for Clara (*Ms Banks*) to take on the task because of her responsibilities anyway. His status is also evident in that he is the only one who speaks during the brief excerpt; raising the topic, proposing who will deal with it and then closing the discussion. From an identity perspective, his contribution reflects the institutional role that he is fulfilling as chair with assigned leadership and also his status as the most senior person present at the meeting. Furthermore, Marra (2015: 8) notes that Smithy "goes some way to mitigate the claim to power that his actions invoke", with the use of humour enabling him to do this. Humour allows him to enact an identity as "one of the team" and as a "good bloke" while also enacting his authority.

Smithy's enactment of his identity in (12) draws on his expectations and beliefs about what it means to be a competent and professional leader in this organisation, and what behaviours are normal and appropriate within the context of this team's meetings. Humour is a common feature of their interactions and an acceptable strategy for him to use in this context. Beliefs, expectations, group knowledge and taken-for-granted assumptions about appropriate behaviour in context are important considerations when examining social norms. Training in a field or area creates expectations and introduces norms for behaviour in any type of work role. Social expectations and social norms also exist when someone needs to access services, as Kim did in (1). We expect people to behave and communicate in ways that are consistent with their roles and the situations they are in, whether as a leader, a police officer, a service assistant, a father or the prime minister of a country.

A social constructionist perspective also emphasises the idea that meaning must be coordinated and negotiated (Foster and Bochner 2008: 89). An important aspect of this is that meaning is jointly produced when people interact. It is important for instance in (12) that Smithy makes his decision in response to an agenda item in a meeting and also that he does this in front of the team. His team also construct him as the leader in the way they behave, by allowing him to hold the floor and to make the decision without any opposition.

Using a social constructionist approach, discourse analysts can explore how language creates knowledge, and how people assert, negotiate, reject and align with social stances through social interaction. Social constructionism informs and enhances our understanding of how people communicate and the role of language in identity construction. Discourse analysis research has investigated the social construction of (among other things):

- leadership
- gender, and
- ethnic and cultural identity

Identity construction is explored in more detail in Chapter 5.

1.5 OUTLINE OF THE REST OF THE BOOK

Chapter 2 continues to introduce discourse analysis, providing a brief survey of approaches to exploring language that were influential on the development of discourse analysis in the latter half of the twentieth century. This includes theories from key academics working in this area – John L. Austin, John Searle, Paul Grice, Dell Hymes, Geoffrey Leech, and Penelope Brown and Stephen Levinson – and the emergence of pragmatic approaches to exploring language data. The work of these scholars provided the foundation for future development and approaches to analysing discourse. Some other key figures whose work was important to specific approaches to discourse analysis will be considered in Part II.

Part II of the book explores four key approaches to analysing discourse, examining their defining characteristics and findings. These approaches each demonstrate a different perspective on analysing discourse. Each chapter in this part of the book introduces the main concepts of the approach covered, with illustrations. This begins in Chapter 3 with Corpus Approaches to Discourse Analysis. Corpus approaches utilise collections of texts, which can be analysed using computer software, and give a broad, big picture view of the discourse. Typically, this means that the texts can be explored using quantitative methods, although this has been increasingly supplemented by qualitative analysis of the discourse, allowing closer exploration of patterns identified.

Conversation Analysis (CA) is the subject of Chapter 4. This approach involves micro level analysis, considering only what is evident within an interaction and focusing very closely on the discourse. CA views talk as organised and orderly and provides systematic ways of identifying and explaining the patterns and structures that "make coherent, mutually comprehensible communication and action possible in interaction" (Drew 2005a: 79).

Chapter 5 considers Interactional Sociolinguistics. Interactional Sociolinguistics is a discourse analysis approach which looks closely at authentic interactional data, while also considering wider contextual factors in interpreting what is going on. Its broader aims are to investigate linguistic and cultural diversity as well as the challenges these may raise for intercultural communication.

The final chapter in this part of the book, Chapter 6, explores Critical Discourse Studies (CDS). Taking a CDS approach can look very much like an Interactional Sociolinguistics approach in terms of analysis. A close analysis of authentic discourse may be informed by looking at wider contextual factors. However, CDS adds another layer, as the beginning point is typically a social problem of some kind. Researchers taking a CDS approach aim not only to analyse authentic data but also intend to help bring about change where language use reflects inequality and discrimination (Fairclough 2015), or where a lack of knowledge about language use in a particular context results in prejudices or biases against a group.

In Part III of this book, Chapter 7 compares and contrasts the four approaches, considering the types of data each typically investigates, the analytical methods employed and the issues focused on. This chapter also explores some applications of discourse analysis research, providing examples of ways it has been used to provide practical input and advice on a range of communication issues.

CHAPTER SUMMARY

This chapter has provided a definition of **discourse** as "*language use* in *context*" and of **discourse analysis** as "*the study of how people communicate*". The discourse samples explored can be spoken, such as interviews, speeches and conversations, or written, such as emails, newspaper articles and rally slogans. We will also see some examples later in this book where other forms of communication are considered. All and any aspects of language may be the focus of discourse analysis, including vocabulary, syntax and turn-taking. Other features of communication such as gestures or visual components may also be examined.

Understanding discourse begins with understanding some of the goals that we have when we communicate – that is, what we *do* with language. Practical goals are an aspect of this, but also how people use language to foster or challenge relationships. Identity construction has become a major focus of discourse research more recently with social-constructionist perspectives prominent in this area, highlighting the vital role of how people communicate in this process, rather than treating aspects of identity such as gender and age as static categories.

Discourse analysis can help us understand how we use language to achieve different types of goals, *why* we interact the way we do, and *why* and *how* this varies from one context to another. Discourse analysis is a useful tool for understanding communication across a range of genres and settings, and is utilised by researchers across a range of disciplines.

FURTHER READING

There are many introductory textbooks on discourse analysis, for example, Paltridge (2012), Gee (2014), Johnstone (2018), Jones (2019) and Waring (2018). Each takes a different approach to exploring what discourse analysis is. Gee (2014) introduces his own integrated methodology and is a great resource for anyone wanting a more grammatically focused approach. An interesting perspective is provided in Waring (2018) who organises her book around the types of questions that discourse analysts ask, and how they are answered by different approaches and in different disciplines. For a concise introduction to social constructionism see Lazzaro-Salazar (2018), or for a more detailed one see Burr (2015).

There are also a number of handbooks which are useful resources. This includes *The Routledge Handbook of Discourse Analysis* (Gee and Handford 2012) and *The Handbook of Discourse Analysis* (second edition) (Tannen, Hamilton and Schiffrin 2015). For a focus on Chinese discourse see *The Routledge Handbook of Chinese Discourse Analysis* (Shei 2019).

EXERCISES

These exercises present two short transcripts of authentic data for you to analyse while considering the aspects discussed earlier. There are notes at the end for feedback and guidance. As you go through you could also think about whether any aspects you identify are consistent with your own communication practices or whether they demonstrate contrasting norms.

Consider discourse samples (A) and (B). For each, answer the following questions.

1. What are some distinctive features of the discourse? You might look at vocabulary, syntax, turn-taking and/or the use of discourse strategies.
2. What do you think the speakers' transactional or practical goals are?
3. Are there any features in their speech that orient to relational goals?
4. Are there any features of the discourse that you would highlight when exploring issues of identity?

(A)   Informal workplace interaction   (Samoan)

Context: Seasonal workers from Samoa working onsite at an orchard in New Zealand.

MOE: sole se sui aku ia a ga mea +++ ua kiga a kaliga i ga pese
SW1: sole se ki mai gi pese kakou ke malamalama ai
      [laughter in the background]
MOE: //sole sui mai gi pese Samoa\
SW1: /sole se ki mai gi pese Samoa\\
SW2: [loudly]: ea la le pese lea:
SW1: [laughs]: pule a oe DJ:
SW2: a fia faalogo le kagaka i pese Samoa +
      sau ma aumai laga laau
      [loud burst of laughter]

Translation

MOE: *change the music +++ I'm getting sore ears already*
SW1: *yes change the music please to songs we understand*
     [laughter in the background]
MOE: *//change to Samoan songs*

SW1: /play some Samoan songs\\
SW2: [loudly]: how about this one?:
SW1: [laughs]: up to you DJ:
SW2: if you wish to listen to Samoan songs +
bring your own stereo the next time we come
[loud burst of laughter]

> Adapted from Salanoa (2020: 120). Used with permission of the author.

(B) Workplace meeting

Context: Helen has made a brief presentation about a report she has written to the senior leadership team in an organisation. Connor, a senior manager, is responding. There are nine people present at the meeting. Recorded in New Zealand.

CONNOR: and Helen you know I love your work
and that I understand it
the detail is ( )
my personal preference um would be maybe
to see a little bit of expansion here
on just what these three things are about
even if it's just a paragraph
and even you know we keep this to a page
and that's where we might draw out a little bit
of what you're saying

> (Source: LWP)

NOTES ON EXERCISES

These notes give some reflections on issues you might focus on in answering the questions but are not meant to be definitive answers. There may be other things that stand out for you in each sample.

A distinctive feature of (A) is the use of humour – the way the workers joke around as they work. Moe and SW1 have a practical goal in wanting SW2 to change the music and they utilise humour and imperatives to get him to do this. When considering turn-taking, there is a section of overlapping speech where Moe and SW1 both request the same thing. The humour and joking contributes to the team's bonding, showing an orientation to relational goals. When considering identity, an important point is that the men are speaking Samoan, and that they are requesting Samoan songs. The use of humour also allows the participants to each enact a friendly, good-humoured identity.

In (B), a distinctive feature is the use of hedging: Connor says for example, *a little bit* and *just* twice, as well as *maybe* and he uses the pragmatic marker *you know*. His transactional goal is to ask Helen to add more detail to the report; he is providing constructive criticism. The way he begins by mentioning that she knows how much he loves her work, along with the hedging, show attention to maintaining a good relationship with her when he does this, orienting to relational goals. Another distinctive feature is that, as with (12), one speaker holds the floor and no one else says anything while he does this. Connor is a senior manager and even in this short turn we can see him enacting a particular leadership identity that suggests he is not authoritarian in the way he leads, but that he will still provide criticism and ask for changes.

2

The foundations of discourse analysis

INTRODUCTION

The foundations of discourse analysis lie in approaches to exploring language data that emerged in the latter half of the twentieth century. This chapter provides a brief survey of some of the influential theories from key academics – John L. Austin, John Searle, Paul Grice, Dell Hymes, Geoffrey Leech, and Penelope Brown and Stephen Levinson – and the emergence of pragmatic approaches to analysing language data. The work of these scholars provided the foundation for the future development of discourse analysis. Some other key figures who were working during this time and who were influential in relation to specific discourse analysis approaches are introduced in Chapters 3 to 6.

2.1 THE BIRTH OF DISCOURSE ANALYSIS

In the first half of the twentieth century, linguists were mainly concerned with studying the organisation of the sound system of languages and the internal structure of words and sentences. Structural linguists were developing sophisticated methods of grammatical analysis and a great deal of effort was also going into studying languages that had never been written down; analysing discourse was typically restricted to describing the grammar of languages.

The call to linguists to study language use in context has been credited to Zellig Harris. Beginning in 1952, Harris published a series of research papers using the term **discourse analysis** (Harris 1952, 1963). Though Harris mentioned the idea of analysing discourse, he did not work out a comprehensive system for doing this. In Europe, the French philosopher Michel Foucault is seen as one of the early key theorists in this area, referring to **discourse** in his book *The Archaeology of Knowledge* (1969).

Linguists were slow to respond to Harris' call and it was philosophers who had a significant impact on linguistics during this time, as they turned their focus to language. In the 1950s this included the work of John L. Austin who developed Speech Act Theory.

2.2 SPEECH ACT THEORY

2.2.1 What is Speech Act Theory?

Speech Act Theory considers language as action rather than just a medium to state information. It attempts to capture people's intentions when they communicate.

DOI: 10.4324/9781003184058-3

Several speech act taxonomies have been proposed, beginning with the work of the British philosopher of language, John L. Austin (Austin 1955/1962, 1975). Austin explored the idea that people not only use language to *assert* things but also to *do* things.

2.2.2 Searle's taxonomy of speech acts

Other academics have developed Speech Act Theory further. John Searle, an American philosopher, developed aspects of the theory more fully and proposed a new taxonomy. The taxonomy he proposed is the most influential (see Searle 1969, 1975, 1976, 1979). Searle's taxonomy is based on **illocutionary point**, that is, the intentions of the speaker. Searle takes the **illocutionary act** (what a speaker *intends* to *do*), rather than the word or sentence, to be the fundamental unit of communication.

Searle's taxonomy contains five major categories of illocutionary acts: **assertives**, **directives**, **commissives**, **expressives** and **declarations**.

Assertives

Assertives commit the speaker to something being the case. The different kinds of assertives include suggesting, putting forward, swearing, boasting, concluding. In (1), a teacher makes a statement about the compositions of her students. This is followed by a statement asserting that students' accomplishments come about because of great teachers. This is an assertive; in particular the writer's intention seems to be to boast that she is a great teacher.

(1) Weibo microblog (Chinese)

Context: Comment by a teacher on a social networking site.

我教的这仨学生作文写得是真不赖，到底是名师出高徒啊，哈哈。

Translation

The compositions of the three students I taught are really good. It is true that an accomplished disciple owes his accomplishment to his great teacher. Haha

Adapted from Journal of Pragmatics 169, Ren, Wei and Guo, Yaping, Self-praise on Chinese social networking sites, p. 184, © 2020, with permission from Elsevier.

Directives

Directives are attempts to make the addressee perform an action. The different kinds of directives include asking, ordering, requesting, inviting, advising, begging. In (2), the caller issues a directive, inviting her friend to come to a party.

(2) Telephone call (French)

Context: Phone call between two friends.

JULIE: er d'acc okay er quais j'voulais t'demander
er du coup j'fais une petite soirée la s'maine prochaine
avec er ben //t'sais les\ filles là qu t'avais vues
SARA: /ouais\\
JULIE: et j'voulais savior si ça t'intéressait de venir du coup

Translation

JULIE: er alright okay er yeah I wanted to ask you
er then I'm having a little party next week
with er well //you know the\ girls who you saw
SARA: /yeah\\
JULIE: and I wanted to know if you'd be interested in coming then

Adapted from Journal of Pragmatics 125, Traverso, Véronique, Ticca, Anna Claudia, and Ursi, Biagio, Invitations in French: A complex and apparently delicate action, p. 170, © 2018, with permission from Elsevier.

Commissives

Commissives commit the speaker to doing something in the future. The different kinds of commissives include promising, planning, vowing, betting, opposing. In (3), the caller uses commissives, leaving two messages promising to ring again.

(3) Telephone answer-phone message (Bulgarian)

Context: A caller leaves two messages when the person she is calling does not answer.

A: tam li si? ne iskaš li da vdigaš?
ajde az šte zvănna po-kăsno da ti
kaža kakvoto imam da ti kazvam
ne šta da go izdavam v săobštenie
[Later]
A: pak săm az opitvam se da se svărža
javno ošte ne si se vărnala
sigurno praznuvaš
ajde po-kăsno pak šte zvănna čao

Translation

A: are you there? don't you want to pick up the phone?
okay I'll call you later to tell you what I have to tell you
I don't want to say it in a message
[Later]

A: it's me again I'm trying to reach you
obviously you're not back yet
you are probably out celebrating
okay I'm gonna call you back later bye

Adapted from Journal of Pragmatics 37, Tchizmarova, Ivelina K.,
Hedging functions of the Bulgarian discourse marker xajde, p. 1155,
© 2005, with permission from Elsevier.

Expressives

Expressives express how the speaker feels about a situation. The different kinds of expressives include thanking, apologising, welcoming, deploring. In (4), there are a number of expressives; a woman apologises for not thanking someone, expresses shame for not doing this, and then thanks the person.

(4)   Interaction in the street   (Akan)

Context: Kwadwo (KW), 36, had given Maame Akua (MA), 70, two thousand cedis. Maame Akua did not go to Kwadwo's house to thank him as tradition demands and meets him in town. Maame Akua rushes to Kwadwo, bends down slightly in deference, and apologises. Recorded in Ghana.

MA: Kwadwo yei deɛ mafa wo aseda adi
anka mefiri me nua panin no hɔ a
na anka wo hɔ na mereba yi
nnora ɔkɔɔ wiram no ɔpiraeɛ ɛna mekɔhwɛɛ
no anɔpa yi yei deɛ woama m'ani awu
KW: o Maame Akua ɛnyɛ hwee
ɛnha wo ho mma fie
kakra yi nti na anka woreha wo ho yi?
MA: ei Kwadwo sidi mpem mmienu nsua
meda wo ase asɔna

Translation

MA: I have taken thanking you for granted
I would have come to you from my brother's house
he went to the woods and hurt himself yesterday
and I had to go and see him
I'm ashamed {for not coming to thank you}
KW: well Maame Akua this is nothing
you don't have to come home
this was only a small gift
MA: what?! Kwadwo two thousand cedis isn't small
thank you one who belongs to the respectable Asona lineage

Adapted from Journal of Pragmatics 31, Obeng, Samuel Gyasi, Apologies
in Akan discourse, p. 719, © 1999, with permission from Elsevier.

Declarations

Declarations change the state of the world in an immediate way. The different kinds of declarations include excommunications, hirings and firings, court rulings and declarations of war. Austin called these types of speech acts **performatives**, which is a term often still used. Example (5) comes from a court judgement; a judge in 1954 overrules and rejects an influential ruling from 1896, this overruling in turn representing a significant and influential judgement.

(5) Judge overruling

Context: Court judgement rejecting and overruling an earlier ruling.

We conclude that, in the field of public education, the doctrine of "separate but equal" has no place. [...] Any language in Plessy v Ferguson contrary to this finding is rejected.

(Brown v Board of Education of Topeka 1954, per Warren CJ)

> Adapted from Journal of Pragmatics 41, Charnock, Ross, Overruling as a speech act: Performativity and normative discourse, p. 411, © 2009, with permission from Elsevier.

The judgement here had an immediate and wide-spread effect. Charnock (2009: 411) notes that

> [b]ecause of its profound social repercussions, Brown v Board of Education of Topeka (1954) was perhaps the most important case decided by the US Supreme Court during the 20th century. In a unanimous opinion, the court held that racial segregation was unconstitutional.

2.2.3 Why is Speech Act Theory useful?

Speech Act Theory is useful for thinking about the functions of language, and what we do when we communicate. Searle's taxonomy is the most influential one that has been proposed with its five broad functions of language as seen earlier: **assertives, directives, commissives, expressives** and **declarations**. Searle's work built on Austin's ideas, expanding the theory and carefully defining the importance of speaker intention. Understanding speaker intention and how hearers derive meaning from utterances was the focus of another philosopher, Paul Grice.

2.3 GRICE'S COOPERATIVE PRINCIPLE, IMPLICATURE AND CONVERSATIONAL MAXIMS

2.3.1 Grice's cooperative principle and implicature

Paul Grice, another British philosopher, explored the way that people derive meaning from utterances. He was interested in the connection between what is said and what is implicated. Often the literal meaning of something is not the same as the intended meaning. In (1) for instance, how do we know that the writer is boasting? They did not directly say "I am a great teacher". In (4), how do we know Maame Akua is apologising? She did not directly say "I apologise". In both cases the speech act, as a boast and an apology, is understood, but how? This was the issue that Grice explored.

Grice concluded that the connection between what is said and what is meant cannot be arbitrary, otherwise people would not be able to effectively communicate; it must be rule-governed to a significant degree. Grice was the first person to describe the characteristic features of implicatures, and also the first to propose a systematic explanation for how they work. His work in the 1960s inspired a great deal of research in this area, resulting in a new field of **pragmatics**, that is, the study of meaning in context.

A fundamental aspect of Grice's approach to exploring implicature was that conversation is a cooperative activity. For effective communication, each party in a conversation must assume that the other(s) are participating in a meaningful way, whether that is to agree or disagree. Grice proposed the **cooperative principle** and four **maxims of conversation** to account for this.

The cooperative principle (Grice 1975: 45):

> "Make your conversational contribution such as is required, at the stage at which it occurs, by the accepted purpose or direction of the talk exchange in which you are engaged".

An important point to note here is that although Grice uses the term *cooperative*, he is not using it to highlight how people *cooperate* in the sense of working together to achieve a common goal as smoothly as possible. In fact, they frequently do not. He is instead interested in how people work out what is meant from what is said, as the hearer must often infer the intended meaning. The writer's statement in (1) is understood as a boast because it comes directly after a statement about how well her students did. The speaker in (4) can be understood to have apologised because she has commented that she has taken thanking someone for granted and expressed shame.

There is a relationship between the literal meaning of an utterance and any implicit meaning it might have, and this is the core of the cooperative principle. When we communicate, we assume that the people we are talking to will be conversationally cooperative, that speakers cooperate to achieve mutual understanding, whatever the overall goals of an interaction might be. The cooperative principle is not about making the task of the hearer in understanding the intended meaning straightforward; it allows the speaker to make their contribution harder to interpret, rather than easier. A speaker can omit information, for example, and expect the hearer to do the extra work necessary to understand (see Davies 2007). The reasons they may communicate in this way include considerations of politeness, for instance (see sections 2.5 and 2.6).

2.3.2 Grice's maxims of conversation

Grice's (1975: 45–46) four maxims of conversation are:

Maxim of quality: Be truthful.

- do not say what you believe to be false
- do not say that for which you lack adequate evidence

Maxim of quantity: Be as informative as required.

- make your contribution as informative as is required (for the current purposes of the exchange)
- do not make your contribution more informative than is required

Maxim of relation (or relevance): Be relevant.
Maxim of manner: Be clear.

- avoid obscurity of expression
- avoid ambiguity
- be brief (avoid unnecessary prolixity)
- be orderly

Consider (6):

(6) Informal workplace meeting

Context: Workplace meeting between a manager, Len, and a member of his team, Eleanor. At this point in the meeting, they are discussing any ways in which they can make Eleanor's job easier, as she has a large workload. Recorded in New Zealand.

ELEANOR: oh and the other thing the other thing is those um remember how you spoke to me about those forms enrolment forms? I don't like them . . .
LEN: oh okay what's the problem with them?
ELEANOR: the font's too small it's hard to read
it's only because I know where everything's laid out
that I can //see\ things but it's hard +
LEN: /right\\

(Source: LWP)

In (6), Eleanor brings up an issue related to forms that she needs to fill in as part of her job. She says she does not like them. Len asks her *what's the problem with them?* and Eleanor replies. This is a fairly straightforward exchange and in answering Len's question, Eleanor obeys all four maxims. Her answer addresses the question and is truthful (as far as we know), informative, relevant and clear.

Communication is often not so straightforward. Consider (7):

(7) Twitter (French)

Context: Tweets between a customer, CC, and the SNCB (Belgium National Railway Company).

CC: Bsr @SNCB pouvez-vous me confirmer que le 8446 à [sic.] circulé ce jour ? Merci ! #SNCB

SMA:	Bonjour NAME CUSTOMER, selon mes infos le 8446 n'a pas circulé en tant que train de voyageurs. Celui-ci a bien cependant fait son pacours [sic.] à vide, afin que le matériel soit au bon endroit pour un trajet ultérieur. NAME RESPONDING SOCIAL MEDIA AGENT
CC:	Dès lors, il serait opportun de mettre à jour les données dans l'attestation de retard qui indique que le train a circulé normalement #SNCB #8446 [screenshot showing journey from Bruxelles midi to Visé without any announcements of delays]
SMA:	Effectivement NAME CUSTOMER, merci pour ce feedback. Je remonte celui-ci vers le service concerné.

Translation

CC:	Good evening @SNCB can you confirm that 8446 has been running today? Thank you! #SNCB
SMA:	Hello NAME CUSTOMER, according to the information I have the 8446 did not run as a passenger train. However, the train did the journey empty, so that the equipment is in the right place for a later journey. NAME RESPONDING SOCIAL MEDIA AGENT
CC:	It would therefore be appropriate to update the delay overview according to which the train ran as usual #SNCB #8446 [screenshot showing journey from Bruxelles midi to Visé without any announcements of delays]
SMA:	Indeed NAME CUSTOMER, thank you for this feedback. I will pass it on to the relevant department.

Adapted from Journal of Pragmatics 171, Depraetere, Ilse, Decock, Sofie and Ruytenbeek, Nicolas, Linguistic (in)directness in twitter complaints: A contrastive analysis of railway complaint interact, p. 219, © 2021, with permission from Elsevier.

In (7), the customer has contacted the railway company to enquire about whether a particular service has been running. The railway company representative answers the question, complying with the maxim of quality as we assume the information provided is truthful, but responds with an extra statement that does not seem to be particularly relevant and which provides more information than the customer requires. This could be seen to challenge the maxims of quantity, relevance and manner. The customer ignores this extra information, orienting to the part of the response that answers their question. In asking their question in the first place we can reasonably interpret the customer as making a complaint since we assume they asked because they already knew that the answer was *no*. The representative's response therefore could be seen to deliberately orient away from this, making the company sound good because the train is ready for the return trip. This is of course of no help to the customer, but the representative has avoided directly acknowledging the implied complaint and therefore has avoided apologising.

Grice's maxims are not a "code of conduct" and speaker's may either obey or break the maxims, depending on their intentions. Grice did not assume that people constantly follow the maxims. Rather he found it interesting when the maxims were not respected, either **flouted** (with the listener being expected to do some cognitive work to interpret the message) or **violated** (with the listener not being expected to note this). Flouting would imply some other hidden meaning, with the importance conveyed by what was not said. Hence, the Gricean maxims serve a purpose both when they are followed and when they are not.

In (8) we do not know if the suspect is violating the maxim of quality or not (he may be lying), but the police officer is treating him as if he is violating it.

(8) Police interview (Dutch)

Context: Police interview with a suspect about credit card fraud. Recorded in the Netherlands.

POLICE: zijn jullie er de hele tijd bij elkaar geweest?
SUSPECT: gisteren ja //gis\teren wel ja
POLICE: /ja?\\ . . .
 je zegt dus dat je de hele tijd bij je vriendin bent geweest
SUSPECT: hm

Translation

POLICE: were you er together the whole time?
SUSPECT: yesterday yes //yes\terday we were yes
POLICE: /yes?\\ . . .
 so you say that you were with your girlfriend the whole time
SUSPECT: hm

Adapted from Journal of Pragmatics 105, Sliedrecht, Keun Young, van der Houwen, Fleur, and Schasfoort, Marca, Challenging formulations in police interrogations and job interviews: A comparative study, p. 119–120, © 2016, with permission from Elsevier.

Example (8) shows a context where one of the participants is required to suspect that the maxim of quality is not being obeyed; the police officer is interrogating a suspect to determine whether they committed a crime or not so must be suspicious of answers that seem to be cooperative. This highlights the importance of context. In this case, it is the specific context of a police suspect interview which makes a participant doubt the other participant is obeying a maxim, but other contextual factors have implications for how maxims may apply. In some cultures, for instance, it is not appropriate to refuse a request directly and what is regarded as appropriate in terms of quantity can also vary. As Grice notes though, it is the deviations from his maxims that provide useful insight into how people effectively communicate across a range of social and cultural contexts.

2.3.3 Why was Grice's work important?

Grice's work on implicature explained another important aspect of human communication. Speech Act Theory had provided insights into the functions of language, and Grice's cooperative principle and maxims provided a means of understanding how we derive meaning when often what people say and write is not directly what they mean. Another important issue, however, is what aspects of context influence how people communicate? This was the question explored by Dell Hymes.

2.4 HYMES' ETHNOGRAPHY OF COMMUNICATION, SPEAKING MODEL

2.4.1 Hymes and the *Ethnography of Communication*

Dell Hymes, an anthropologist and linguist, first published his work on analysing speech in the 1960s. He was interested in studying how people communicate within the context of social and cultural practices and beliefs. He used the term **Ethnography of Speaking** initially to describe his approach, modifying this to **Ethnography of Communication** because he wanted to also take account of non-verbal aspects of communication.

Hymes believed that language should not be studied in isolation. Any language is not just a set of grammatical rules, and when people use it there are many contextual factors that influence how they communicate. Language use needs to be studied in the wider context of social and cultural aspects: whenever people communicate, individual and cultural norms, beliefs and expectations are important.

Hymes began with the concept of **speech community**, referring to a group who share norms in terms of speaking and writing. Within a speech community there are many situations "associated with (or marked by the absence of) speech" (Hymes 1972: 56). These **speech situations** involve different types of **speech events**, which in turn are made up of **speech acts**.

Consider (9), which presents a speech event, in this case a narrative episode, in a longer news report (the speech situation).

(9) News report

Context: Section of a war news report highlighting mail delivery day in a marine camp. CBS, 4 April 2003.

Verbal text	**Visual text**
Reporter (voice-over): with the heat building and fatigue from the long road march setting in marines were desperately in need of a physical and emotional recharge before launching what may be their final battle of this war	*marines resting, shirtless in heat*

Verbal text	Visual text
what they needed came today in the form of mail	soldier walks through area, carrying letters
Soldier: letter from my sweetheart ah yeah smells good	soldier holds up envelope to camera
good stuff good stuff	kisses envelope and smells it
	looks through several envelopes in hand
Reporter (voice-over): hundreds of letters from loved ones	piles of letters on blanket on ground soldiers squatting searching
Soldier 1: I got a letter	soldier to camera
Reporter: news from back home what'd you get?	soldier kisses letter and smiles in mid shot to Reporter (off camera)
Soldier 2: three letters from my girlfriend	
Reporter: how long's it been?	
Soldier 2: er three weeks she wrote these about over a month ago	
Reporter (voice-over): and when you're this far from home a lot can happen in a month . . .	
for many of these marines	several soldiers standing or kneeling around piles of letters
it was just the tonic for the dangerous road ahead	soldier sitting cross-legged looking through several envelopes

Adapted from Journal of Pragmatics 43, Piazza, Roberta and Haarman, Louann, Toward a definition and classification of human interest narratives in television war reporting, p. 1546, © 2011, with permission from Elsevier.

In (9), the speech situation is that of a televised news report. Example (9) is just one part of one section of the news report, a speech event within the wider speech situation. Exploring (9) in more detail we can see the individual speech acts that are included in this excerpt. We first have **assertives**, as the reporter begins with a voice-over describing the situation that has led to the visual footage presented of a group of soldiers resting. The report goes on to provide a brief narrative episode related to the delivery of mail to the soldiers. A soldier speaks to the camera, recounting that he has received a letter from his *sweetheart*, and there is then an **expressive** as he expresses how he feels about this, *good stuff good stuff*. More **assertives** follow, then, as this brief story about the soldiers receiving mail continues, the reporter uses a **directive**, asking a soldier what mail he got and the soldier replies with another **assertive**. There is then another **directive-assertive** pair, as the reporter then asks another question and again the soldier replies. The excerpt then continues with another voice-over from the reporter, with more **assertives**.

As noted earlier, language use needs to be studied in the wider context of social and cultural aspects, so we can also explore this example by considering relevant contextual factors.

2.4.2 The SPEAKING model

To try and capture the contextual factors that are important when people communicate, Hymes developed the **SPEAKING model**. In Hymes' approach, a speech situation can only be understood if aspects of the wider context are taken into consideration. He captured the factors he saw as being relevant in the acronym SPEAKING: setting, participants, ends, act sequences, key, instrumentalities, genre (Hymes 1974). These factors are:

S	Setting and scene	where and when is the speech taking place? what is the psychological setting or cultural definition of the occasion?
P	Participants	who is involved?
E	Ends	what are the goals and outcomes?
A	Act sequences	what speech acts occur and in what order?
K	Key	what is the tone and manner in which the speech is carried out? is the situation formal or not?
I	Instrumentalities	what medium and forms of communication are used?
N	Norms	what are the norms for speaking/writing and the norms for interpretation?
G	Genre	what "type" of speech is present and what are its cultural contexts?

The **setting and scene** for (9) refer to when and where this interaction took place. The excerpt comes from a televised news broadcast so this is an aspect of the setting. Also important is the soldiers' camp where the footage of the soldiers is recorded; they are shown delivering and receiving mail, as well as talking to the reporter (and to the camera) during a rest period at the camp.

When considering **participants**, this shifts throughout the excerpt although the report has been recorded and edited with its audience in mind. At the beginning the reporter is addressing the audience in the voice-over and also does this at the end. At other points in the excerpt the reporter interacts directly with the soldiers. The reporter and the soldiers at this point take on specific roles as interviewer and interviewees. The soldiers are not only replying to the reporter's questions, however; they are aware of the audience who will view the report. A recording crew are also present although not speaking. In addition, it is important that it is being recorded for a US audience and the soldiers are American. It is not recorded with the intention of being viewed by those on the other side of the war.

The **ends** in terms of this example were to give viewers a human interest story and to focus on emotions; there is scant news value in this section of the news broadcast. **Ends** refers to the conventionally recognised and expected outcomes of an exchange as well as to the personal goals that participants seek to accomplish. The soldiers may also have personal goals in agreeing to be interviewed, hoping their friends and family may see them, as well as wanting to remind the audience of the fact that they are overseas serving their country.

The basic **act sequence** in this excerpt, was described earlier. There were several assertives, as it began with the voice-over from the reporter, followed by the brief story about mail delivery. The story included assertives, an expressive and then two directive-assertive sequences involving the reporter's questions and the soldiers' answers. The excerpt concluded with more assertives, another voice-over putting the episode shown into the context of the war.

The **key** of this excerpt is reasonably serious in the voice-overs at the beginning and end while the reporter highlights the context of the mail delivery story. The soldiers are in a camp because they are fighting in a war. The tone is more light-hearted in the sections focusing on the mail delivery. **Key** may also be marked non-verbally for instance by gesture or facial expression and in this example the visual text information notes soldiers kissing letters and one smiling at the camera.

The **instrumentalities** of this particular example involve a televised broadcast and the speakers are presumably all speakers of varieties of American English. The reporter and the soldier are interacting face-to-face but the presence of a camera crew adds an element of formality.

The use of voice-overs and the brief interviews with people are fairly typical aspects of this type of segment in a news report, conforming to the **norms** for the speech event and situation. The brief interaction within the report includes the reporter asking questions and the soldiers answering, again an expected occurrence in this type of report.

Considering the **genre** of the excerpt, this is a brief narrative adding human interest to a news report. There is nothing here that marks it as being inappropriate given the setting and the goals of the excerpt.

2.4.3 The importance of Hymes' work

Hymes' approach brought into focus the importance of context. In particular, Hymes' **SPEAKING model** attempted to capture the range of contextual aspects which are important when people communicate. Hymes proposed his model as a framework, as well as a methodological and research tool. Importantly, he also highlighted the significance of both the social and cultural context on how people communicate.

Philosophers had inspired linguists to explore the functions of language use in context more closely, and how meaning is derived. Hymes' work extended this by exploring the aspects of context that may impact communication. Another aspect that linguists began to explore at this time was politeness.

2.5 LEECH'S POLITENESS THEORY

2.5.1 Leech's approach to politeness

Politeness research looks beyond the form and basic function of utterances to explore the many ways that the *same* thing can be said in a language and what the different ways tell us about the relationships between people. Addressing this issue, Geoffrey Leech, a British linguist, proposed a **politeness principle**:

> Minimise (other things being equal) the expression of impolite beliefs . . . maximise (other things being equal) the expression of polite beliefs.
>
> (1983: 81)

Leech saw this as complementary to Grice's cooperative principle. Leech's politeness principle, like Grice's cooperative principle, involves a number of conversational maxims.

2.5.2 Leech's maxims

Leech lists six maxims which deal with polite behaviour:

- **tact** and **generosity** (applying to directives and commissives)
- **approbation** and **modesty** (applying to expressives and assertives)
- **agreement** (applying to assertives) and
- **sympathy** (applying to assertives)

The way these maxims are expressed varies from culture to culture: what may be considered polite in one culture may be impolite or rude in another.

The tact maxim: Minimise the expression of beliefs which express or imply cost to other; maximise the expression of beliefs which express or imply benefit to other (Leech 1983: Chapter 5).

An example of a speaker complying with this maxim can be seen in (10).

(10) Doctor training simulation

Context: Training simulation involving a trainee doctor, Jason, a nurse, Linda, and a doctor, Jim. Recorded in the UK.

LINDA: h- he's possibly been in a RTC ["road traffic collision"]
he's been found next to a a (smashed) car
he's <u>definitely</u> got a head injury he's got low GCS ["Glasgow Coma Scale"]

	and his his BP's ["blood pressure"]
	//about ninety sixty\
JASON:	/okay have we got a\\ trauma team here?
LINDA:	do you want to give them a call?
JASON:	can we put a trauma //call out first please?\
LINDA:	/alright okay\\
JASON:	can you get IV ["intravenous"] access for me please?
JIM:	yeah no worries

> Adapted from Journal of Pragmatics 160, Chałupnik, Małgorzata and Atkins, Sarah, "Everyone happy with what their role is?": A pragmalinguistic evaluation of leadership practices in emergency medicine training, p. 90, © 2020, with permission from Elsevier.

In (10), Jason allocates tasks to specific members of the trauma team primarily through indirect means. He asks two questions: *can we put a trauma call out first please?* and *can you get IV access for me please?* These requesting forms literally check the other person's ability to perform an action and, in doing so, identify any potential obstacles. In English using a question like this with *can* is a conventional way to make requests. Wording a request in this way leaves room for an addressee to opt out of performing the requested task, meaning that less imposition is placed on the hearer, and therefore this complies with the tact maxim.

The generosity maxim: Minimise the expression of beliefs which express or imply benefit to self; maximise the expression of beliefs which express or imply cost to self (Leech 1983: 133–134).

Unlike the tact maxim, the maxim of generosity focuses on the speaker and says that others should be put first instead of the self. In (3), the caller promised to ring back the person she was trying to reach, placing the task of making contact on herself, rather than expecting the other person to ring her. In doing so, she is complying with the generosity maxim.

The approbation maxim: Minimise the expression of beliefs which express or imply dispraise of other; maximise the expression of beliefs which express or imply approval of other (Leech 1983: 135–136).

Complimenting someone is a way of fulfilling this maxim. Consider (11):

(11) Conversation between friends (Colloquial Algerian Arabic)

Context: Dinner conversation between four male teachers at Farid's house. Farid has done the cooking. He is unmarried but is keen to get married. Recorded in Algeria.

AHMAD:	baṣṣah awwel marah dug//ṭyyaab teʕ Farid?\
FARID:	/[laughs]\\
AMIR:	a hada awwel marrah
AHMAD:	awwel marrah was rayyek?
AMIR:	(ʔa sehbi) qulna ʕlih ha- haada ma- maḥdaas yezewwej hada

Translation

AHMAD: *it's the first time you taste //Farid's cooking?*
FARID: */[laughs]*
AMIR: *yeah it's the first time*
AHMAD: *first time what do you think?*
AMIR: *(oh mate) it's history now*
he- he'll never ever marry

Adapted from Journal of Pragmatics 172, Dendenne, Boudjemaa, Complimenting on-the-go: Features from colloquial Algerian Arabic, p. 274, © 2021, with permission from Elsevier.

Here Ahmad asks Amir what he thinks of Farid's cooking. Amir compliments Farid, who is a good cook, albeit in an indirect way. Farid wants to get married, but Amir jokes that he will never do this, as he is a good cook so does not need a wife. In Algerian culture wives are expected to do the cooking. Amir's compliment shows him complying with the approbation maxim.

The modesty maxim: Minimise the expression of beliefs which express or imply praise of self; maximise the expression of beliefs which express or imply dispraise of self (Leech 1983: 136–138).

In (4), a speaker (Maame Akua) apologised and expressed shame about not coming to thank someone (Kwadwo) for his gift. The response of Kwadwo to this demonstrates Leech's modesty maxim. In responding to Maame Akua's apology, Kwadwo shows modesty and minimises praise of self by telling Maame Akua not to worry about the "small gift" he has given her, also saying "this is nothing". He insists that he has done nothing extraordinary that requires Maame Akua to thank him. Obeng (1999: 720) notes that the money Kwadwo gave was not a small amount.

The agreement maxim: Minimise the expression of beliefs which express or imply disagreement between self and other; maximise the expression of beliefs which express or imply agreement between self and other (Leech 1983: 132; 138).

The agreement maxim suggests that people generally try to be agreeable. This does not mean that people totally avoid disagreement though. Consider (12):

(12) Informal workplace meeting

Context: Meeting between Kiwa, manager, and Nathan, senior policy analyst, in a government department. They are discussing another organisation whose work impacts on them, although the people who work there have not always shown an understanding of government processes. Recorded in New Zealand.

KIWA: I think with Benjamin there
they're going to be much more aware of the importance
of working within the within the policy process
the appropriate policy process i e //um\
NATHAN: /yeah\\ yeah but don't-
yeah I know but you're arguing personality here right? ++

KIWA: yeah but even in principle I think I think that
they would be aware that um they
one they haven't ha- had as much influence as they should have
in the political processes
two one of the ways of doing that
is to become much more involved in the policy process

(Source: LWP)

The two men here are problem-solving. Disagreement can be an important aspect of problem-solving as it can result in more robust decisions (Vine 2020: 133). In the interaction that (12) is taken from, the two men have been discussing how to deal with another organisation, and Kiwa has mentioned someone new in this organisation, Benjamin, who he believes will help them work together more effectively. Nathan's first turn shows him acknowledging Kiwa's point, but he goes on to question what Kiwa has said, *yeah yeah but don't yeah I know but you're arguing personality here right?*, disagreeing with Kiwa's statement. In responding to this, Kiwa also says *yeah yeah but*, disagreeing with Nathan's assessment. The men both disagree with each other, although they use initial expressions of agreement when they do this. This is a common strategy to argue and disagree in a more agreeable way, and illustrates compliance with the agreement maxim.

The Sympathy maxim: Minimise the expression of beliefs which express or imply antipathy between self and other; maximise the expression of beliefs which express or imply sympathy between self and other (Leech 1983: 132; 138).

This maxim covers a small group of assertives such as congratulations, commiserations and expressing condolences, as in (13).

(13)   Expression of sympathy role play   (Peruvian Spanish)

Context: The speaker had to respond to a scenario where they have just heard that their boss was involved in a very serious accident. They have gone to the hospital and when they got there they were informed that he had died. They see his wife and talk to her. Recorded in Peru.

A: hola señora cómo estás
acabo de enterarme que tu tu esposo ha fallecido
y por eso he venido acá al hospital
para darte el sentido pésame por esta pérdida

Translation

A: hello ma'am how are you
I have just found out that your husband has passed away
and that's why I have come here to the hospital
to offer you my sympathy for this loss

Adapted from Journal of Pragmatics 42, García, Carmen,
"Cuente conmigo": The expression of sympathy by Peruvian
Spanish speakers, p. 413, © 2010, with permission from Elsevier.

The speaker here expresses sympathy to the person role playing as the wife of someone who has died in an accident. Other examples of complying with the sympathy maxim would include commiserating with someone who received a bad grade or failed to achieve another goal.

2.5.3 The importance of Leech's work

Leech's approach to politeness built on the work of Grice and drew on Searle's speech act taxonomy. Leech's politeness principle and maxims set out the factors he saw as influencing how people take account of relationships when they communicate. He was concerned with exploring the constraints on conversational behaviour brought about by the need to effectively manage relationships. He felt that the **tact** and **approbation** maxims appear to be more powerful constraints on conversational behaviour than the **generosity** and **modesty** maxims because politeness is typically focused more strongly on others than on self (1983: 133). This is of course all highly culturally constrained and it has been pointed out that Leech's work is based on British English, white, middle-class norms. Around the time that Leech developed his approach to politeness in the UK, Brown and Levinson were working on their politeness theory in the United States.

2.6 BROWN AND LEVINSON'S POLITENESS THEORY

2.6.1 Brown and Levinson's approach to politeness

A very influential theory in terms of understanding politeness was proposed by Penelope Brown (an anthropological linguist) and Stephen Levinson (a linguist) (Brown and Levinson 1978/1987). Politeness is defined in their approach as a complex system for softening threats to face, with a **threat** being anything that impinges on someone in some way. Brown and Levinson claimed that their theory is universal, applying across languages and cultures. The theory arose out of the observation that interaction is:

(a) the expression of social relationships and

(b) crucially built out of strategic language use

(1987: 56)

This is a social constructionist approach as outlined in Chapter 1, with politeness being understood as essential to "the production of social order", as well as being "a precondition of human cooperation" (Gumperz 1987: xii). The theory is elaborated in detail by Brown and Levinson, but here I outline just some of the main aspects.

2.6.2 Key concept: face

Brown and Levinson's politeness theory is built on the concept of **face** as introduced by the sociologist Erving Goffman. Goffman defined **face** as the "positive social value a person effectively claims for himself" (1956: 268). The image of self depends on both the norms and values of a particular society and the situation a person is in. Maintaining face feels good and threats to this, "losing face", are undesirable. Face saving is a process that people who interact can cooperate in achieving.

A central concept therefore of Brown and Levinson's politeness theory is that people have a social self-image (face) that they consciously project and try to protect. People use various politeness strategies to protect the face of others when addressing them, as well as protecting their own face. It is in the mutual interests of people when they interact to maintain each other's face (Brown and Levinson 1987: 60).

Brown and Levinson propose two types of face:

- **Negative face** – the want to be unimpeded, and
- **Positive face** – the want to be approved of in certain respects (1987: 58)

2.6.3 Threats to face

Some speech acts intrinsically threaten face: they are **face threatening acts (FTAs)**. One distinction Brown and Levinson make is between FTAs that threaten negative face and those that threaten positive face (1987: 65). Threats to negative face include requests such as the one in (14).

(14) Conversation after a committee meeting   (Japanese)

Context: Nomura, president and director of the committee, asks Okano, a committee member and a friend of his outside this context, to have dinner with them. Recorded in Japan.

NOMURA: Okano san konya gohan dokkade goissyo shimasen ka?
OKANO: [with smiles and giggles]: iya iya konya wa goenryo shitokimasu:
NOMURA: iya sonna enryo shinaide kudasai yo
OKANO: iya honto kyouwa kazokutono yakusoku ga aru node
enryo sasete itadakimasu
NOMURA: aa soudesuka
sorejyaa mata jikai ni zehi

Translation

NOMURA: *Mr. Okano why don't you come out to dinner with us somewhere tonight?*
OKANO: *[with smiles and giggles]: no I will refrain myself from going out tonight:*
NOMURA: *please feel free to join us*
OKANO: *really I have a previous engagement with my family tonight
so I won't be able to go*
NOMURA: *oh I understand
then let's definitely go next time*

Adapted from Takita (2012: 192). Used with permission from the author.

Here, Nomura asks Okano to have dinner after the committee meeting has finished. His request can be seen to impinge on Okano's negative face as it will impede on any actions Okano has already planned. Negative FTAs are speech acts which potentially impinge on participants' autonomy. They include requests like this, and other speech acts such as advice, warnings or offers which potentially impede the hearer's or the speaker's actions.

Threats to positive face include criticism, as in (15).

(15) Interaction in the street

Context: A dispute has arisen between a resident, S1, and a student who also lives in the area, S2, over one parking space. They are in the street discussing incidents which have occurred on previous occasions. Recorded in Wales, UK.

S1: why is it that you get out of the car with this attitude?
S2: [sighs and shakes head]
S1: [raises his hands triumphantly] no no you've been seen doing it
S2: have I //+\ really?
S1: /yes\\
S1: with this attitude and your language is foul
S2: phew //right let me\ just turn that one around on you
S1: /so it's foul\\
S1: oh right
S2: you were the one who has been shouting and swearing at me I haven't been //( )\
S1: /ah aye aye\\

Reprinted with permission. From Bousfield, Derek. Impoliteness in interaction, p. 103, © 2005, John Benjamins Publishing.

Here, the resident and the student both criticise each other. S1 impinges on S2's positive face with his criticism that S2 swears, using *foul* language, and S2 in turn impinges on S1's positive face when responding with criticism aimed at S1, that he shouts and has been swearing at S2. Positive FTAs indicate that the speaker does not care about the hearer's want for approval. Positive FTAs include criticism like this, and other speech acts such as reprimands, disagreements and insults. They may also damage the positive face of the speaker.

2.6.4 Politeness strategies

Brown and Levinson's politeness theory identifies a whole range of strategies that people use to take account of face when they interact. At a broad level they identify five politeness strategies a speaker uses when dealing with FTAs. This does not depend on the type of FTA, rather it focuses on the particular strategies that speakers can use with any type of FTA. The five strategies are:

1. bald on-record
2. negative politeness
3. positive politeness

4. off-record, and

5. don't do the FTA

(1987: 69)

The strategy used will depend on a number of factors, including the relationship between the speaker and hearer. In (15), the resident and the student have an antagonistic relationship and are openly criticising each other. S1 **baldly on-record** criticises S2, *your language is foul,* and S2 does the same to S1, *you were the one who has been shouting and swearing at me.*

In (14), Nomura and Okano hold different status positions within the committee, but are also friends outside this, so Nomura phrased his request as a question using a **negative politeness strategy**. Negative politeness strategies are used when speakers know they are imposing on a person in some way and want to show respect. Using a question gives Okano the option of saying "no", which he does. Negative politeness strategies address negative face, that is, the want to be unimpeded. Strategies to address this include questioning, the use of apologies and hedging (for instance, using *just* to hedge/soften a directive, *would you mind just ta- copying one photocopy of that?* (Vine 2009: 1402), implying that the task being requested is not a big imposition).

Example (16) presents an example of a speaker using a **positive politeness strategy**.

(16) Interaction between friends (South Indian Tamil)

Context: A speaker asks a friend for money.

S: periya visaysham!
kaacu veenum
tampi naan Vellakovilukku pookanum
naalekeki taareen

Translation

S: *big news!*
I need cash
younger brother I've got to go to Vellakovil
I'll give it back tomorrow

Reprinted under an STM licence from Brown, Penelope and Stephen C. Levinson. 1987. Politeness: Some Universals in Language Use, Cambridge University Press, p. 108.

The speaker in (16) uses an ingroup identity marker to claim ingroup membership, *tampi* "younger brother". This softens the FTA, using a **positive politeness strategy**. Positive politeness strategies are used when speakers know they are impinging on someone and want to emphasise closeness and solidarity. The use of an ingroup address form in (16) marks the speaker and hearer as part of the same ingroup; they are not brothers but *tampi* is a form used between people to index their closeness. This addresses positive face wants, that is, the want to be approved of. Positive politeness strategies include ingroup address forms and seeking agreement.

Going off-record is a politeness strategy which involves the speaker being indirect. This includes, for example, giving someone a directive without directly asking the listener to do the required task, as in (17).

(17) Workplace interaction

Context: Interaction between a manager, Sonia, and her personal assistant, Beth. Recorded in New Zealand.

SONIA: that needs to be couriered up to [name] + today

> Adapted from Journal of Pragmatics 41, Vine, Bernadette, Directives at work: Exploring the contextual complexity of workplace directives, p. 1399, © 2009, with permission from Elsevier. (Source: LWP)

In (17), the speaker refers to something that *needs to* happen, but does not explicitly ask the hearer to complete the task. The relative roles of the two participants here and their job responsibilities mean that Beth easily infers that it is her job to organise the couriering of the item. In examining how such utterances work, Brown and Levinson draw on Grice's maxims and the effect of disobeying them (Brown and Levinson 1987: 214). **Going off-record** means doing an FTA in such a way as to avoid responsibility for doing it, leaving it up to the hearer to interpret the intended meaning.

(18) shows a speaker using the fifth strategy, by **avoiding the FTA** altogether.

(18) Service encounter

Context: Service encounter in a café in New Zealand.

[A customer realises that although she specifically asked if bean sprouts are an ingredient in the noodle soup and then requested that they be omitted from her order, her order contains bean sprouts. She does not say anything to the staff at the café.]

> Reprinted under an STM licence from Vine, Bernadette. 2020. Introducing Language in the Workplace, Cambridge University Press, p. 126. (Source: LWP)

The customer could have complained, but instead leaves the café thereby avoiding the FTA. She commented that she just took her order back to her office and picked out the bean sprouts.

2.6.5 The importance of Brown and Levinson's theory

Brown and Levinson's theory of politeness was one of the first attempts to develop a detailed theory of politeness and it has been extremely influential. The preceding discussion has highlighted and illustrated some of the main aspects of Brown and Levinson's politeness theory. **Face** is central to their theory, with two types of face identified – **negative** and **positive**. Speech acts can threaten negative or positive face, and threats to face result in the utilisation of a range of politeness strategies.

There have been many criticisms of this theory. Examples of criticisms include the questioning of how "universal" it really is, that is, whether it applies across cultures as Brown and Levinson claim, as well as a criticism that analysis takes utterances out of their discourse context, that is, utterances are typically analysed without considering the surrounding talk. However, as with the other theories outlined in this chapter, it represented a substantial step forward at the time in the development of approaches to analysing discourse.

CHAPTER SUMMARY

Chapter 2 has provided a brief survey of approaches to analysing language which were influential in the development of discourse analysis. This includes important theories from key academics working within philosophy, anthropology and linguistics: John L. Austin, John Searle, Paul Grice, Dell Hymes, Geoffrey Leech, and Penelope Brown and Stephen Levinson. The work of these scholars has been influential across a range of approaches, providing the foundation for future developments.

The work of Austin and Searle in the area of Speech Act Theory highlighted the functions of language. Grice's cooperative principle and maxims provided a means of understanding how meaning is derived from what people say and write, especially when their intended meaning is often implied and not directly stated. Hymes' Ethnography of Communication and SPEAKING model explored the contextual factors that influence communication, while Leech's work on politeness built on the theories of Austin, Searle and Grice in order to explore how people manage relationships. Brown and Levinson's theory also explored the expression of politeness, with the concept of face being central to their approach. Their detailed exploration of how people manage face threats focuses in on the strategies people use to do this.

In the late 1960s, the 1970s and 1980s, a variety of approaches to a new cross-discipline of **discourse analysis** began to develop, influenced by the work of these scholars. Many of these approaches favoured a more dynamic study of interaction than was typically used at the time. The next four chapters will explore four of these.

FURTHER READING

Each of the scholars whose work is included in this chapter have publications outlining their work. For Speech Act Theory see Austin (1962), *How to Do Things with Words*, which provides a collection of essays based on his lectures in this area, along with Searle's (1976) or (1979) publications. Grice's lectures on his approach to implicature were published, see for example, Grice (1975), and Hymes (1974) is a useful resource for exploring his work. Leech outlined his politeness principles and maxims in his 1983 book, *Principles of Pragmatics*, which was updated and expanded in his 2014 book, *The Pragmatics of Politeness*. Studying Brown and Levinson's (1987) book, *Politeness: Some Universals in Language Usage*, is the best way to come to grips with their approach.

EXERCISES

These exercises present three short transcripts of authentic data for you to analyse while considering the theories and concepts discussed earlier. There are notes at the end for feedback and guidance. As you go through you could also think about whether the samples seem familiar and are consistent with your own communication practices or whether they demonstrate contrasting norms.

Consider each discourse sample and answer the questions.

1. Use Searle's Speech Act labels to identify the speech acts in (A).

   (A) Informal interaction   (Norwegian)

Context: Interaction between two people from the Norwegian version of the TV reality series *Big Brother*, 2001. Anette has been standing in front of the kitchen bench making breakfast for herself, buttering slices of bread on the cutting board. Lars approaches her and while she goes to fetch something, he takes her place, moves the slices away, and starts cutting bread. Anette waits a bit and then asks Lars to let her finish.

ANETTE:	kan'kke jeg få lage ferdig a Lars?
LARS:	jeg syns //det er så ++\ unødvendig å bruke skjærebenken som pålegg
ANETTE:	/det er så strevsomt å\\
ANETTE:	//hæ?\
LARS:	/kan\\ ta en asjett +
ANETTE:	ja men kan du ikke vante til folk er ferdig da?
	[Lars does not move and continues to cut the bread]
LARS:	nei
ANETTE:	du har det ikke så forbanna travelt
LARS:	det plager meg faktisk

Translation

ANETTE:	*can't I finish Lars?*
LARS:	*I think //it is so ++\ unnecessary to use the cutting bench as a spread*
ANETTE:	*/it is so exhausting to*
ANETTE:	*//what?*
LARS:	*/you can\\ take a plate +*
ANETTE:	*yes but can you not wait until folks are ready then?*
	[Lars does not move and continues to cut the bread]
LARS:	*no*
ANETTE:	*you're not so damned busy*
LARS:	*it bothers me actually*

Adapted from Journal of Pragmatics 139, Urbanik, Paweł and Jan Svennevig, Managing contingencies in requests: The role of negation in Norwegian interrogative directives, pp. 112–113, © 2019, with permission from Elsevier.

2. a. Do any of the speakers in (B) obviously violate or flout Grice's maxims?

   b. If so, which maxim and why?

   (B) Workplace meeting

Context: Six men in a regular meeting of a project team in a large commercial organisation. Callum has failed to update a document header leading Barry to think he has the wrong document. Recorded in New Zealand.

CALLUM: I definitely sent you the right one
BARRY: [laughs]
ERIC: yep Callum did fail his office management [laughs] word processing lesson
CALLUM: I find it really hard being perfect at everything

> Adapted from Journal of Pragmatics 34, Janet Holmes and Meredith Marra, Having a laugh at work: How humour contributes to workplace culture, p. 1688, © 2002, with permission from Elsevier. (Source: LWP)

3. Is there evidence in (C) that the speaker adheres to Leech's politeness maxims?

   (C) Speech transcript

Context: Excerpt from a speech by British Lord Chancellor (Earl of Selborne) in The House of Lords, UK, when considering an appeal to a case, Foakes v Beer 1884. The Lord Chancellor expresses his reluctance to overrule an earlier decision, which would be required to accept the appeal.

LORD CHANCELLOR: the doctrine itself as laid by Sir Edward Coke
may have been criticised as questionable in principle
by some persons whose opinions are entitled to respect
but it has never been judicially overruled
on the contrary I think it has always since the sixteenth century
been accepted as law
if so I cannot think that your Lordships would do right
if you were now to reverse as erroneous
a judgment of the Court of Appeal
proceeding upon a doctrine which has been accepted
as part of the law of England for two hundred and eighty years

> Adapted from Journal of Pragmatics 41, Charnock, Ross, Overruling as a speech act: Performativity and normative discourse, p. 404, © 2009, with permission from Elsevier.

4. a. Do any of the samples contain any acts that Brown and Levinson would categorise as face-threatening acts (FTAs)?

   b. If *yes*, do they threaten positive or negative face?

   c. Are any politeness strategies employed and if *yes*, what type are they?

5. Using Hymes' SPEAKING model explore the aspects that we know about the context of each sample.

NOTES ON EXERCISES

Applying Searle's Speech Act taxonomy to sample (A) we can identify some different types of speech acts. There are a number of directives, for example, *kan'kke jeg få lage ferdig a Lars?* "can't I finish Lars?", where the function of Anette's utterance is to get Lars to move so she can finish what she was doing. The speakers also use assertives, for example, *du har det ikke så forbanna travelt* "you are not so damned busy", while Lars' last turn *det plager meg faktisk* "it bothers me actually" can be interpreted as an expressive.

For sample (B), we assume that Callum is not flouting (or violating) any maxims and that he did send Barry the correct version of the document. Eric flouts the maxim of quality, "be truthful", when he asserts that Callum failed his word processing lesson. He is doing this to make a joke, and humour is a strategy where speakers may often flout maxims. You could also argue that Callum also flouts this maxim when he says he finds it hard being perfect at everything, again doing this to make a joke.

The speaker in (C) demonstrates some adherence to Leech's politeness maxims. Although he is disagreeing with others, he adheres to the approbation maxim and agreement maxims in the way he does this. He praises the opinions of those he is disagreeing with and refers to outside sources to justify his disagreement. His reason for disagreeing seems to be that he does not want to overrule something that has been accepted in law for 280 years rather than considering whether there is a valid reason to overrule it or not on moral grounds (see Charnock 2009: 404).

All three of the samples contain FTAs. In (A), Anette and Lars are having a disagreement about the use of the space and neither seems willing to accommodate to what the other wants. Lars is impeding Anette and his resistance to her directive to let her finish threatens her negative face. Anette's directives to him also threaten his negative face as he wants to carry on what he is doing unimpeded. In (B), Eric's humour threatens Callum's positive face because it is aimed at Callum and suggests he has failed at something. In both these samples the speakers do not use strategies to protect the face of others. This contrasts with (C), where there is an FTA (since the speaker is resisting the appeal which would overrule an earlier judgement), but he uses politeness strategies to soften his statements, for example, when he notes that opposition to his position comes from *some persons whose opinions are entitled to respect*. This is a positive politeness strategy since it expresses approval of the people and their opinions, even though he is not agreeing.

Question 5 – Work through the features that make up the SPEAKING model for each sample. You may find some aspects more useful than others or may think of other features of the context that you think are important. Treat Hymes' model as a starting point for exploring contextual factors.

Part II

Some key approaches to analysing discourse

3

Corpus approaches to discourse analysis

INTRODUCTION

When taking a Corpus Approach to Discourse Analysis, collections of texts, **corpora**, are explored using quantitative methods, and this is supplemented by qualitative analysis allowing closer exploration of patterns found. Corpus tools and techniques can highlight how frequently an item or phrase is used and they can also indicate potentially interesting items. These can then be analysed by exploring how they fit in larger sequences and with reference to the wider context. A Corpus Approach to Discourse Analysis allows the bigger picture to be viewed, seeing how the aspects that make up individual texts contribute to the overall distinctiveness of a genre or a variety of a language.

This chapter introduces Corpus Approaches to Discourse Analysis. The chapter begins with a brief overview of the origins and development of corpus linguistics. In Section 3.2, definitions of some basic terms and concepts are provided. Corpus linguistics uses a range of tools and some of these are examined in Section 3.3, with illustration from some studies in this area. Section 3.4 briefly explores how analysis can move beyond these tools, while Section 3.5 outlines some benefits of using a Corpus Approach to Discourse Analysis.

3.1 THE ORIGINS AND DEVELOPMENT OF CORPUS APPROACHES TO DISCOURSE ANALYSIS

Corpus studies use computer software, allowing a large amount of language to be analysed at once. Technological advances enabled the expansion of the field of corpus linguistics in the 1960s, 1970s and 1980s with computers making this type of approach to analysis relatively easy and fast.

Collecting texts and transcribing data was initially still a very labour- and time-intensive process, so not many corpora were compiled for many years. Two of the early corpora include the Brown Corpus of Standard American English (Brown) and the Lancaster-Oslo/Bergen Corpus (LOB). The Brown Corpus was the first of the modern, computer readable, general corpora and was compiled at Brown University in Rhode Island, USA. It consists of one million words of American English written texts printed in 1961. The LOB corpus was compiled by researchers in Lancaster, Oslo and Bergen. It consists of one million words of

DOI: 10.4324/9781003184058-5

British English written texts from 1961 and was designed as the British counterpart of the Brown Corpus.

Nowadays it is much easier to compile corpora and many large corpora exist, particularly of web-based or written data that can be easily sampled and processed. It is also much easier to compile a small individual corpus with a particular focus for a project. Examples of research drawing on both large and small corpora from a range of languages will be provided later. The majority of research in this area does, however, still focus on English.

With technological advances, specialist software was developed to analyse corpora, including various tools. Although I do not refer to specific software in this chapter, there are now many options, including freeware, or software that comes with specific corpora. As well as providing tools to analyse corpora such as word lists, software typically produces basic descriptive statistics, and in more recent software more sophisticated statistical analysis is also often built in.

Initially analysis of corpora was undertaken by researchers interested in describing "reliably the lexicon and grammar of languages" (Kennedy 1998: 9). The frequency of forms was important, as was the ability to study meaning in use, that is, how words were used in naturally occurring data. The potential of corpus linguistics and discourse analysis methods to complement each other began to be explored in the early 2000s (Partington 2004).

3.2 INTRODUCING CORPUS APPROACHES TO DISCOURSE ANALYSIS

3.2.1 Some basic terms and concepts

A key term of course in corpus approaches is **corpus**. A **corpus** is a collection of texts that can be analysed by computer software. Corpora may be large, containing millions or even billions of words and characters, with representative samples of naturally occurring language. The International Corpus of English (ICE) project, for instance, aims to include at least 26 one million word components from different varieties of English. The British National Corpus (BNC) totals around 100 million words representing spoken and written British English from the late twentieth century, while the Corpus de Referencia do Galego Actual (CORGA, Reference Corpus of Present-day Galician Language) contains 40.2 million words as of 2020. Other large corpora include the corpus of Global Web-based English (GloWbE; pronounced "globe"), which contains about 1.9 billion words in total from 20 different countries, and the Beijing Language and Culture University Chinese corpus (BCC), which contains 15 billion Chinese characters.

Another key term in corpus approaches is **genre**, that is, the different types of talk that people engage in or the different types of writing that they produce (cf. Hymes' slightly different use of **genre** noted in Chapter 2). A **genre** is situation specific talk or writing. Examples of genres include broadcast interviews, sports commentaries, newspaper editorials and comic books. Each genre is distinctive and involves recurrent and recognisable patterns specific to the genre. Corpus techniques help identify what makes genres distinctive.

Corpora can be written, spoken or multi-modal. Some genres of written data which are utilised in the studies highlighted include:

- popular and academic science articles
- Twitter and Facebook comments, and
- Shakespearean texts

Some genres of spoken data utilised in the studies highlighted here include:

- family conversations
- telephone calls to a medical advice call centre, and
- business meetings

Large corpora tend to include several different genres. The ICE components for instance include a range of genres, such as classroom lessons, parliamentary debate, private phone calls, student essays, business letters and short fiction. The BCC corpus includes news, literature, nonfiction books, blogs and Weibo entries, as well as classical Chinese.

Corpus studies also make use of smaller, specialised corpora, which may represent a specific genre and/or variety of a language. Often researchers compile these for specific research projects and there are some examples of corpora of this type mentioned later in the chapter (see Section 3.3 – e.g., Adolphs et al. 2004; Kim 2009; Plappert 2019).

3.2.2 Utilising corpora in discourse analysis research

Approaches to analysing corpora have been categorised as either **corpus-based** or **corpus-driven** (Tognini-Bonelli 2001). Tognini-Bonelli defines a **corpus-based** approach as one which uses a corpus "as a repository of examples to expound, test or exemplify given theoretical statements" (2001: 10). Researchers using this approach have a focus in mind before they begin. The corpus then functions as a database that can be searched for examples. A **corpus-driven** approach on the other hand, involves exploring items that emerge as interesting through analysis of a corpus.

Large corpora may be utilised for corpus-based or corpus-driven analysis and can be used in a range of ways. For instance:

- the whole corpus may be analysed
- the whole corpus may be analysed but then a random sample taken for closer analysis
- a section of a larger corpus may be selected for closer exploration. This may focus on one genre, compare one genre to another, or compare a section of a corpus to a larger reference corpus

With smaller corpora, the whole corpora tends to be examined, and comparisons may be made to larger reference corpora.

Deciding whether to use a large or small corpus depends on the focus of a study. In Chapter 1, different aspects of discourse that can be analysed were highlighted, for example vocabulary or syntax, and corpus linguistics makes it easy to focus in on specific words or phrases and on how frequent these are in different genres or varieties of a language. If an item of interest is infrequent then it may be necessary to use a large corpus in order to find enough examples. If an item is very frequent then a smaller corpus may suffice. Smaller corpora are also used when a very specific situation may be of interest, for instance development in the use of apology strategies by second language speakers who have undertaken study abroad (see Barron 2019 in Section 3.3.3).

Some corpora that are available for research have been tagged, that is, the words have each been categorised and tagged for grammatical information, making such corpora easy to explore for specific parts of speech. This is also helpful to differentiate words with multiple uses, for example, *search* and *book* as nouns, or *search* and *book* as verbs. Corpora may also be annotated in other ways, for instance, a version of the Hong Kong Corpus of Spoken English (HKCSE) is available which includes prosodic transcription (Cheng, Greaves and Warren 2008), and in other cases writing or speech is encoded according to the social characteristics of the person who produced it so that researchers can easily analyse the speech of, for example, children (see the CHILDES project data which was used by Jones 2007 in Section 3.3.4 and which is encoded for whether the speech is produced by a child or an adult).

A number of corpus tools and techniques enable corpora to be easily explored for specific words or tags. Often studies draw on a range of these tools and techniques. Research using a range of approaches and utilising different tools and techniques are described in the following sections in order to demonstrate some of the varied ways corpora can be used for discourse analysis.

3.3 EXPLORING WORDS AND PHRASES

3.3.1 Basic searches and exploring frequencies

Corpora can be searched for particular words. Wichmann (2004), for instance, investigated the use of *please* in the British component of the ICE corpus (ICE-GB). Her initial approach in this study was to search for all occurrences of *please*. *Please* is a relatively infrequent word, so in the one million words included in ICE-GB there were only 208 tokens (Wichmann 2004: 1529). Only 88 of these were in the spoken genres of the corpus so Wichmann then focused in on these 88 tokens for closer analysis to see which were used in requests. The utterance in (1) from this study demonstrates the specific use of *please* Wichmann investigated.

(1) ICE-GB spoken sample

so Mr Lehrer if I can take you back please to page one of the the er agreement

Adapted from Journal of Pragmatics 36, Wichmann, Anne,
The intonation of Please-requests: a corpus-based study, p. 1531,
© 2004, with permission from Elsevier. (Source: ICE-GB)

With such a small number of tokens, Wichmann (2004) was then able to explore the utterances *please* occurred in in close detail, examining syntactic, pragmatic, prosodic and contextual factors.

Five bilingual interjections and their use in Nigerian English were the focus of a study by Unuabonah and Daniel (2020). Their research utilised the 42.6 million word Nigerian component of the GloWbE corpus. (2) presents some of their results. The figures compared are expressed as words per million. This is a normalised figure which treats each sample as if it is the same size and is a useful way of showing a frequency since it means samples of different sizes can be easily compared. It also demonstrates a standard way for referring to frequencies within corpora, although with low frequency items studies may specify normalised counts per 10,000 words instead or use raw counts.

(2) Origins, meanings, frequencies, and spelling variants of five interjections in the Nigerian component of the GloWbE corpus

Interjection	Origin	Meaning	Frequency (per million words)	Spelling variants	Pragmatic function
haba	Hausa	*you can't be serious*	5.8	haba, habba, habaa, haaba, haabaa	expresses surprise, shock, anger, disapproval, disgust, disbelief, disappointment, and disagreement
kai	Hausa	*oh my God*	2.4	kai	expresses feelings of surprise, sympathy, anger, pain, sadness, disapproval, and shock
chai	Igbo	*oh my God*	1.2	chai	same as *kai*
chei	Igbo	*oh my God*	1.2	chei	same as *kai*
mtchew	different Nigerian cultures	*suck-teeth/ kiss-teeth*	5.9	mtchew, mschew, mtschew, mstcheew, etc	expresses sadness, anger, utter disgust, despair, derision, and disinterest

Adapted from Journal of Pragmatics 163, Unuabonah, Foluke Olayinka and Daniel, Florence Oluwaseyi, Haba! Bilingual interjections in Nigerian English: A corpus-based study, p. 74, © 2020, with permission from Elsevier.

The most frequent of the five interjections was *mtchew* (5.9 occurrences per million words of text) followed by *haba* (5.8 occurrences per million words). *Kai* was the next most frequently used of the terms (2.4 occurrences per million words), while *chai* and *chei* both occurred with frequencies of 1.2 tokens per million words. The study concluded that these emotive bilingual interjections add to the distinctiveness of Nigerian English. This is an example of a study that explored a large corpus because an initial search in the one million word Nigerian component of the ICE corpus did not produce enough tokens for closer exploration. In fact, there were no occurrences of *mtchew* in ICE-Nigeria, which as with all the ICE corpora only includes 20% of its texts from informal interaction, the main context where such interjections are used.

Frequencies for items may also be compared across genres or corpora. An example of research taking this approach is Kim (2009). Kim (2009) compared the use of first and second person pronouns in Korean and in British English using two small corpora of popular science articles. Kim was interested in the use of these pronouns to involve the reader, so each token was checked to make sure the referent was the reader, as illustrated in (3) and (4). Precise use of an item is an aspect that can be verified reasonably easily with small corpora, but which is difficult with large corpora where thousands of occurrences may need to be checked.

(3)   Popular science article

It is no longer safe to assume that **we** know everything about lions and that **we** can be confident of their survival. It is hard to believe that the king of the jungle has frailties but that is precisely what **we** must do if **we** are to protect him.

(4)   Popular science article   (Korean)

wuli-nun salam-man-i tokwu-lul ssu-ko kakonghanta-nun sayngkak-ey salocaphye sa-n-ta

Translation

We are obsessed by a thought that only human beings can use implements and manufacture something

Adapted from Journal of Pragmatics 41, Kim, Chul-Kyu,
Personal pronouns in English and Korean texts:
A corpus-based study in terms of textual interaction,
pp. 2094 and 2091, © 2009, with permission from Elsevier.

The total number of second and first person plural pronouns used in the English corpus was about 3.8 times more than found in the Korean corpus; see (5). In addition, there was a clear distributional difference. In English, second person *you* and first person plural *we* were employed with almost equal frequency, whereas in Korean, *wuli* "we" was the predominant choice. Kim points out that the difference in the results here are due in part to syntactic differences between the two languages, but he also argues that the results seem to be affected by the socio-cultural context; the preference for indirectness in Korean society is influential, as well as the writer's attitude towards the reader and scientific phenomena in British culture (Kim 2009: 2086).

(5) The number and percentage of personal pronouns for indicating reader involvement in two corpora of popular science articles

Pronoun	British English	Korean
2nd person	681 (49.24%)	4 (1.1%)
1st person plural	702 (50.76%)	353 (98.88%)
Total	1383 (100%)	357 (100%)

Adapted from Journal of Pragmatics 41, Kim, Chul-Kyu, Personal pronouns in English and Korean texts: A corpus-based study in terms of textual interaction, p. 2092, © 2009, with permission from Elsevier.

Kim's (2009) study is also an example of research on function words, in this case pronouns. Pronouns and articles are function words rather than content words and are consequently shared across many genres. This is not to say that they do not serve an important and varied function in different genres or texts, as Kim (2009) demonstrated.

Because Kim's study utilised a small corpus, he was able to check each token to make sure it was functioning with the purpose that was the focus of his research. Another way that a researcher can check the function of items when using a large corpus and finding a high frequency is to take a sample. In a study comparing metaphor use in Hungarian and English, Simó (2011) used written texts from two large corpora to identify 500 examples from each language that could then be explored in more depth. The corpora in this case – the Magyar Nemzeti Szövegtár (Hungarian National Corpus, HNC) and the Corpus of Contemporary American English (COCA), both large corpora of many millions of words at the time (and even larger now) – were used as sources for sampling. The samples were based on the word *blood* in English and the equivalent in Hungarian involving the root *vér* "blood" and any suffixed forms. The samples were then read through to identify all metaphorical uses, as illustrated in (6) and (7).

(6) Written corpus sample

For Christopher Petty, the military was in his **blood**. Petty's grandfather commanded artillery troops during World War II. Another relative led militiamen against the British during the Revolutionary War. Uncle Ralph Petty said that for Christopher, being an Army officer came quite naturally. (NPR Morning, 2006–01–17)

(7) Written corpus sample (Hungarian)

Nemhiába, ahogy a tavalyi, hazai mérkőzésekre időzített halaszthatatlan üzleti tárgyalások megmutatták, Komorának a **vérében** van a menekülés. (Népszava, 1997–08–05 [nonfiction])

Translation

*And in fact, as the timing of last year's immutable business trips, overlapping with the home games showed, Komora has escape in his **blood**.*

Adapted from Journal of Pragmatics 43, Simó, Judit, Metaphors of blood in American English and Hungarian: A cross-linguistic corpus investigation, pp. 2900 and 2901, © 2011, with permission from Elsevier. (Sources: COCA and HNC)

The analysis showed that both languages make extensive use of *blood* metaphors, mostly to represent the same two target themes. One theme was *blood* to signal emotion and the other as "essence", that is, "as a fundamental factor contributing to the essence of a person" (2011: 2899), as in (6) and (7). At the same time, there was a marked difference in the frequencies and usage patterns of the expressions, especially within the theme where *blood* signals emotion.

Frequencies from corpora can also be analysed through **frequency lists**, that is, lists of items ranked according to how frequent they are in a corpus. The aforementioned studies are all corpus-based and the researchers knew what they wanted to focus on. Frequency lists are helpful for corpus-driven research since scrutiny of such lists can highlight items for closer investigation.

3.3.2 Keywords and exploring distinctiveness

Frequency lists highlight the words that occur most frequently in a corpus. **Keyword lists** show which words are distinctive in a genre, and exploring **keyness** is a tool that is utilised in corpus-driven research. This is done by comparing the frequency list from a specialised dataset with one from a larger reference corpus, thereby showing which words are significant in the specialised dataset. Keyword analysis demonstrates how many of the most frequent words from a corpus, such as pronouns and other function words, are not keywords because they are shared across many genres. Instead, it is typically content words that are more specific to a genre or variety.

Declercq, Tulkens and Jacobs (2021) explored keywords in a small corpus of Twitter and Facebook comments about a Belgium Dutch language television show about food. They were interested in how food-related social media content is produced in dialogue with traditional media content. In order to explore keywords in this study, a statistical tool called a log-likelihood test was used. This identifies words that are unexpectedly infrequent in a sample compared to a reference corpus, as well as those that are unexpectedly more frequent. Declercq, Tulkens and Jacobs (2021) found 141 items which were highlighted as being significantly more frequent than a reference general Twitter corpus. After removing emoticons and words that were names, for example, of the show or presenters on the show, they identified the first significant keyword as *gezond* "healthy". It occurred 75 times in the corpus, while a combined search of all forms of the adjective *gezond* "healthy" and the noun *gezondheid* "health" yielded 131 occurrences. The researchers saw this as an indication that health is a dimension of eating that the audience was interested in and something they commented on in social media as a response to segments of the show, whether to express surprise at content presented about the healthiness (or not) of some food, or to provide extra insight and information about health aspects.

Sometimes function words do turn out to be keywords. In a study of the works of Shakespeare, Hope and Witmore (2014) used keywords in order to explore what makes the language of *Macbeth* distinctively unsettling, as commented on over the years by many scholars and actors. They found that *the* was used significantly more often than expected when compared to a reference corpus containing all of Shakespeare's work. Being a function word, Hope and Witmore did not initially pay much attention to *the*, even when it was flagged as unexpectedly frequent when applying the log-likelihood test. The other more "interesting" words identified, however, did not explain the impression that the language of Macbeth is very unsettling. *Thane*, for example, was tagged as the most unexpectedly frequent word in *Macbeth*, but two factors are important here. Firstly, that it only appears in this play so will of course generate a high log-likelihood score, and secondly that its exclusive use in this play is not surprising given it is the only play set in Scotland, a *thane* being a Scottish lord.

Returning to the puzzle of *the* as an unexpectedly frequent keyword, Hope and Witmore (2014) noticed that *the* occurred 422 times, which was approximately 150 more uses than expected when examining figures for the reference corpus. Whilst at first this did not seem to explain the creepiness of the play, closer examination identified specific ways that *the* was being used which could be regarded as contributing to this feeling. Consider the quotes in (8):

(8)   Shakespearean quotes

    a.   Lady Macbeth: It was the owl that shrieked, the fatal bellman. (Macbeth II.ii.3)

    b.   Macbeth: The eye wink at the hand; yet let that be,

        Which the eye fears, when it is done, to see. (Macbeth I.iv.50–53)

> Adapted from Hope, Jonathan and Michael Witmore, The Language of *Macbeth*, pp. 201 and 203, © Ann Thompson, 2014, "Macbeth: The State of Play" The Arden Shakespeare, an imprint of Bloomsbury Publishing Plc. (Source: Macbeth by William Shakespeare)

Hope and Witmore (2014) concluded that the use of the definite article when the indefinite would be expected, as in (8a), gives "definiteness to reference that is general" (2014: 203). Hence *the owl* could perhaps be considered more ominous than *an owl*. In (8b), *the* is used instead of *my* as it is Macbeth's own eyes and hand that he refers to. This has the effect of making him seem disassociated from his own body and evokes the way he is beginning to be tormented by his own decisions. Both uses of *the* here are not typical and help contribute to the unsettling quality of the language in the play.

Hope and Witmore's (2014) study also demonstrates another important contribution that using corpus techniques can make to better understanding a genre, or in this case a specific play. Scholars have studied the works of Shakespeare for centuries but the prevalence of *the* as a keyword brought into focus a pattern that had previously remained hidden.

In another study of keywords, Adolphs et al. (2004) also found function words to be significant in a corpus of staged calls to a medical advice line. Callers rang the National Health Service (NHS) Direct help line in the UK and requested advice on a problem. The person providing the advice did not know if a call would be genuine or staged, so had to treat every call as a genuine request for help. The corpus of consultations that was collected was then analysed. A first step in this study was to undertake keyword analysis, comparing the NHS Direct corpus with the much larger Cambridge and Nottingham Corpus of Discourse in English (CANCODE). Two pronouns that were identified as keywords were *you* and *your*. In Kim (2009) *you* and *we* were studied for the way writers used these pronouns to involve readers. In the NHS Direct corpus *you* and *your* were found to be used by the medical advisers in a similar way, to secure callers' involvement in the early phases of phone calls. An example can be seen in (9).

(9)   Phone call to a medical help line

Context: Staged phone call to the NHS health help line in the UK.

HEALTH ADVISER:	yeah **you** see **you** have to do the whole course **you** see #
	right # what I'm gonna do is just take some details of **you**
	for our confidential files . . .
	if I may and then get a nurse to call **you** back
	it will be
PATIENT:	okay
HEALTH ADVISER:	approximately around about forty forty five minutes at the moment
	or a little later . . . thank **you** very much
	right have **you** called us before about **yourself**

Adapted and reprinted with permission from the Journal of Applied Linguistics 1, Adolphs, Svenja, Brian Brown, Ronald Carter, Paul Crawford and Opinder Sahota, Applying corpus linguistics in a health care context, p. 17 © Equinox Publishing Ltd 2004.

The use of *you* in this example helps to maintain the focus on the patient and the patient's actions. A closer discourse analysis of keywords in Adolphs et al. (2004) showed that many were related to specific phases of the telephone consultations and to developing rapport and mitigating the asymmetry between the call taker and the caller. Some of the keywords and key phrases were found in the process of assessment at the beginning of calls, others in the phase of advice giving and others were predominantly used in the "wrap up" phase of the phone calls.

Keyword lists are useful as they highlight which words are distinctive in a text, genre or corpus. Often these are content words and may provide insight on terminology or ways of talking associated with a specific field or genre. At other times they may be function words which may be playing an important role that may otherwise remain unnoticed.

3.3.3 The use of phrases and formulaic language

Frequency and keyword lists can be compiled of **phrases** or **strings of words** (also called **lexical bundles, clusters** or **multi-word units**). One of the most significant findings from corpus linguistics is that much of language use is formulaic. Speakers do not simply take single words and put them into slots to form sentences. Language is typically made up of preformed chunks, many of which perform specific pragmatic functions.

In a workplace corpus of Brazilian meetings, Berber Sardinha and Barbara (2009: 114) explored pronoun clusters. A high frequency of pronouns in their meeting data prompted them to explore clusters involving the key pronouns *eu* "I", *você* "you" and *nós* "we". Common clusters for *eu* included *eu acho* "I think", *eu tenho* "I have", *eu estou* "I am", *mas eu* "but I", *eu quero* "I want", and *deixa eu* "let me". Berber Sardinha and Barbara (2009) concluded that the high frequency of pronouns in the meetings suggested the importance of interaction. Further exploration of clusters demonstrated "the important role of the interpersonal metafunction, revealing some of the ways in which participants built relationships with one another" (2009: 113).

Barron (2019) explored a small corpus of elicited apologies from Irish learners of German which she compared to data from native German speakers. She wanted to map the learning of strategies for apologising by the Irish learners of German over time, gathering data at the beginning and end of ten-month study abroad experiences. Her approach was corpus-driven and she utilised a number of corpus tools and techniques. One of her findings was the common use of the phrase *tut mir leid* "I'm sorry" by learners. This was constant across time, and the learners used this phrase significantly more frequently than the native speakers (2019: 92). Barron suggested that this was a result of transfer from the learners' first language, as well as the communicative security of being able to fall back on a routine (2019: 93).

Another study which explored phrases was undertaken by Plappert (2019) who used a corpus-driven approach to explore scientific writing on genetics. In order to study this genre of scientific discourse he compiled a corpus (called *genecorp*) containing 2979 texts from the journal *Nature Genetics* published from 2000 to 2010. Plappert began by finding the keywords in this corpus, based on comparison with the BNC, and *gene* was identified for further analysis because of the high frequency of *gene* and *genes*. He then identified a number of frequent phrases which included *gene(s)*, see (10).

(10) Phrases between three and six tokens in length containing the keyword *gene* in *genecorp*

Phrase	Frequency
gene expression data	218
gene expression patterns	191
mutations in the gene encoding	175
gene expression profiles	158
tumor suppressor gene	154
changes in gene expression	122
analysis of gene expression	97
variation in gene expression	93
gene expression profiling	89

Adapted from Journal of Pragmatics 139, Plappert, Garry, Not hedging but implying: Identifying epistemic implicature through a corpus-driven approach to scientific discourse, p. 166, © 2019, with permission from Elsevier.

Through utilising first keywords and then frequent phrases using the most frequent keyword, Plappert (2019) was able to identify distinctive terminology within the field. This then provided him with a focus for further investigation of how writers express and nuance claims in genetics.

Formulaic language in expressing negative evaluation was the focus in research by Taboada, Trnavac and Goddard (2017). They investigated two small online corpora: one comprised comments posted in response to newspaper opinion articles and one involved reviews of movies, books and consumer products. One of their findings was the use of phrases that seemed to be frequently used to convey negative opinion. Examples include, *nothing but, nothing short of, nothing more than, anything but* and *so much for*. Sentence starters that tended to be used to express a negative opinion included *The trouble/issue with . . .* and *It's hard to believe that . . .* (2017: 65). The corpora used for this study were small, but they provided some useful insights that could be explored in larger corpora.

3.3.4 Collocations and exploring words that frequently occur close to each other

Examining strings of words that occur in set phrases is one way to explore words that occur close to each other. Another way to do this is to look at **collocates**, that is, words that co-occur with each other. The **collocation tool** (or similar) in corpus analysis software allows other items that occur around the item of focus to be easily identified. This can be words that occur either immediately before or after, but also within a certain number of words of the target word, say for example five words each side of the focus word.

Butler and Simon-Vandenbergen (2021) explored the use of the terms *social distancing, social distance, physical distancing* and *physical distance* and their collocates in samples from four corpora of British English – BNC, ukWaC (the UK component of the WaCky Wide Web project), NOW 2019 and NOW 2020 (UK components of the News on the Web corpus for each year). As well as studying the frequency and usage of these phrases in the different corpora which represented texts created both before and during the worldwide Covid-19 pandemic, they also wanted to determine whether the recent spread of the phrases in the Covid-19 context has entailed any shifts in the collocates for these words. Sudden and radical shifts in the collocational profile of these words were found for *social distance/distancing*. For *social*, for instance, there were eight unique collocates found in the NOW 2020 corpus: *contact, distance, distancing, gatherings, insurance, interaction, protection, restrictions*. Butler and Simon-Vandenbergen (2021) conclude that the semantic fields of the key items have shifted in terms of synonymy, antonymy and associated concepts, as well as there being evidence of shift in the grammar of some of the items. The data excerpt in (11) provides an example of use from the NOW 2020 corpus.

(11) UK web news sample

Social or physical distancing has affected billions of people around the world during the past weeks. The Government has told us to stay at least two metres away from each other, "to stop the spread" of the coronavirus.

Adapted and reprinted under Creative Commons from p. 64 of Butler, Christopher and Anne-Marie Simon-Vandenbergen 2021. Social and Physical Distance/Distancing: A Corpus-Based Analysis of Recent Changes in Usage. *Corpus Pragmatics* 5: 427–462. (Source: NOW 2020)

Metaphor is an aspect of language use that is often explored through the aid of collocation data. In a study utilising the online BCC corpus, for instance, Shi, Liu and Jing-Schmidt (2020) examined verbal constructions in Chinese that encode metaphorical manual object manipulation, for instance, the equivalent of "grasp" when applied to abstract concepts, as in English when we say "grasp an idea" or "grasp an opportunity". German and Korean also have similar uses (Shi, Liu and Jing-Schmidt 2020: 127). One of the aims of Shi, Liu and Jing-Schmidt's study was to explore for Chinese the semantic categories of the objects which occurred as collocates in such constructions. In the BCC corpus the verb construction 抓紧 *zhuājǐn* "grab tightly, clutch" plus noun phrase was used metaphorically in 91% of the sample of 1000 tokens identified. When exploring collocations through the nouns in the noun phrases, there were 196 different types found. The top three items made up nearly 80% of the dataset, however, with the top-ranked item being 时间 *shíjiān* "time". The concept of time or timing stood out as the dominant semantic category that the noun phrase collocates fell into. Other collocates referred to opportunity. 时机 *shíjī* "opportunity" and 机会 *jīhuì* "opportunity, chance", were the second and third ranked nouns. Two instances from the data are shown in (12):

(12) Corpus examples (Chinese)

    a.   抓紧时间, 学习, 学习, 再学习

          zhuājǐn shíjiān xuéxí xuéxí zài xuéxí

          Translation: *Hurry up, study, study, and study some more (lit. grab tightly time to study, again study)*

    b.   要提高, 就要抓紧一切机会学习

          yào tígāo jiù yào zhuājǐn yíqiè jīhuì xuéxí

          Translation: *If we want to improve, we must grab every opportunity to study*

> Adapted from p. 134 of Shi, Heidi Hui, Liu, Sophia Xiaoyu, and Jing-Schmidt, Zhuo. 2020. Manual action metaphors in Chinese. In Bianca Basciano, Franco Gatti and Anna Morbiato (eds.). *Corpus-Based Research on Chinese Language and Linguistics.* 122–141. Venezia: Edizioni Ca' Foscari – Digital Publishing. (Source: BCC)

Shi, Liu and Jing-Schmidt (2020) conclude that the results from their analysis demonstrate that the two types of metaphor are used to convey a keen sense of urgency and/or importance.

An interesting approach to collocation is demonstrated in Jones (2007), which explores the use of antonyms in English across four types of discourse. The first two, adult-produced writing and adult-produced speech, are taken from the BNC. The second two, child-produced speech and child-directed speech, are taken from the English section of The Child Language Data Exchange System database (CHILDES). Based on a list of antonyms, Jones identified 4370 antonym co-occurrences which were then explored in more depth to identify functions. Some examples of the antonym pairs he found in child-produced speech are provided in (13).

(13) Child-produced speech

    a.   that other man turned into a **bad** hulk and Doctor David Banner turned into a **good** hulk

    b.   let's put all my **new** toys and all my **old** toys into my bag

    c.   and the man **standed up** and then **fell down** in the water

> Adapted from Journal of Pragmatics 39, Jones, Steven, "Opposites" in discourse: A comparison of antonym use across four domains, pp. 1110–1112, © 2007, with permission from Elsevier. (Source: CHILDES)

An aspect of Jones' work on antonyms that has been considered important is his approach to collocation (Hoey 2002: xv). Jones explores the function of collocations, an aspect of collocation that is often overlooked. He is not interested in demonstrating that antonyms are collocates, but rather that these collocations have regular functions within the discourse, for instance to impart a sense of opposition between two other words or phrases, as in (13a) where *the other man* is *a bad hulk* but *Doctor David Banner* is *a good hulk*. A major finding of his study was that the semantic fields of the antonyms in the adult and child corpora were quite different, but the functions they served were similar.

3.3.5 Concordance lines and exploring the immediate discourse context further

One of the benefits of corpus linguistics is that a large amount of data can be analysed, but this also creates challenges. If a corpus is untagged, for instance, how can a researcher know how many instances of an item, for example, *search, book*, are associated with each part of speech? Even in tagged corpora, words have many different meanings and functions in context, so how can a researcher know how any item is being used without reading through each of the texts it appears in? A tool to aid in this is the use of **concordance lines**. With concordance lines, it is possible to read vertically through a list containing the terms, with part of the utterance, phrase or sentence they occur in included. This enables specific uses of items to be identified, along with potential patterns of use.

A small section of a concordance for the word *word* from the BNC is provided in (14). This comes from research by Ädel (2014) who explored the use of the word *word* for its metonymic meanings, that is, for when it is used to stand for units of communication of varying scope. Because the BNC is so large and the combined frequencies of *word* and *words* was over 40,000 tokens a random sample comprising 10% of the occurrences was examined more closely. From this, concordances were checked for occurrences which had a metonymic meaning.

(14)   Some concordance lines for *word* from the BNC

Not a	**word**	about the Heber scandal has appeared
make a mistake, or cannot think of a	**word**	beginning with their letter, drop
At least in its given application, a	**word**	which is forced into service.
Then I don't think they spoke another	**word**	to each other for the rest of the
He asked if he could have a discreet	**word**	with me. To put it in another way,

Adapted from Journal of Pragmatics 67, Ädel, Annelie, Metonymy in the semantic field of verbal communication: A corpus-based analysis of WORD, p. 76, © 2014, with permission from Elsevier. (Source: BNC)

In a study of German borrowings in English, Schröter (2021) checked concordance lines to ascertain the way terms were being used. Schröter (2021) also compared the English uses to the way the words are used in German. The corpora utilised in this study were the English and German components of the Ten-Ten web corpora. Over 15 billion words are included in each of the Ten-Ten components. Schröter (2021) extracted concordance lines from the Ten-Ten English component, for instance, to illustrate the use of *nix* (verb) in English. *Nix* is based on the German pronoun *nichts* "nothing" and its colloquial and phonetically shortened version *nix*. Pronouns are a closed set and as such are not open to lexical innovation and borrowing. This is consistent with its borrowing into English not as a pronoun but as a verb, which is a marked departure from its use in German. The semantic link is still there though, "*to nix* implies the process of turning something (back) into nothing" (Schröter 2021: 68). Schröter (2021: 68) provided the following concordance lines as examples.

(15) Some concordance lines illustrating the use of *nix* in English

one user complained. It wasn't only men who wanted the article **nixed**. LOL, my thoughts exactly.
lawmakers are not planning to try and override. Her decision to **nix** the bill that would allow the simulcasting of OTB events
the gains made in Britain since Kyoto in reducing emissions had been **nixed** by increased carbon loss from soils
BuzzFeed News reported recently that crowdfunding site Kickstarter was **nixing** its unlimited vacation policy, in part because workers were not sure

Adapted from Journal of Pragmatics 182, Schröter, Melani, The wanderlust of German words and their pragmatic adaptation in English, p. 68, © 2021, with permission from Elsevier.
(Source: enTenTen15)

In Vine (2021b) the use of the New Zealand pragmatic marker *eh* was explored in a corpus of one-to-one workplace meetings recorded in white collar workplaces in New Zealand from the Wellington LWP corpus. Some concordance lines for *eh* are shown in (16). The concordance lines in this case were used to foreground the issue of use in context (see further discussion of this point later). They were presented after quantitative analysis had identified who in the sample was using *eh* the most, in this case it was men rather than women. The first three examples are from women, while the other four were produced by men. The next section of the paper moved on to a discourse analysis of *eh* and gender at work using an Interactional Sociolinguistics approach (see Chapter 5).

(16) Some concordance lines for *eh* from a meeting dialogue sample

that's good though	eh	that's good
cos he's terrible	eh	cos he doesn't have eftpos
overnight or something	eh	just let it calm down a little
over a thousand hours	eh	yeah
I know them	eh	know them way back

he's a hard case	**eh**	yeah so
in a good mood	**eh**	not running around

Republished with permission of Taylor & Francis Informa UK Ltd – Books, Spoken workplace discourse, Bernadette Vine, in: Eric Friginal and Jack A. Hardy (eds.) The Routledge Handbook of Corpus Approaches to Discourse Analysis, 2021, p. 12; permission conveyed through Copyright Clearance Center, Inc. (Source: LWP)

Concordance lines allow the utterance or sentence in which an item occurs to be easily viewed without needing to go back to each text. Concordance lines also allow analysts to infer the meanings of linguistic items by viewing them in their discourse context.

3.3.6 Summary

Corpus tools provide a range of ways to explore collections of texts. **Word searches** are useful when a particular word is of interest and **frequency lists** can be analysed both to see how frequent a word is compared to others or to see which words might warrant further investigation. **Frequency lists** can also be utilised to highlight **keywords** in a corpus or genre in comparison to a reference corpus. This can help us better understand the language of specific genres or specialised corpora and what makes them distinctive. These tools can also be used to explore **phrases**. **Collocation** tools enable examination of surrounding discourse, expanding the focus beyond words or phrases. A final tool briefly outlined was the use of **concordance lines**, which allows the functions a word has to be analysed without going back manually to check each text in which it appears.

3.4 BEYOND WORDS AND PHRASES

Understanding how items are actually being used, requires moving from quantitative to qualitative analysis, from frequency to meaning in context. Exploring collocates and concordance lines are two ways of doing this, but they provide only a small amount of the surrounding discourse. As seen in the other chapters in this book, discourse analysis requires looking beyond words and phrases. We have seen earlier some examples from research that do this, for example, Simó (2011), Butler and Simon-Vandenbergen (2021) and Adolphs et al. (2004) who explore longer sequences in order to understand how items are used in context.

The concordance lines shown earlier from Vine (2021b) in (16), come from a chapter exploring the use of the pragmatic marker *eh* in one-to-one workplace meetings by women and men. The aim of the paper was to demonstrate one way a corpus approach can be integrated with discourse analysis. The quantitative results presented showed that men use *eh* more than women in the meetings examined; women only accounted for 23% of the tokens found. Men also used *eh* more when speaking to other men than when interacting with a woman, although women's use did not seem to be influenced by the gender of their addressee. An Interactional Sociolinguistic analysis of the data in Vine (2021b) then demonstrated the way interactants skilfully utilise this pragmatic marker to respond to a range of contextual factors. Consider (17):

(17) Workplace one-to-one meeting

Context: A manager, Kiwa, is meeting with a member of his team, Jill, a policy analyst. They are discussing Jill's workload. She has too many projects, so they are working out how to deal with this. Kiwa will need to report on this to his own manager. Jill suffers from occupational overuse syndrome (OOS). Recorded in New Zealand.

JILL:	well I don't want that OOS situation
	and the fact that my projects are behind [slowly]: to: work against me **eh**
KIWA:	yeah
JILL:	[slowly]: because: when we made those plans
	we made those plans on the assumption that er
	//nothing\
KIWA:	/all things\\ being equal **eh**
JILL:	yeah
KIWA:	mm
JILL:	and it wasn't . . . if I can just keep working on those three
KIWA:	yeah I reckon yeah okay so I'll make a recommendation
	[taps pen]: for you to do that **eh**:

> Republished with permission of Taylor & Francis Informa UK Ltd – Books, Spoken workplace discourse, Bernadette Vine, in: Eric Friginal and Jack A. Hardy (eds.) The Routledge Handbook of Corpus Approaches to Discourse Analysis, 2021, pp. 15–16; permission conveyed through Copyright Clearance Center, Inc. (Source: LWP)

Jill is under a great deal of stress and Kiwa, as her manager, mentors her as he goes through the ways he can support her. Kiwa has a non-authoritarian management style and *eh* is one device he draws on at times as he adopts an informal style to build and maintain rapport and express solidarity. Jill's use of *eh* in this extract also suggests that she perceives Kiwa as predisposed to support her. The achievement of transactional goals is a defining feature of workplace talk, and effective communicators do this while also achieving relational goals. Examination of longer sequences of talk in Vine (2021b) demonstrates how *eh* allows speakers to attend to relational goals by claiming common ground, reducing status differences, showing support for what others are saying, and agreeing and aligning with the people they are interacting with.

Studies integrating a corpus approach with closer discourse analysis may draw on a range of approaches to analysing discourse. Chapters 4 to 6 in this book outline some of the approaches that may be utilised for this purpose.

3.5 WHY TAKE A CORPUS APPROACH TO DISCOURSE ANALYSIS?

A Corpus Approach to Discourse Analysis provides another perspective on data, enabling better understanding of how people communicate and why. The use of corpora enables researchers to identify patterns and there are a number of benefits from using a corpus-based approach to discourse analysis. Baker (2006: 10–17) notes four advantages:

3.5.1 Reducing researcher bias

With a corpus approach all examples of something can be identified, or at least a random sample can be used, not just the ones that the researcher notices. Simó's (2011) study of *blood* metaphors was inspired by earlier research where she had used small manually searched specialised corpora. She wanted, however, to avoid "the problems of relying too much on researcher intuition" (2011: 2898) so she assessed larger corpora to verify her conclusions. The quantitative results in her corpus-based study justified her caution since they did not confirm the results from her earlier study (Simó 2008) that Hungarian made greater use of *blood* metaphors than American English. Both languages make extensive use of *blood* figuratively, mostly to represent the same target themes. A finding across both studies, though, was the at times different connotations of metaphors between the two languages; for instance, both *in cold blood* and expressions of *boiling blood* appeared to be dominated by one negative sense in American English, while being split between negative and positive connotations in Hungarian (2011: 2909).

3.5.2 Understanding the incremental effect of discourse

Because corpora tend to provide many examples this may then demonstrate that a pattern goes beyond an individual and is something that may be shared (and potentially constrained) by a community or within a culture. In Unuabonah and Daniel's (2020) study of bilingual interjections, they identified use of the interjections across speakers of Nigerian English, and not just by speakers of the languages the interjections come from; they had spread beyond these groups and represented a distinctive feature of Nigerian English.

3.5.3 Understanding resistant and changing discourses

A fundamental fact about language is that it is subject to change. Comparing large corpora collected at different times brings into focus changing patterns, or features that are resistant to change. Butler and Simon-Vandenbergen's (2021) research, for instance, demonstrated a sudden and radical change in the collocational profile of certain words which was brought about because of the Covid-19 pandemic.

3.5.4 Triangulation

Corpora can provide another perspective on data and also enable researchers' hunches to be confirmed. Schröter (2021: 65), for example, states that an aim in conducting her study on German borrowings in English was to seek "to provide evidence that borrowing may lead to 'new opportunities for variation and innovation . . . adding to the native repertoire as opposed to replacing elements within it' (Peterson and Beers Fägersten 2018: 106)".

Vine (2021b) explores gender differences because closer discourse analysis of transcripts from the LWP corpus over the years had given the impression that there was a gender difference in the frequency of use of the pragmatic marker *eh*. The corpus results confirmed this impression.

Another advantage that is evident in some of the research taking a Corpus Approach to Discourse Analysis cited in this chapter is:

3.5.5 Unexpected patterns emerge

At times, the results that a corpus analysis produces are surprising and unexpected, for example, as found by Hope and Witmore (2014) when examining the language of *Macbeth*. Other surprising results include a study on mixed metaphors in newspaper articles by Kimmel (2010). Metaphors that occur in close textual proximity in journalism, but that do not emerge from the same concepts, were reasonably frequent, and were used in "well-formed arguments on a regular basis" (2010: 97). Seventy-six percent of all metaphor clusters were of this type, challenging the view of mixed metaphors as awkward and distracting. (18) shows an example from this study, where although there is no conceptual integration of the metaphors, all five of the metaphors here (in bold) contribute to creating a coherent argument.

(18) News report

Tony Blair's criticism of EU regulations [. . .] would be laughable if it were not so **two-faced**. While **preaching the pro-business gospel**, he has done nothing **to stop the tide of EU rules** and **red tape** from **choking Britain**. (*Guardian* PD 175)

> Adapted from Journal of Pragmatics 42, Kimmel, Michael, Why we mix metaphors (and mix them well): Discourse coherence, conceptual metaphor, and beyond, p. 109, © 2010, with permission from Elsevier.
> (Source: Guardian)

CHAPTER SUMMARY

Corpus tools and techniques include the use of basic searches and counting the frequency of items. Keyword analysis is a way of exploring the distinctiveness of a genre or specialised corpus and is a useful starting point in identifying language patterns that are specific to a particular group of people or type of interaction or writing. This procedure provides a more quantitative and arguably systematic point of entry into a dataset. Frequency and keyword analysis can also be expanded to explore phrases and formulaic language.

Discourse analysis aims to explore meaning-in-use so the function of items is important. Examining collocations and concordances are two corpus tools that can aid in this. Discourse analysis techniques on data from corpora expands this, going beyond words and phrases, which is a limitation with corpus techniques. Qualitative analysis of tokens through closer discourse analysis allows deeper examination of the way items function and how speakers may strategically use items. Corpus analysis and discourse analysis can be usefully combined to gain a broader understanding of how people communicate across a range of contexts.

FURTHER READING

For relatively brief introductions to corpus linguistics see Kennedy (1998) and Barth and Schnell (2022), while *The Routledge Handbook of Corpus Linguistics* (O'Keeffe and McCarthy 2022) provides a comprehensive survey of this methodology. Flowerdew (2012) is a good overview of Corpus Approaches to Discourse Analysis and Baker (2006) is a useful and highly accessible guide to combining corpus linguistics and discourse analysis. Friginal and Hardy's (2021) *The Routledge Handbook of Corpus Approaches to Discourse Analysis* provides an excellent and wide-ranging selection of chapters exploring different ways corpus linguistics and discourse analysis can be integrated.

EXERCISES

These exercises present three short samples of authentic data for you to analyse while utilising the corpus tools just outlined. There are notes at the end for feedback and guidance.

1. (A) presents the collocates that were found for the word *Malaysia* in a corpus of Malay speeches by Tun Dr Mahathir Mohamad (Prime Minister of Malaysia 1981–2003, 2018–2020). Examine the data and then answer the questions:

    a. What do you notice about the type of meanings of the words that collocate with *Malaysia*?

    b. What does this tell us about the focus of the speeches and the concerns of the speaker?

(A) Collocates for the word *Malaysia* in political speeches (Malay)

Word	Translation	Frequency	Rank
negara	*nation*	1269	4
kita	*we*	1146	5
rakyat	*people*	1035	7
Islam	*Islam*	399	18
kerajaan	*government*	395	19
kaum	*race/ethnic group*	351	25

Adapted from Don, Zuraidah Mohd, Gerry Knowles and Choong Kwai Fatt, "Nationhood and Malaysian identity: A corpus-based approach"; in: Text & Talk 30/3, 2010, p. 278. Used with permission of De Gruyter.

2. A list of keywords is provided in (B). The list was generated by comparing a small collection of spoken transcripts (around 10,000 words) to a larger reference corpus (around 775,000 words). Both corpora included data from workplace meetings, with the smaller sample comprised of the speech of just one person. All recordings were made in New Zealand.

Consider the keyword list and answer the following questions.

   a. What types of words are showing up as keywords?
   b. Which words do you think are interesting and would like to examine more closely, and why?
   c. Which words do you think are not so interesting, and why do you think they show up?

(B) Keyword list

Rank	Word	Frequency
4	AND	476
5	EH	71
7	ALBERT	20
8	THEY	140
9	CALEB	17
10	OH	117
14	HE	75
15	YOU	264
16	BOARD	27
17	THERE	107
18	DIRECTORS	13

(Source: LWP)

3. Examine the concordance lines in (C). They come from the study mentioned earlier which analysed calls to a medical help line and all occur in the speech of the medical advisers (Adolphs et al. 2004, see (9)). An interesting word that was flagged as a keyword in their corpus was the modal verb *may*. Answer the questions:

   a. What function does *may* have in each case?
   b. What does this tell you about the way the advisers present information?

(C) Some concordance lines for *may* from the NHS Direct sample.

| and they also say cool baths **may** help itching and just gently pat your skin and um |
| it may be that there **may** be some other course for it |

it said taking with this medication **may** cause flushing nausea vomiting abdominal pain
Tetracycline **may** discolour developing teeth if it is taken by children
they **may** dry the skin out and they make the itching worse
stopping it tonight **may** not reduce your symptoms tonight

Adapted and reprinted with permission from the Journal of Applied Linguistics 1, Adolphs, Svenja, Brian Brown, Ronald Carter, Paul Crawford and Opinder Sahota, Applying corpus linguistics in a health care context, p. 18 © Equinox Publishing Ltd 2004.

NOTES ON EXERCISES

The words that collocate with *Malaysia*, as shown in (A), are related to the Malaysian people, religion, ethnic groups and the government. The speaker seems to be focused on people and does not treat *Malaysia* as a geographical concept, which might be expected when examining the use of a country name. They suggest that the Prime Minister is concerned with emphasising people and national unity (Don, Knowles and Fatt 2010: 275). The exception to this is *kerajaan* "government" which treats Malaysia as an administrative unit.

There are some function words in the keyword list presented in (B), including *and*, *they* and *you*. Names also feature – *Albert* and *Caleb*. Some words that show up indicate topics that are discussed in the smaller sample – *board*, *directors*. An interesting word that warrants further investigation is the New Zealand English pragmatic marker *eh*. It might also be interesting to explore *oh* and the way it is being used. The names and specific topic words would not be so interesting. The function words may not be so interesting either, although given the findings of some of the studies seen in this chapter, for example Kim (2009), Hope and Witmore (2014) and Adolphs et al. (2004), it might be worthwhile to explore how they are being used. For instance, does the speaker use *you* to involve meeting participants more than other speakers from the larger corpus and if so, why?; or, does the use of *you* as a keyword mean the pragmatic marker *you know* has a high frequency? This keyword list was generated for research reported in Vine and Holmes (forthcoming) which explored the use of *eh* and *you know*.

The concordance lines in (C) show *may* is mainly used to soften the listing of side-effects of certain treatments or conditions or to suggest further optional actions that patients could take. Adolphs et al. (2004) interpreted *may* as being used to mark politeness by introducing optionality.

4

Conversation analysis

INTRODUCTION

Conversation Analysis (CA) is the name given to a particular discourse analytical approach which focuses on talk at the micro level, like picking up a magnifying glass to carefully examine the details of a text. In this approach, talk is viewed as organised and orderly, and CA provides systematic ways of identifying and explaining the patterns and structures that "make coherent, mutually comprehensible communication and action possible in interaction" (Drew 2005a: 79). This chapter introduces this approach to discourse analysis. The chapter begins with a brief overview of the origins and development of CA, with Section 4.2 then exploring and illustrating some key concepts in CA. Section 4.3 examines the use of CA to investigate data from institutional settings, while Section 4.4 expands this to consider new mediums of communication.

A difference between CA and many other discourse analysis approaches is that CA only treats contextual factors as relevant if they are oriented to by the participants in an interaction. External contextual factors are not considered unless they are foregrounded in some way in interaction. CA analysts do not focus on how gender, ethnicity, social roles or power affect participants; instead, they focus on *what* is being accomplished and *how* in a specific interaction from moment to moment. Social roles may be important, but to merit consideration they must emerge through the talk.

CA analyses originally focused very much on spoken English data, especially face-to-face personal conversations and telephone calls in particular, and this type of data was the main focus for CA researchers for many years. Telephone calls rely only on speech, and so non-verbal signals are irrelevant, making the analyst's focus more "authentic". More recently, however, there have been a growing number of studies exploring other languages and a broader range of settings. Often these studies compare the patterns found to those found in earlier studies of conversational English. In this chapter I draw on research on different languages and this includes data from a range of types of settings.

Before going further, it is important to note that CA transcripts include a great deal more information than the transcripts presented so far in this book. CA transcription conventions note in detail not just *what* is said but also *how* (see Jefferson 2004), capturing features of intonation, volume, silence and laughter. In the discussion that follows simplified transcription conventions are still used for ease of

DOI: 10.4324/9781003184058-6

reading, but there is often some extra detail noted. This includes information about pauses:

(0.5) pauses timed in tenths of seconds
(.) micro-pause

4.1 THE ORIGINS AND DEVELOPMENT OF CONVERSATION ANALYSIS

CA as an approach began with the work of Harvey Sacks, a sociologist, and was further developed by his colleagues Emanuel Schegloff and Gail Jefferson. Like many new approaches, it arose from a desire to engage with language data in a way that was not possible with other approaches at the time. Sacks was interested in the detail of how social relationships are enacted in everyday conversation and he focused in on talk in a way that had not been done before. In the 1960s and 1970s larger scale research methods were typically employed in sociology, utilising surveys and statistics. Sacks, Schegloff and Jefferson's micro-level approach was thus revolutionary and their paper describing the turn-taking system of ordinary conversation was groundbreaking (Sacks, Schegloff and Jefferson 1974).

Other figures who were influential in the development of CA were Erving Goffman and Harold Garfinkel. Goffman whose concept of "face" was central to the development of Brown and Levinson's theory of politeness (see Chapter 2), also provided inspiration for Sacks. Sacks and Schegloff were students of Goffman and his focus on face-to-face interaction opened up a whole world of possibilities for research for his students. Garfinkel, however, is seen as the major influence on CA, with his re-conceptualisation of social order as "a practical problem of social action" (ten Have 2007: 6), with individual's actions in everyday activities being a primary means by which social order is achieved. He would encourage his students to violate the expected norms in order to better understand them, for example, by bargaining in stores where merchandise is a fixed price (Garfinkel 1967: 69).

Most of the early work in CA focused on **ordinary conversation**, that is, interaction not occurring in specialised settings or in completing particular tasks. The exception to this was telephone calls to a suicide hotline which Sacks had access to as he had worked there in the 1960s. In studying recordings of these calls, he observed the structure in such conversations. Ordinary conversation is often not viewed positively, but it is the practices of this type of talk that are adapted for other contexts, and it can be viewed as the basic form of human interaction. Research applying CA to institutional talk, such as doctor-patient or lawyer-client interaction, began to emerge in the late 1970s and the 1980s with the work of analysts such as J. Maxwell Atkinson and Paul Drew (e.g., Atkinson and Drew 1979), John Heritage (e.g., Heritage 1985) and Steven Clayman (e.g., Clayman 1988).

4.2 WHAT ARE SOME KEY CONCEPTS IN CONVERSATION ANALYSIS?

Key concepts in CA include:

- action and sequence
- turn-taking

- adjacency pairs
- sequence organisation
- preference
- repair

4.2.1 Action and sequence

Central to a CA approach are the notions of **action** and **sequences**. **Action** refers to the things people *do* with words (cf. Austin 1962, see Chapter 2). **Sequences** are "courses of action implemented through talk" (Schegloff 2007: 3). CA therefore focuses on how actions, such as directives or commissives, are realised and recognised in interaction. How are actions evident and what resources are used for constructing action? And how do participants jointly coordinate the construction of social actions as visible in sequentially ordered displays of understanding?

CA argues that the social order is talked into being by social actors as they orient to a social context which is constructed through talk. Social order is both a result of and resource for action/talk. Consequently, interaction is not about people saying something and others passively receiving the message: meaning and social order are co-constructed. If a speaker makes a statement about needing something, for example, only through seeing how the hearer responds and how the interaction unfolds can we tell if the action involved is a directive.

4.2.2 Turn-taking

A central concept in CA is that talk and people's orientation to who has what speaking rights and obligations to say what, to whom and when, talks into being the social order. This construction of the social order is related to **turn-taking**. A feature of the turn-taking in an interaction may be frequent overlapping talk, or people may talk one at a time. Consider (1):

(1) Telephone call (Finnish)

Context: Sepe has called his friend Simppa's home in order to check whether he and his partner can come over for coffee. Simppa is not home. Vera, who has answered the phone, has suggested they come later. Sepe asks her to ring and let them know when Simppa is back.

```
SEPE:   mno //[slowly]: soit:\tele [quickly]: t (.) tännepäin sitte ku:
VERA:          /(vai)\\
        (.)
VERA:   [slowly]: joo:=
SEPE:   =ku se on ö paikalla ni [slowly]: m: (.)
        //me tul\laan
VERA:   /joo:\\
SEPE:   //jeh\
VERA:   /[quickly]: selvä:\\
SEPE:   tehään näin
```

Translation

SEPE: well give us a //call\ here when
VERA: /(or)\\
(.)
VERA: [slowly]: yeah:=
SEPE: =when he's back and //we'll co\me
VERA: /[slowly]: yeah:\\
SEPE: //yeah\
VERA: /okay\\
SEPE: let's do it that way

> Reprinted with permission. From Couper-Kuhlen, Elizabeth and Marja Etelämäki. On divisions of labor in request and offer environments. In: Requesting in Social Interaction, edited by Paul Drew and Elizabeth Couper-Kuhlen, p. 118, © 2014, John Benjamins Publishing.

In this example, Sepe asks Vera to call when Simppa gets home and Vera confirms that she will do this. There is overlapping talk, but it is brief and there is minimal silence between turns. This was seen as a broad rule for how turn-taking works. Through the turn-taking system, participants in an interaction "administer rights" (Heritage 2008: 305) to take turns at talk, and this is often unconscious; interactants only really become aware of the rules when they are violated, such as by disruptive interruptions or when a participant fails to take a turn when one is allocated to them. In CA, the turn-taking system is seen as having moral implications, as well as accounting for the technical aspects of interaction. Each participant in an interaction has the right to be heard and to speak, along with the obligation to listen and to provide appropriate talk and responses as required. If participants do not fulfil these obligations, then communication can break down.

The universality of the turn-taking system seemed to be generally accepted. Stivers et al. (2009) explored a sample of ten languages, showing that all of the languages tested provided "clear evidence for a general avoidance of overlapping talk and a minimization of silence between conversational turns" (Stivers et al. 2009: 10587). However, other research has shown that this may not hold true for all languages and communities. Example (2) presents data from |Gui, an African language, that seems to demonstrate a different pattern.

(2) Informal interaction (|Gui)

Context: Four adult men, CR (about 30 years old), GR (about 45 years old), TM and SK (both about 60 years old) are sitting around a fire. SK, the eldest, and GR have been talking about the physical difference between the Bakgalagadi agro-pastoralists (‡kêbe) and themselves (kúa). Kúa children tend to physically grow more slowly than ‡kêbe children because of child-rearing practices. CR appears to talk about different matters. Recorded in Botswana. Overlaps are in bold in this excerpt.

SK: ǁnâmka ʔaa-si-xo kà yá ǁgǎeǁgàre ǁgǎeǁgàre //[**slowly, prolonged**]: -kx'ai:\
CR: /**Tara-xa -ǁkù ǀqx'are -kx'ai cema**\\

	cì ǁnàwa ʔíǀkàe ǀxòa ǁkǎa-ku cì cía //**kîiǁkà -kaxo**\
SK:	/**yá kxʼawa !kári-xò**\\ kà hana-hana-hana-hana
CR:	káxōre Tara-m̀ ǁkâm
	//**chú ǀnèxo ǀnè ʔee ǁkâsi ǁkâõ-sì-wà kà ǀʔui-sì ǀxòa ǁʔanaha**\
SK:	/**yá ǁkōõ-m̀ǀkui-kéma chú ǁnâmka ǀnàa-ǁgò-mà suai-suai yá cì ǀnàa-ǁgò-mà**\\
	ǀkui-kí-máʔkà ǀnàa-ǁgò-ma suai-suai

Translation

SK: and then you go nowhere staying over there
 //*for a long long long time*\
CR: /*Tara and other boys are very young but*\\
 why! saying they are in the same age as us
 and //*astonish*\ me
SK: /*and the difficult things*\\
 will continue for a long time
CR: namely Tara was living
 //*there with his female affine in that deserted house*\
SK: /*and the parents at once will fill the big stomach*
 fill the big stomach\\ {of the children}
 fill the big stomach swelling it at once

Adapted from Journal of Pragmatics 44, Sugawara, Kazuyoshi,
Interactive significance of simultaneous discourse or overlap in
everyday conversations among |Gui former foragers, pp. 596, 612
© 2012, with permission from Elsevier.

Sugawara (2012: 597) notes that the younger man, CR, had tried to intervene in the talk between SK and GR, but his attempt was ignored. (2) comes after this as CR seems to direct his speech towards TM (who does not speak here). This resulted in prolonged overlapping and the participants were not bothered by this. Based on the analysis, Sugawara proposed a rule for |Gui which contrasts with those provided for English. This is that each participant in an interaction "is disposed to satisfy [their] own desire to speak or to explore [their] memory, sometimes without caring whether [their] words are heard by the others" (2012: 600). This is not perceived as disorderly or chaotic. On the contrary, it allows all participants to satisfy "the most fundamental desire to be a social being endowed with vocal language" (2012: 600).

CA research has noted that a general avoidance of overlapping talk is a feature of many languages, with minimal silence between turns at talk. This is seen as fundamental because it is part of what makes communication coherent and comprehensible. The transition between speakers during conversation and who talks when is also not arbitrary. Through examining a corpus of interactions, Sacks, Schegloff and Jefferson (1974) came up with a set of rules about turn-taking. They proposed that turns are constructed from basic building blocks called **turn constructional units**, which allow the projection of a possible completion point. The moment when the possible completion is detectable to the hearer constitutes a potential **transition-relevance** place. This projectability (and predictability) allows changes in speaker to occur with minimal gaps and overlaps, as in (1).

At the first transition-relevance place, the next turn is assigned according to the following rules:

(a) If the current speaker selects the next speaker, the party so selected has the right and obligation to take the next turn
(b) if the current speaker does not select the next speaker, the next speaker may self-select, and
(c) if (a) and (b) are not followed, the current speaker may continue

(Sacks, Schegloff and Jefferson 1974: 704)

Example (3) demonstrates these rules, as a mother and son take turns at talk.

(3) Family conversation

Context: A mother and son are discussing the son's purchase of textbooks for university. Recorded in New Zealand.

MOTHER: well tell me again about these books
why are they cheaper if you pay cash?
SON: [inhales] um it's just- (0.8)
I don't know- I don't- it must be like (1.1)
you know how they- isn't there a cheque clearance thing now? (0.8)
MOTHER: [tut] only twenty five cents
SON: well e- um I don't know (0.8) perhaps they want cash
cos cash is more easier to handle so
MOTHER: [tut] have they got a cashflow problem dear? (0.9)
SON: possibly (0.7)
MOTHER: who are th- who are these people?

(Source: Wellington Corpus of Spoken New Zealand English)

The mother selects her son to speak, asking him a question. During his answer he pauses for over a second, but his mother does not take a turn here and he eventually continues to try and answer the question. He then selects when his mother will take her next turn, again using a question. After she answers this, he self-selects to continue answering her first question. His mother then self-selects asking him another question, although his response is a little slow here, there being nearly a one second pause as he thinks about his answer before he begins to speak. His mother then self-selects again, asking another question. The turn-taking here involves both self and other selection.

The precise mechanisms of turn-taking may vary between languages given the different resources that languages have. These resources may be syntactic (relating to grammar), prosodic (relating to intonation), pragmatic (relating to meaning in context), or when participants are interacting face-to-face, gaze or gestures may also play a part. For example, the syntactic structure of a language is an important resource that participants in interaction draw on to project the shape of an emerging turn (Schegloff 1987: 71). In English, for instance, the relatively stable word order of Subject-Verb-(Object) means hearers can predict when a turn might end and where they might therefore begin a new turn. In other languages with different word order and varying syntactic resources, turns may be built differently. Tanaka notes that the differences between English and Japanese in terms of syntactic resources "can be expected to have profound ramifications on how participants go about building turns" (2006: 152). This means for example that in Japanese, unlike English, the beginnings of turns do not necessarily project what their shape and type will be (Tanaka 2006: 178).

4.2.3 Adjacency pairs

Related to turn-taking (and specifically to *who* speaks *when*) are adjacency pairs. An **adjacency pair** is an ordered pair of utterances spoken by two different participants in an interaction. Once the first has been spoken, the second is required. For instance, when someone asks a question, it is expected that their addressee will answer the question and thus provide what is known as a conditionally relevant response, that is, a reply that is considered to answer the question. In (1), Sepe requests that Vera lets them know when Simppa gets home. This request for her to ring, as the first part of a request-and-answer adjacency pair, clearly requires a conditionally relevant response. Vera directly agrees to do this; she says *joo* "yeah" firstly part way through Sepe's request and then again at the end. In (3), the mother asked a number of questions which her son attempted to answer, and at one point he also asked her a question which she answered.

Some other types of adjacency pairs are shown in (4) and (5).

(4)   Face-to-face interaction   (Samoan)

Context: An inspection committee has been going around a village meeting dozens of people. The chief of the committee greets a woman.

CHIEF S: tālofa Kelesia!
            (0.2)
KELESIA: tālofa!

Translation

CHIEF S: hello Kelesia!
            (0.2)
KELESIA: hello!

Republished with permission of John Wiley & Sons – Books, from Universal and culture-specific properties of greetings, Alessandro Duranti, Journal of Linguistic Anthropology 7(1), 1997, p. 73; permission conveyed through Copyright Clearance Center, Inc.

(5) Family meal time (Polish)

Context: Dorota, her sister Kasia, her father and nephew are having breakfast.

DOROTA: ten- daj kawalek tego ogóra
KASIA: a proszę

Translation

DOROTA: *this- give me a piece of that gherkin*
KASIA: *here you are*

> Reprinted with permission. From Zinken, Jörg and Deppermann, Arnulf. A cline of visible commitment in the situated design of imperative turns: Evidence from German and Polish. In Imperative turns at talk: The design of directives in action, p. 49, © 2017, John Benjamins Publishing.

In (4) a greeting is followed by a greeting. In (5) Dorota requests that Kasia give her some of the gherkin she has on her plate. Kasia replies positively to this and gives Dorota some of the gherkin. Her response here is both verbal and non-verbal, although she could have just completed the action without a verbal response.

Sometimes there are inserts or embedded adjacency pairs within another pair, called **side sequences** by Jefferson (1972) or **insert expansions** by Schegloff (2007). In (3), the son struggled to answer his mother's first question, and asked her a question which she answered before he continued to try and provide an answer to her first question. In (10), there is an insert between an invitation and its acceptance. Again, the second speaker is seen as having an obligation to provide the second pair part once the first is spoken, even when other talk intervenes.

At other times an additional utterance may seem to belong with the pair, for example if Dorota has said "thank you" to Kasia in (8), so the concept of a **three-part exchange** or an **adjacency triplet** has also been proposed. Adjacency pairs (or triplets) can stand on their own but are often part of larger sequences.

4.2.4 Sequence organisation

Expansion beyond the adjacency pair, brings into focus the way adjacency pairs may feature as part of larger sequences, and the way these sequences are organised. Sequences of utterances are an important focus in CA. Analysts using a CA approach want to answer questions such as:

- how does interaction unfold across a sequence of talk as different participants contribute?
- what evidence is there in the interaction of how the hearer has interpreted an utterance and how does the first speaker respond to this?

Consider (6):

(6) Telephone conversation

Context: Two women are talking on the phone. Robbie has just started teaching at a school where Lesley has taught in the past. Robbie is talking here about one of her new colleagues. Recorded in the UK.

ROBBIE: [slowly]: I: find her I get to the [slowly]: stage:
where [slowly]: I I: come out of staff room
cos I feel like saying to her [inhales] (0.2)
if you don't wanna put anything into teaching
then why don't you get out=
LESLEY: =that's [slowly]: righ//t:\
ROBBIE: /did\\ you f- (.)
di//d you (feel the same)\
LESLEY: /[slowly]: yes: yes she's\\ just ticking over
isn't she=
ROBBIE: =[slowly]: oh: it's ridicu//lous\
LESLEY: /[slowly]: yes:\\

Adapted from Journal of Pragmatics 41, Drew, Paul and Walker, Traci,
Going too far: Complaining, escalating and disaffiliation, p. 2401,
© 2009, with permission from Elsevier.

In (6), Robbie complains in a phone call to Lesley about someone that she is currently working with. Lesley used to work with this person, so knows them. Robbie's indirect complaint is followed by agreement from Lesley, *that's right*, as she aligns with Robbie. Robbie then directly asks Lesley a question, *did you feel the same?*, which she answers, *yes yes she's just ticking over*. Lesley uses a tag question at the end of her turn here, *isn't she?*, eliciting an answer from Robbie.

Robbie's question and the related utterances that precede and follow are all part of a longer sequence within the interaction. Robbie's question had been preceded by her complaining about another teacher, and Lesley had also responded to this with agreement, again aligning with Robbie. Drew and Walker (2009: 2401–2402) comment that these sequences are also part of a larger sequence, in which the two participants have been collaboratively talking and complaining about several of Robbie's colleagues. Sequence organisation captures the fact that when people communicate they produce a series of coherent, orderly and meaningful utterances.

4.2.5 Preference

In (4) and (6), there is what is referred to as a **preferred** response. The preferred response to a greeting is to also provide a greeting. The preferred response to an indirect complaint (from the complainant's point of view) is for the second speaker to agree (show affiliation) and support the first speaker. In (1), Vera agreed to let Sepe know when Simppa returned, the preferred response in this case.

In CA, taking turns at talk is viewed as a way participants cooperate and jointly construct interaction. Breaches become accountable, so **dispreferred** responses are often avoided or mitigated. Examples (7) and (8) show dispreferred responses.

(7) Informal conversation (English and Chinese)

Context: A man offers to get his son to drive a woman home. Recorded in the UK.

A: Manhing drive you home
B: (1.0) ngaw daap basi hoei
A: yiga m ho hoei yan daw (.) ho naan daap basi a
B: [waits for A to call Manhing]

Translation

A: Manhing drive you home
B: (1.0) I'll take a bus
A: don't go now so many people (.) very difficult to get on a bus
B: [waits for A to call Manhing]

Adapted from Journal of Pragmatics 23, Wei, Li and Lesley Milroy, Conversational code-switching in a Chinese community in Britain: A sequential analysis, p. 290, © 1995, with permission from Elsevier.

In (7), A offers to get his son to drive B home. B declines the offer saying she can get the bus and thereby giving a dispreferred response. There is a one-second pause before she gives her response, a frequent indicator that a dispreferred response is coming.

(8) Interaction between a couple in a car

Context: Minna has proposed they go buy a bike and thereby delay grocery shopping. Henrik is hungry and just wants to buy food. Recorded in Finland.

MINNA: we can go to //the\
HENRIK: /[tiredly]: then\\
we'll never get [slowly]: home:
(1.5)
MINNA: so what do you wanna do?
(1.4)
MINNA: you wanna skip the bike because you're hungry?
(1.0)
HENRIK: [exhales] want to skip the bike for food
[slowly]: er: for buying food

Adapted from Journal of Pragmatics 129, Pietikäinen, Kaisa S., Silence that speaks: The local inferences of withholding a response in intercultural couples' conflicts, p. 80, © 2018, with permission from Elsevier.

Henrik's response to Minna's question in (8), *so what you wanna do?*, is to remain silent – a dispreferred response. The preferred response to a question is to directly answer the question, as seen in (1) and (6). Henrik has remained silent though because a direct response saying what he wants to do, will be at odds with what he knows Minna wants to do. Minna then goes on to provide an answer to her own question, *you wanna skip the bike because you're hungry?* Again, there is a pause after she says this before Henrik confirms what he wants to do, which he knows does not align with Minna's wishes.

Preference can relate to a number of aspects of interaction and is therefore a complex concept. In (3), the son struggles to answer his mother's questions and cannot give her the preferred response by directly answering her because he does not know the answers. In (8), Henrik knows that a direct answer will be problematic for him because it will go against Minna's wishes. The form of a preferred response can also vary across cultures. The appropriate response to a compliment, for instance, in some cultures is to graciously accept it, while in others refusing to accept it is preferred.

4.2.6 Repair

Schegloff, Jefferson and Sacks (1977) maintained that it is crucial when people interact that there are systematic ways for repairing troubles in hearing, speaking or understanding since these are intrinsic characteristics of interaction. So, if someone for example says something they know is wrong or mispronounces something, there are ways to correct it. This leads on from the CA principle that there is little point in interacting if participants cannot understand each other. **Repair** is therefore an important aspect of communication and the basic interactional organisation of repair was set out by Schegloff, Jefferson and Sacks (1977). In this paper they make a distinction between repair initiation (indicating there is a problem) and the task of providing the repair solution (fixing the trouble). They further distinguish between who carries out these tasks – whether **self** or **other**.

Self-repair

The first opportunity for repair is within a speaker's ongoing turn and self-initiated same-turn repairs are the most common. Consider (9):

(9) Telephone conversation

Context: Penny is talking to her boyfriend Stan on the phone. She works as a part-time waitress and this is the opening of a story she tells about two of her bosses.

PENNY: [clears throat] [inhales] [tut] right you know [slowly]: um:
[inhales] (0.5)
[slowly]: um: y- you know I've got two bosses
well I've got loads but (.) my main two
like Reanne and Trudie
STAN: [slowly]: yeah: [exhales]=
PENNY: =and Trudie's just like really sort of really sort of
re- horrible and moody and stuff [inhales]

and Reanne's like really nice
but she doesn't do any work right

Adapted from Journal of Pragmatics 47, Jackson, Clare and Jones, Danielle, Well they had a couple of bats to be truthful: Well-prefaced, self-initiated repairs in managing relevant accuracy in interaction, p. 29, © 2013, with permission from Elsevier.

Penny's claim to have two bosses turns out to be inaccurate, and she self-repairs here, adding that she actually has *loads of bosses*, a point which she knows Stan knows. She has modified her claim with a *well*-prefaced repair, replacing *two* with *loads* – *well I've got loads*. She reasserts the relevance of her original claim though by naming two bosses who are her main ones. The core of her original claim is maintained and is treated as being "'essentially correct' for the purposes of the interaction" (Jackson and Jones 2013: 30).

Other-repair

Jefferson (1987) notes that other-correction is rare and often avoided. This is not just because of lack of opportunity, however, but also because of concerns about social rights: self-initiated same-turn repair respects the rights of speakers to own what they say (Heritage 2008). Other-correction impinges on those rights. Its occurrence depends on the type of trouble that has arisen. Consider (10):

(10)   Telephone conversation   (Korean)

Context: Two friends who live in different cities are talking on the phone. Min asks Yoo to come and see him sometime since Yoo has a car.

MIN: ney-ka cha-ka iss-unikka com (.) hanpen wa
YOO: mwe?
MIN: ney-ka cha-ka [slowly]: iss-unikka:
YOO: ung kulay=
MIN: =hanpen o-la-ko
YOO: kulay kulem

Translation

MIN: *since you have a car try and come by some time*
YOO: *what?*
MIN: *[slowly]: since: you have a car*
YOO: *yeah okay=*
MIN: *=come by once {I} said*
YOO: *okay will do*

Adapted from Journal of Pragmatics 87, Hayashi, Makoto and Kim, Stephanie Hyeri, Turn formats for other-initiated repair and their relation to trouble sources: Some observations from Japanese and Korean conversations, p. 201, © 2015, with permission from Elsevier.

In (10), Yoo responds to Min's invitation to visit him with *mwe?* "what?". In response to this, Min repeats his invitation, showing that he has treated Yoo as having indicated a problem of hearing. In his repair Min also adds the quotative particle *ko*, which indicates that the utterance has been said earlier and is being repeated. Min has treated *mwe?* as a repair initiator which does not specify a particular part of the trouble-source unit as problematic. Here, *mwe?* initiates an insert expansion (Schegloff 2007), which serves to resolve trouble so that a larger course of action, an invitation-acceptance sequence, can be completed.

There is a complex relationship between turn design used for repair and the type of trouble being addressed; repairs may be made for a range of reasons. And again, as noted in regard to turn-taking, the syntactic resources in different languages also influence how turns are built when repair is needed. Research has demonstrated that repair harnesses the grammatical resources of languages, as well as the prosodic and pragmatic resources that are available (see Kitzinger 2013).

4.2.7 Summary

Key concepts in CA include **action and sequence, turn-taking, adjacency pairs, sequence organisation, preference** and **repair**. These features of talk all involve close examination of texts. Because discourse is viewed as organised and orderly in CA, researchers have explored patterns in the way each of these aspects are utilised by speakers. Initially research focused on English and mainly on informal conversation and telephone calls, but the applicability of rules across different languages has also been explored. This includes the ways the different resources available in different languages influence the precise realisation of these rules.

Because CA allows close examination of discourse, this approach enables researchers to identify how speakers draw on a whole range of resources to effectively communicate. The preceding examples have only illustrated a few of these, such as the strategic use of silence to manage questions which are difficult to answer because someone does not know the answer (as in (3)) or because they know their response is not what the person who asked the question wants to hear, as in (8).

4.3 BEYOND "CONVERSATION": INSTITUTIONAL SETTINGS

The examples presented so far in this chapter have been from conversational data, that is, they have not involved people interacting in institutional settings. Conversational data has been a major focus of CA research, with studies examining conversation between family and friends, both face-to-face and via telephone. As noted earlier, most of the early work in CA focused on **ordinary conversation**, that is, interaction not occurring in specialised settings or in completing particular tasks.

CA has expanded however, to explore **institutional talk**. This includes medical, legal and media discourse. These settings involve language use which is different from ordinary conversation in a number of ways:

(i) the goals of the participants are more limited and are specific to the institution

(ii) there are restrictions on the nature of contributions that participants can make, and

(iii) there are often institution and activity specific inferential frameworks at play

(Drew and Heritage 1992)

4.3.1 Medical settings

CA investigations of medical discourse began at a time when researchers were wanting to explore how ordinary talk is adapted in specialised settings and how participants orient to the role of either medical expert or patient. Initial interest was in physician-patient interactions but has expanded to include a whole range of medical contexts, from psychotherapy consultations to home-care visits to medical training simulations.

The general organisational features of consultations have been identified, such as the progression of the different activity phases within the interaction. Recurrent features of medical consultations include the medical history phase and the problem presentation phase, both involving question-answer sequences. The construction of turns of talk within these sequences has also been explored, for example, how questions are asked and responded to. The power asymmetry between the doctor and patient is seen to emerge through the interaction. Example (11) shows a sequence from a doctor-patient consultation.

(11) Doctor-patient consultation

Context: Opening sequence in a doctor consultation. Recorded in the US.

DOCTOR:	[inhales] [slowly]: a:lrighty (.) mm well they were talking (0.2) the nurses told me a little bit about //your (.)\ [slowly]: pro:blem
PATIENT:	/yeah\\
	(.)
DOCTOR:	[inhales] doesn't sound like fun
PATIENT:	[slowly]: no:
DOCTOR:	[inhales] (d-) is this something you had [slowly]: before:? //or is\ it brand new //problem\
PATIENT:	/no\\ /just [slowly]: some:\\thing [slowly]: new:
DOCTOR:	[softly]: hm: (0.2) mm [tut] [inhales] tell me a little more about it they wrote down //a couple of\ notes but er
PATIENT:	/n- kay\\
PATIENT:	[slowly]: well: (.) it started like Wednesday I started like f- feeling a pull in my [slowly]: neck:
DOCTOR:	mm hm

Adapted from The structure of patients' presenting concerns:
Physicians' opening questions, Heritage, John and Jeffrey D. Robinson,
Health Communication 19(2), p. 90, 2006, reprinted by permission of
the publisher (Taylor & Francis Ltd, www.tandfonline.com).

In the study which (11) is drawn from, Heritage and Robinson (2006) explore how the form of physicians' initiating questions affect the way patients present the problem. In the US, where this example was recorded, patients are generally seen by nurses or medical assistants before meeting with a doctor. In these preliminary interactions, information is collected about why the patient needs to see a doctor. This information is normally then provided to physicians prior to their consultations with patients. This complicates the process of problem solicitation as physicians must decide how much of that knowledge to display. Patients must also decide how much repetition is appropriate. In (11), the physician manages this by setting out what they know, indicating that the nurses have given them some information from the pre-consultation interaction. The doctor then asks if this is a new problem, before asking the patient to *tell me a little bit more about it*. Heritage and Robinson (2006: 90) note that the physician's question here encourages the patient to repeat possibly known "news", relieving any concern about this.

4.3.2 Legal settings

Legal discourse is another area which has been the focus of CA research. This includes courtroom data and police interviews. The courtroom is a context where participants are concerned with establishing such matters as what has happened, the seriousness of some offence and who did it. Also important in this situation are the constraints that exist around interaction, such as who can ask questions and what kind of answers are allowed. This can vary between different countries and different judicial systems. In the Netherlands, for instance, judges typically examine suspects, and this is an important part of trials (Komter 1998). When they do this, they refer to the case file provided by the prosecution. Example (12) comes from the section of a trial where this is happening.

(12) Courtroom interaction (translated from Dutch)

Context: Trial of a suspect accused of theft. Recorded in the Netherlands.

JUDGE:	what do you think of that accusation?
SUSPECT:	er yes what do I think of that accusation?
	but he himself also knew that //it was a joke\
JUDGE:	/can you try\\ and speak up a little?
SUSPECT:	he himself also knew that it was a joke
	and he got it back
	we were just fooling around
JUDGE:	yes
SUSPECT:	it is not so that we have stolen it
JUDGE:	yes so you say it is right that I've done that
	and you've also- on page twenty in the case file
	you also say right that you did it
	only you said like

	[slowly]: yeah: it was not a robbery
	it was just foolishness
SUSPECT:	*(yes)*
JUDGE:	*well he got it back I read that too*
	[slowly]: um: but yes
	he apparently did not think it was foolishness
	for he did file a complaint
	(5)
JUDGE:	*right?*
SUSPECT:	*yes you could see it like that*

Adapted and reprinted under STM guidelines from Komter,
Martha. 2012. The career of a suspect's statement:
Talk, text, context. Discourse Studies 14, p. 743.

Komter (2012: 743) notes that judges often begin their examinations by asking suspects what they think of the accusation, or whether they agree with it, and here the judge does this, asking for the suspect's perspective on the accusation. The suspect answers, asserting that it was just a joke, that the victim knew this and got his money back and so therefore they had not stolen the money. He downplays his actions and denies the charges against him. The judge then reads from the summary of the police interview, quoting the suspect and thereby contradicting what has just been said, since on the earlier occasion the suspect admitted taking the money.

Another legal setting which has received a great deal of attention is police interviews of suspects. In fact, in the study (12) comes from, Komter (2012) tracks the process from the police interview to the written statement to the use of this statement in court. The judge's way of questioning the suspect is different from the suspect's interrogation by the police: in the police interview the focus is on what the suspect did when the alleged crime took place, but in the judge's questioning, although this aspect is important, so is "what the suspect *said he did* to the police" (Komter 2012: 744).

A range of aspects of police interviews have been explored, including the way police question suspects. In (13), the police ask several questions.

(13) Police interview   (Serbo-Croatian)

Context: Detectives are questioning a factory mechanic who is a suspect in a case involving a theft from a factory. The detectives are asking about the suspect's brother who also worked at the factory but considered quitting his job after the theft. The detectives are suspicious about this. Recorded in Montenegro.

DETECTIVE 1:	pa [quickly]: je li tebe nešto tu glupo
	da on sad odjednom oće da napušti: [slowly]: posa:
	//[quickly]: posle: ovog?\
DETECTIVE 2:	/a zbog ćega\\ je? (.) koji mu je razlog
	(0.9)
SUSPECT:	ne [exhales] [slowly]: snam: bogomi (0.1)
	pitajte njega (1.5)

	//[quickly]: šta ć- šta: [slowly]: ja znam:? [softly]: (čuš):\
	/[background noise]\\
	(0.3)
DETECTIVE 1:	kako mu ti ka <u>brat ne</u> rečeš <u>šta</u> //đešnapu(šta)\
SUSPECT:	/a i\\ <u>viko</u> sam
	[quickly]: bogomi:

Translation

DETECTIVE 1:	well [quickly]: is it somewhat stupid to you in there that he now suddenly wants to quit his: [slowly]: job: //[quickly]: after: this?\
DETECTIVE 2:	/and why\\ is it? (.) what <u>is his reason</u>?
	(0.9)
SUSPECT:	I don't [exhales] [slowly]: know: by God (0.1) ask him (1.5)
	//[quickly]: what w- what: [slowly]: do I know? [softly]: (listen to this):\
	/[background noise]\\
	(0.3)
DETECTIVE 1:	how come you as a <u>brother do not</u> tell him //not to quit\
SUSPECT:	/and\\ {I} <u>did</u> tell him [quickly]: by God:

Adapted from Journal of Pragmatics 105, Cerović, Marijana, When suspects ask questions: Rhetorical questions as a challenging device, p. 28–29, © 2016, with permission from Elsevier.

Detective 1 constructs his inquiry about the suspect's brother quitting his job as a positive yes-no question (with a preference for a *yes* answer) and embeds this in a question about whether the suspect thinks this is stupid. He implies that there must be a reason behind the suspect's brother's sudden decision to quit and that it might somehow be theft-related as its timing coincides with the time of the theft. The detective is here inviting the suspect to agree with what is implied. There is no space for the suspect to speak however as Detective 2 comes in, overlapping and producing two wh- interrogatives *a zbog čega je? koji mu je razlog?* "and why is it? what is his reason?" aligning with Detective 1's request for agreement; they indicate the suspect should know why his brother wants to quit his job, and invite him to elaborate on his brother's reasons for quitting.

The delay of 0.9 seconds following these questions indicates the suspect's reluctance to answer the detectives' questions, possibly because answering them might incriminate his brother. He then denies having any knowledge of why his brother wants to quit, which is then followed by the colloquial *bogomi* "by God" which he uses to vouch for his truthfulness. Neither of the detectives comes in to take over the turn – there is a one and a half second pause during which any of the participants could have started speaking. The suspect then reformulates his denial as a question *šta ja znam* "what do I know?". Detective 1 then asks another question which challenges the suspect in his role as a brother, implying that the suspect's brotherly duty is to advise his brother not to quit his job.

4.3.3 Media settings

Another type of institutional talk investigated by CA researchers is the broadcast news interview. Again, this is a more formal context for communication than everyday conversation and there are more restrictions on turn-taking. An important feature of news interviews is the fact that they are being conducted for an audience; their purpose is to provide information, opinions and perspectives on a range of issues of interest to the public.

Aspects of news interviews that have been investigated by CA researchers include the turn-taking system, how participants orient to the audience, and question and answer design. Example (14) demonstrates the way interviewers set agendas with their questions, both topically and in terms of the action that is called for in the interviewee's response (Clayman 2013: 641).

(14) News interview

Context: Interview with then British Prime Minister Edward Heath. The interviewer asks him if he likes the leader of the opposition, Harold Wilson. Recorded in the UK.

INTERVIEWER:	do you quite [slowly]: like: him?
	(0.1)
EDWARD HEATH:	[inhales] [slowly]: well: I th- I think in politics you [slowly]: see: i- it's not a question of going about (.) [slowly]: liking: people or not [exhales]
	it's a question of dealing with people [exhales] [inhales]
	[slowly]: and er: (.) I've always been able to deal perfectly well with Mister Wilson as [slowly]: indeed: er- he has with me
	(0.4)
INTERVIEWER:	[slowly]: but do you like: him?
	(0.1)
EDWARD HEATH:	[inhales] well again it's not a question of er (.)
	[slowly]: likes or dislikes
	it's: a question of [slowly]: working together:
	with other people who are in politics
	(0.6)
INTERVIEWER:	but do you like him?
	(0.4)
EDWARD HEATH:	[inhales] (.) that'll have to remain to be [slowly]: seen: won't it

Republished with permission of John Wiley & Sons – Books, from Conversation Analysis in the news interview, Steven E. Clayman. In Jack Sidnell and Tanya Stivers (eds.) The Handbook of Conversation Analysis, 2013, p. 641; permission conveyed through Copyright Clearance Center, Inc.

The interviewer asks here if Edward Heath likes Harold Wilson, setting the topic, and in being a yes-no question it is designed to solicit a particular response, either *yes* or *no*. Edward Heath does not provide a preferred response, however, instead talking about how in politics it is not about liking people but *dealing with people* and that he thinks he and Harold Wilson deal with each other *perfectly well*. Because he does not provide a preferred response the interviewer repeats the question twice, pressing Edward Heath for a response that directly answers the question in a preferred way, but Edward Heath continues to evade a direct response (a strategy stereotypically associated with politicians).

4.3.4 Summary

CA studies undertaken on interaction in institutional settings have shown that features of everyday conversation are utilised in different contexts, but adapted to accomplish particular tasks and to address the specific dilemmas that arise in those contexts. The joint accomplishment of actions and activities has also been discussed, with research demonstrating how all participants in an interaction are involved in producing the characteristic features of talk in each specific context. This includes medical, legal and media discourse, as illustrated earlier, but other types of institutional talk have also been explored, such as business meetings (see e.g., Clifton 2017; Svennevig and Djordjilovic 2015) and talk in educational settings (see e.g., Mehan 1979; Seedhouse 2004).

4.4 NEW MEDIUMS OF COMMUNICATION

Another way that CA research has expanded is by considering communication using new types of mediums, such as mobile text chatting and online communication mediums. Collister (2011), for instance, extends examination of repair to an online community, that of *World of Warcraft* players. This involves text chatting and she explores the use of the asterisk as a repair marker. The asterisk is used to repair a typographical error (typo) in a previous line of chat. When a player makes a typo in chat, the next message sent by this player may contain an asterisk and the corrected version of the error, as in (15).

(15) Online text chat

Context: A player indicates their action in an online role-playing game

11/27 21:14:52.750 [Party] Aniko: when i run ot
11/27 21:14:54.765 [Party] Aniko: out*

Adapted from Journal of Pragmatics 43, Collister, Lauren Brittany, *-repair in online discourse, p. 919, © 2011, with permission from Elsevier.

The player, Aniko, mistypes *out* as *ot*. Immediately following this, Aniko types *out**, with the asterisk indicating that this is a repair. In (15), the asterisk is used following the corrected version of the error, although the asterisk can also occur before the correction.

In other research, König (2019) explored the use of laugh particles in data from WhatsApp chats on mobile phones, see (16).

(16) WhatsApp chat   (German)

Context: Sophie posts a hint in a mobile group chat that a local drug store (called "dm") is offering a 20% discount.

SOPHIE: Falls noch jemand was von dm braucht – Jana hat gerade geschrieben bei dem auf der münchner straße gibt es heute auf alles 20% ☺
LENA: Da wollte ich gerade hin Haha wie witzig :;
SOPHIE: ☺

Translation

SOPHIE: *In case anyone should need anything from dm – Jana just wrote the store on münchner straße has a 20% discount off everything today* ☺
LENA: *I was just about to go there Haha how funny :;*
SOPHIE: ☺

Adapted from Journal of Pragmatics 142, König, Katharina, Stance taking with laugh particles and emojis – sequential and functional patterns of "laughter" in a corpus of German WhatsApp chats, p. 162, © 2019, with permission from Elsevier.

Sophie's first post informs the group about the discount. In her reply, Lena first comments on her plans to go to the drug store before she inserts a laugh particle, *Haha*. She then comments on the laughable with her following *wie witzig :;* "how funny ;:". The use of the laugh particle at this precise point relates to the fact that Lena was just about to go there herself, information she has just provided. The laugh particle refers to some element in the preceding discourse, and this is the place where the participants in this group used laugh particles, whether right after a **laughable** posted by themselves or by someone else. Lena's humorous stance is taken up in Sophie's next post with the laughter-indexical emoji ("grinning face" ☺).

The utilisation of laugh particles in this way, demonstrates the development of a practice to accommodate a new way of communicating that differs from spoken interaction. Users tend to deploy laugh particles as responsive rather than as projective tokens, commenting on something which has already been introduced. In conversation too, the varied production and placement of laughter has been found to reveal a great deal about its meaning and use (Glenn 2003; Holt 2013). Laughter plays a highly significant role in how people enact, respond to, and manage identities and relationships and as such is a powerful device to adapt and utilise in new mediums of communication.

In sum, as with CA studies which have shown how features of everyday conversation are utilised in institutional settings, research is now demonstrating how features are being adapted to accomplish particular tasks and to address the specific dilemmas that arise in new mediums of communication. The joint accomplishment of actions and activities is once again evident, as research demonstrates how participants are involved in producing the characteristic features of talk in each specific context.

CHAPTER SUMMARY

CA argues that the social order is talked into being by social actors as they orient to a social context. Interaction is not about people saying something and others passively receiving the message: meaning, and social order, are co-constructed. In this approach, the rights and obligations of participants in an interaction are also crucial; and people are accountable for the way that they participate and interact with others.

CA is an approach that was developed within sociology, from a desire to explore the role of language in enacting social relationships. Ordinary conversation was the primary focus of early studies, with identification of patterns a key concern. Conversation was regarded at the time as chaotic, so the finding that it was orderly and governed by rules was groundbreaking. CA research has generated numerous insights into the organisation of language, action and interaction in a range of different settings and in different types of talk. CA views language as a system and therefore it is important for researchers following this approach to identify patterns, whether in the way turn-taking is designed, or in how sequences unfold, or in the use of repair markers.

Some finer details of interaction which have been focused on across a variety of settings include:

- how speaker turns are managed
- how preference is managed, and
- how speakers and hearers manage repair

The great attention to detail that CA encourages has deepened our understanding of the complexity of speech and communication. Features such as hesitations and false starts have been demonstrated to be a natural and normal aspect of speech, and the important role of intonation, volume and factors such as silence and laughter have been highlighted.

Conversational data and telephone calls were the main focus of CA research in the early days, but this approach soon expanded to include data from institutional settings. As noted in section 4.3, key institutional settings explored include medical, legal and media. Some of the key findings of CA research relate to the way language is used in these different settings, and how ordinary talk is adapted to specialised settings. For instance, questions from doctors to patients in consultations tend to be worded differently and have different goals when compared to those that lawyers use when questioning defendants and witnesses in court. In both situations, however, questions play a crucial role in the achievement of the transactional goals of the workplace. Current research also demonstrates how features of conversation are being adapted to new mediums of communication, such as texting and online communication.

FURTHER READING

On the development of CA, see ten Have (2007: 5–9), Maynard (2013) and Clift (2016: 36–39). Douglas Maynard's chapter comes from *The Handbook of Conversation Analysis* edited by Jack Sidnell and Tanya Stivers (2013), which is a brilliant resource for anyone interested in finding out more about CA. The four volume series on CA edited by Paul Drew and John Heritage (Drew and Heritage 2006) is also a great resource. For a shorter treatment see Rebecca Clift's excellent book, *Conversation Analysis* (Clift 2016), which provides many examples from important studies using CA.

For anyone interested in exploring the work of early CA researchers, Gene Lerner's book (2004) *Conversation Analysis: Studies from the First Generation*, provides a compilation of contributions from Sacks, Schegloff, Jefferson and others who were at the forefront of the development of CA. Paul ten Have's (2007) *Doing Conversation Analysis: A Practical Guide*, is a really useful book for anyone wanting to try out CA for the first time.

EXERCISES

These exercises present three short samples of authentic data for you to analyse while considering the concepts discussed earlier. There are notes at the end for feedback and guidance. Consider each discourse sample and answer the questions.

1. Discuss the following features of interaction in (A):

   a. adjacency pairs

   b. turn-taking

(A) Job interview (Dutch)

Context: An applicant is having an interview for a job as a subway driver. The interviewer has sketched a hypothetical situation: it is a normal working day and suddenly a woman collapses on a platform. The interviewer then asks the applicant what he would do if this happened.

INTERVIEWER:	wat zou jij doen?
APPLICANT:	nou een vrouw in er mekaar gezakt
	en er (1.5)
	ik weet niet of [slowly]: je: direct er (.) een ambulance (.) kan bellen?
INTERVIEWER:	[quieter]: ja:
APPLICANT:	de GGD? [Gemeentelijke GezondheidsDienst]
INTERVIEWER:	bijvoorbeeld maar dat mens kan ook natuurlijk alleen maar gestruikeld zijn
APPLICANT:	ja (2.0) (nou) ja (1.3)
	[quicker]: nou: ik zou eerst er gaan kijken natuurlijk er (1.7)
	wat er aan de hand is er precies (1.0)

Translation

INTERVIEWER:	what would you do?
APPLICANT:	well a woman er collapsed

	and er (1.5)
	I do not know whether [slowly]: you: immediately (.)
	are able to call er (.) an ambulance?
INTERVIEWER:	[quieter]: yes:
APPLICANT:	the GGD? [Municipal Health Authority]
INTERVIEWER:	for example but that person of course might just have stumbled
APPLICANT:	yes (2.0) (well) yes (1.3)
	[quicker]: well: first I would er go have a look of course er (1.7)
	to see what's going on er exactly (1.0)

> Adapted from Journal of Pragmatics 105, Sliedrecht, Keun Young, van der Houwen, Fleur, and Schasfoort, Marca, Challenging formulations in police interrogations and job interviews: A comparative study, pp. 122–123, © 2016, with permission from Elsevier.

2. What observations can you make about preference in sample (B)?

(B) Family interaction

Context: Sisters talking as they play. Anna is five years old and Katy is three years old. They are playing "school".

ANNA:	Katy? so Katy? it's alr – my picture's [slowly]: nearly: done
	soon we can go to [slowly]: school: . . .
KATY:	and take balls cos it's a football class
ANNA:	no (.) not football [slowly]: class: Katy
KATY:	I want to take a [slowly]: ball:
ANNA:	Katy [faster]: you're not allowed to: else the teachers will tell you off
	(0.5) they'll throw it in the dustbin

> Adapted and reprinted under STM guidelines from Discourse Studies 20(3), Friedland, Joanna and Merle Mahon. 2018. "Sister talk: Investigating an older sibling's responses to verbal challenges", p. 345.

3. Discuss aspects of repair as evident in (C)?

(C) Email

Context: email from a closed discussion group

For the central Europeans it is perfectly normal that their mother stayed at home until they went to school, when we in Finland are used to the fact that both of the parents work, basically from the day we are born (well, not exactly but you know what I mean).

> Adapted from Journal of Pragmatics 40, Tanskanen, Sanna-Kaisa, and Karhukorpi, Johanna, Concessive repair and the negotiation of affiliation in e-mail discourse, p. 1592, © 2008, with permission from Elsevier.

4. Are there any features of (A) and (C) that you think indicate adaption of rules of conversation to specialised and new settings?

NOTES ON EXERCISES

The sample in (A) begins with a question-response adjacency pair. In trying to answer the question, the applicant in (A) appeals to the interviewer, an appeal which requires an answer, before he can provide a full second part for the first adjacency pair. The interviewer replies and the applicant then makes a further query. In answering this the interviewer hedges. The whole sequence evolves from the initial question. After the insert sequences, the applicant begins to give a fuller response to the first question. Because of the questions and appeals in this sample, the floor passes back and forth between the two participants, with each selecting the other to speak in turn at different points. There is no overlapping speech shown. There are several longish pauses in the applicant's speech as he thinks about what to say.

There are a number of dispreferred responses in (B). Katy has asserted that they will take balls when they play schools. Anna however challenges this. The preferred response would be to go along with Katy's proposal. Katy then asserts what she wants to do, not accepting Anna's challenge, so this is another dispreferred response. In response to this, Katy again presses her point (a further dispreferred response).

In (C), the writer modifies her statement in a self-initiated same turn repair. The writer has made an overstatement and repairs this; this type of repair has been referred to as a **concessive repair** (Couper-Kuhlen and Thompson 2005). Her repair is a *well*-prefaced repair, as Penny's was earlier in (9).

One way there is evidence of adaption to the specific context in (A) is the long pauses. The interviewer allows the applicant to think about how he would respond and does not start talking in the pauses. In (C), the writer uses brackets to encase the part of her turn that involves her repair and prefaces it with *well* (which is often used in speech).

5

Interactional sociolinguistics

INTRODUCTION

Interactional Sociolinguistics is a discourse analysis approach which looks closely at authentic interactional data, while also considering wider contextual factors in interpreting what is going on. Its broader aims are to investigate the interaction between linguistic and cultural diversity.

The focus of Interactional Sociolinguistics is interactional data, that is, data such as job interviews, conversations between family and friends, or workplace meetings. Ethnographic observations are used to provide contextual information and analysis may also be informed by interviews. This can involve asking participants about their interactions to gain insights which may uncover different perspectives that enrich the analysis.

This chapter introduces this approach to discourse analysis. The chapter begins with a brief overview of the origins and development of Interactional Sociolinguistics, with Section 5.2 then exploring and illustrating some key concepts. Section 5.3 examines some key topics that have been researched using an Interactional Sociolinguistics approach and concepts.

5.1 THE ORIGINS AND DEVELOPMENT OF INTERACTIONAL SOCIOLINGUISTICS

The key concepts and methods of Interactional Sociolinguistics were introduced by John Gumperz, an anthropological linguist. With Dell Hymes, he developed what was at the time a new way of looking at sociolinguistics (see Chapter 2). Gumperz built on Hymes' work by examining power differences between people from different speech communities. In particular, he noted that the *standard* form of any given language, that is, the form that is expected in formal situations, is typically the dialect of the people who have the most power. Two topics that were central in Gumperz' work were intercultural communication in institutional settings (see e.g., Gumperz 2015) and code-switching (see e.g., Gumperz and Cook-Gumperz 2005).

Interactional Sociolinguistics has been applied and further developed by a number of scholars around the world, providing important insights into communication in a range of settings. Inspired by Gumperz' work, three main streams of Interactional Sociolinguistics have emerged centred in three different geographic locations, although other researchers are also working in other places around the world.

DOI: 10.4324/9781003184058-7

Interactional sociolinguistics

Firstly, based in the UK, are Celia Roberts and her colleagues. Roberts had worked with Gumperz. A key topic in her research has been issues related to ethnicity and the disadvantages that people from linguistic and ethnic minorities face when interacting with institutional representatives. This includes interaction in health settings (see e.g., Roberts and Sarangi 2005), and institutional selection processes (e.g., job interviews), and their potential for indirect discrimination (see e.g., Roberts 2011, 2013).

Secondly, based in the US, key important figures in Interactional Sociolinguistics are Deborah Tannen and her students. Tannen had been a student of Gumperz. The focus for this group has been interaction in a range of contexts, from conversation between family and friends (e.g., Tannen, Kendall and Gordon 2007; Tannen 2007, 2014) to workplace interactions (e.g., Yamada 1992; Tannen 1994b). A major issue of interest for Tannen has been gender differences in language use and she has explored communication in different kinds of family relationships, from siblings interacting (Tannen 2010) to mothers and daughters (Tannen 2014), as well as interaction between friends (Tannen 2013) and colleagues (Tannen 2000).

The third stream of Interactional Sociolinguistics is centred in New Zealand with Janet Holmes and her colleagues. Their version of Interactional Sociolinguistics has been developed through the long-running Wellington Language in the Workplace Project (see www.wgtn.ac.nz/lwp). They have explored a range of aspects of workplace interaction, from small talk, humour, narratives and directives (e.g., Holmes and Stubbe 2015) to issues of power, leadership (Marra, Holmes and Vine 2019), gender (e.g., Holmes 2006), and ethnic and cultural identity (e.g., Holmes, Marra and Vine 2011; Vine, Holmes and Marra fc).

All these groups focus on linguistic and social diversity in interaction, although each is operating in a different cultural context, and each has specific interests and issues that they explore. The distinctive qualities of Interactional Sociolinguistics are the focus on diversity within interaction, exploration of inference and contextualisation, along with an interest in social outcomes rather than just social order (Auer and Roberts 2011). Interactional Sociolinguistics research often explores intercultural interactions or other situations where individuals may have differing norms and expectations.

5.2 WHAT ARE SOME KEY CONCEPTS IN INTERACTIONAL SOCIOLINGUISTICS?

Two key concepts of an Interactional Sociolinguistics approach are:

- contextualisation cues and
- conversational inference

Other concepts that have helped in exploring these aspects include:

- framing
- norms and conversational style
- indexicality and stance

5.2.1 Contextualisation cues

Contextualisation cues are features which indicate how speakers intend their utterances to be interpreted, and which listeners use to interpret meaning. These cues are culturally specific and usually unconscious.

Features at a number of levels can act as contextualisation cues, including:

- dialect and style
- vocabulary and syntax
- prosody and non-verbal behaviours (Gumperz 1982: 131)

Consider (1):

(1)   Dinner conversation   (German)

Context: Five friends are having dinner. Hanna has mentioned a Turkish friend of hers, Len, who is also friends with Urs. Urs has then related how Len has received a prize for being a model citizen from the mayor. Urs then imagines what the mayor was thinking when handing out the award.

URS: natürlich sein dorfschultes [laughs] in [laughs]: Bergendorf: hat gedacht u-
       Türke Len der sich gegen Ausländerfeindlichkeit engagiert
       Len und gleichzeitig en Häusle //baut\
GERD: /[laughs]\\
URS: //der sich anpasst\ und gleichzeitig gegen diskriminierung
GERD: /[laughs]\\
URS: //des isch doch ideal\\
KLARA: /[slowly]: au nein:\\
URS: [flüsternd]: und der schafft wie en brunnebutzer
       hot no a gschäft und goht no in d schicht zum:

Translation

URS: *of course his mayor [laughs] in [laughs]: Bergendorf: thought ah a Turk Len
       who is committed to fighting the discrimination of foreigners
       Len and at the same time builds a little //house*
GERD: */[laughs]*
URS: *//who conforms\ to German life and at the same time is against discrimination*
GERD: */[laughs]*
URS: *//this is just ideal*
KLARA: */[slowly]: oh no:*
URS: *[whispery voice]: and he works like a dog
       has his own business and does shift work:*

Adapted from Günthner, Susanne, "Interactional sociolinguistics"; In: Gerd Antos, Eija Ventola and Tilo Weber (eds.) Handbook of Interpersonal Communication, Berlin: De Gruyter, 2008 p. 57–58, transcript (1). Used with permission of De Gruyter.

In (1), Urs starts to reconstruct the mayor's inner monologue by announcing *natürlich sein dorfschultes in Bergendorf hat gedacht* "of course his mayor in Bergendorf thought". He uses an antiquated term *dorfschultes* for the village mayor and laughs throughout this announcement. The use of a specific lexical item, *dorfschultes*, and laughter are contextualisation cues indicating that he is being humorous and satirical, making fun of the mayor. Using direct reported speech, he then creates an imagined world of thought, and does this while switching to a dialect variety (Swabian). This switch in dialect is another contextualisation cue which animates "the quoted dorfschultes" and stylises him as "rather naive and provincial" (Günthner 2008: 59). This is supported by the "cliché-like" thoughts attributed to him; he highly values a Turkish citizen who fights against discrimination and who meets the Swabian ideal of building their own home and working hard.

In (2), non-verbal aspects act as contextualisation cues.

(2) Research group meeting

Context: A microbiology research group at a US university are involved in troubleshooting around their lab experiments. Jihun, a South Korean postdoctoral researcher, is presenting his results to the group. Nick is an Anglo-American and is the primary investigator who runs the research project and the lab.

NICK:	so you're seeing these three bands
	[pointing at image on screen with right hand]
	come up
	[moves pointing finger up and down]
	( ) or four bands
	[moves pointing finger up and down]
	//right\ here
JIHUN:	/yeah\\
NICK:	and those two line up?
	[points at two objects, turns to Jihun]
JIHUN:	I can actually show you
	[reaches to keyboard]
NICK:	[retracts pointing gesture]
JIHUN:	some because
	[looks at screen and searches through files and then opens PowerPoint] (8)
ALL:	[fixate eye gaze on screen until the end of the excerpt]
NICK:	[slowly]: um: (19)
JIHUN:	and this is cesa antibody
	[points at corresponding image with cursor]
	and this is histidine antibody
	[points at corresponding image with cursor] ++

> Adapted from Kimura, Daisuke and Suresh Canagarajah, Embodied semiotic resources in research group meetings: How language competence is framed. Journal of Sociolinguistics 24, 2020, pp. 649–650. With permission of the publisher (John Wiley & Sons).

At the beginning of (2), Nick asks Jihun to clarify what he is seeing in the images. Accompanying his utterances are gestures directed at elements on the screen which act as contextualisation cues, helping him convey his meaning. As he asks Jihun *and those two line up?*, he turns his head to Jihun making it clear that he is addressing Jihun. Kimura and Canagarajah (2020: 651) suggest that this shift in gaze also possibly indicates that he is expecting "a more elaborate response than a minimal token yeah". As Jihun starts to look through his files, Nick stops pointing, marking a shift in activity. Jihun has said *I can actually show you*, and his physical activity and gaze after this serve as contextualisation cues for Nick about his response and decision to take the turn, although it is not a verbal response at this point as he looks for a file with the results which can help answer Nick's question.

5.2.2 Conversational inference

Conversational inference is the context-bound process of interpretation that listeners use to understand what speakers *mean* by what they *say* and *do*. Each participant in an interaction draws upon a set of culturally shaped **contextualisation conventions** to signal and interpret meanings. Conventions involve contextualisation cues, so they too include features at a number of levels:

- dialect and style (and language choice)
- vocabulary and syntax, and
- prosody and non-verbal behaviours

Urs and his friends in (1) share the same conventions and easily interpret the meaning of his utterances. In (2), Nick uses gestures to help signal what he is meaning to Jihun and vice versa. Jihun does not share the same first language and Kimura and Canagarajah (2020: 645) note that he had limited proficiency in English. Conventions at a number of levels are not therefore shared. The group have developed non-verbal conventions, however, and along with the clear understanding that all participants share about the goals of the group and the meeting, they are able to effectively communicate.

In (3), the children share the same set of conventions, which in this case includes the use of two languages, Spanish and English.

(3) Classroom interaction among children (English and Spanish)

Context: Three students, Emmanuel, Davina and Jorge, are busy with a story unit, while Sonia, having finished, is now doing her weaving. Just prior to this excerpt, Emmanuel had asked Davina a question about their schoolwork and Sonia had interjected. Since no one responds to her, Sonia taps Emmanuel on the arm and repeats her statement.

SONIA: [inhales] [taps Emmanuel on the arm] lo acabé ["*I finished it*"]
[Sonia holds weaving up]
. . . just kidding . . .

EMMANUEL:	[slowly]: <u>ou</u>: lo acabaste? ["*you finished it*"]
	[Teacher watches table from a short distance]
JORGE:	qué hizo? ["*what did she do?*"]
EMMANUEL:	[slowly]: solo: bajó más ["*well she made it longer*"]
	+
	[all students look at the teacher, the teacher leaves]
	[Sonia's gaze returns to weaving as Jorge begins speaking]
JORGE:	a verlo Sonia, ["*let's see it Sonia*"]
	. . . [Sonia continues weaving]
	let me see it Sonia
SONIA:	let me s- [quickly]: finish it up: +

Adapted from Gumperz, John J. and Jenny Cook-Gumperz, "Making space for bilingual communicative practice"; In: Intercultural Pragmatics 2(1), Berlin: De Gruyter, 2005 p. 12, excerpt III. Used with permission of De Gruyter.

Gumperz and Cook-Gumperz (2005) use this excerpt to illustrate how code-switching conveys information "by contributing to the situated interpretations about how specific messages are to be understood", that is, how code-switching can be involved in inferencing. At the beginning of the excerpt, Sonia audibly inhales, taps Emmanuel on the arm, and repeats an announcement she has already made (not shown) that she has finished. She holds up her weaving, and after a brief pause, switches to English saying *just kidding*. Interactionally with the switch to English, Sonia indicates that what she is saying departs from the ongoing interaction. The shift to English also marks the talk as a meta comment on what has just been said.

Emmanuel then asks if Sonia has finished the weaving, the topic initiated by Sonia. At this point, Jorge joins in, turning to Emmanuel to ask him about Sonia's work. Jorge, having received an answer from Emmanuel, then turns to Sonia and asks to see her weaving. A few moments later, when Sonia does not respond, Jorge reformulates the request in English. The language shift is positioned as a second attempt, but given its lexical content, it can also be interpreted as an appeal for a response. Sonia follows Jorge's shift to English and responds in English, showing that she orients to the course of action in progress. Here the combination of content and language choice contributes to interpretation: when Jorge speaks, he first uses one mode of speaking and then repeats in another mode, which, as a result, gains more urgency (Gumperz and Cook-Gumperz 2005: 13). Sonia replies with a justification that is potentially not what Jorge is expecting, but its effect is softened because it is delivered in the same mode. The code switch is integral to the business of negotiating throughout the excerpt. The children share the same set of conventions, with code-switching another resource that is available for them in this case to strategically signal meaning.

The data excerpt in (4) is from a job interview where the interviewers and the interviewee do not share the same set of conventions, and in being a one-off high stakes encounter there was no opportunity to develop an understanding of difference and ways to accommodate, as was possible for the interactants in (2). There is apparently not even any awareness that there might be differing norms. In this case, conventions around different styles and their effectiveness to signal meaning are not shared.

(4) Job interview

Context: Tahir is British Bangladeshi who is being interviewed for a receptionist position in a college. Recorded in the UK.

INTERVIEWER 1:	can you tell me about any experiences you have of cash handling?
TAHIR:	obviously you have to do the recon- reconciliation
	and I've done we do that well in my current job and
	before when I've worked as a sales assistant
	I've worked on tills like operated the g- s like as a cashier . . .
	my current job we do like I was saying we do the reconciliation
	and petty cash
	and things that I buy to buy tea coffees and (4)
	I buy the flowers as well [rising intonation]
INTERVIEWER 2:	you buy the //flowers [laughs]\
TAHIR:	/for reception\\ yeah
	but I get refunded though . . .
	//and um\
INTERVIEWER 2:	/yeah\\
TAHIR:	I chose some really nice flowers and then get refunded
	I chose the flowers [laughs] but they give you a budget . . .
	the girls really like it like the flowers they come and pinch it though
	i- i- it doesn't last more than like a couple of hours the new ones
INTERVIEWER 1:	[laughs]
TAHIR:	but they all come and pinch it and they take it [laughs]

> Adapted from Roberts, Celia, "Gatekeeping discourse in employment interviews"; In: Christopher N. Candlin, and Srikant Sarangi (eds.) Handbook of Communication in Organisations and Professions, Berlin: De Gruyter, 2011 p. 420–421, ex. 4. Used with permission of De Gruyter.

The excerpt begins with an interviewer asking Tahir about his work experience with handling cash. Tahir presents a list of administrative tasks in a relatively impartial style, followed by a more personal narrative. This narrative is only loosely connected to the question about cash handling. Roberts (2011: 421) comments that this is a pattern he uses throughout the interview. This second part of the answer is more animated with rising tone and laughter, and it positions him as having fun with *the girls* who feature in his narrative. Roberts suggests that the more institutional discourse of the first part of his answer and the personal discourse of the second part did not mesh well for the interviewers. They expected explicit linking between the sections of his answer according to her analysis, and without this were unsure of the relevance of the personal narrative. The applicant in (4) is a British Bangladeshi and his style of giving information did not conform to the style expected by the British interviewers.

Another aspect that may vary is prosody. Gumperz (2015) points out that the South Asians in an interview dataset he analysed that was recorded in the British Midlands often failed to recognise that accenting or stress is used in English to convey key information. They did not therefore recognise the significance of the way interviewers stressed different words. An important factor here is that people are members of different social and cultural groups. The way they use language therefore conforms to different contextualisation conventions which reflect the groups they belong to and identify with.

5.2.3 Framing

Framing is another concept that has been drawn on by some researchers taking an Interactional Sociolinguistics approach. The concept of **framing** as used by Interactional Sociolinguistics analysts derives from the work of Goffman (1974), who had in turn drawn on work by Bateson (1972). A **frame** is what is going on, which then enables participants to imply and interpret meaning. Gumperz was interested in how frames are built and how they work. The observable elements of frames are contextualisation cues. Conversational inference works when people decode contextualisation cues, interpreting utterances, gestures and actions in a shared frame. Although not sharing many language-based cues and conventions, the participants in (2), for instance, were able to communicate effectively because of their understanding of the shared frame of the research group meeting.

Tannen and Wallat (1993) investigate framing in a video-recorded medical encounter involving a pediatrician, a mother and her cerebral palsied daughter. They demonstrate how the pediatrician uses language and paralanguage to quickly switch between the three primary frames that comprise the situation: the social encounter, examination and consultation. Often the pediatrician manages two frames at once, for example engaging socially with the child while examining her. In (5), shifting frames can be seen in an interaction between a father and his daughter.

(5) Family interaction

Context: A father, Steve, and his nearly three-year-old daughter, Natalie, are interacting. Natalie is pretending that her daughter (her doll, Lucy) is sick and Steve pretends to be a doctor. Recorded in the US.

NATALIE:	you be the daughter and I'll be the mommy okay?
STEVE:	okay
NATALIE:	hi this is my daughter Lucy she's not feeling well
STEVE:	[deep voice]: she's not eh?:
NATALIE:	no
STEVE:	[deep voice]: what are her symptoms?:
NATALIE:	could you check her out please?
STEVE:	[deep voice]: sure
	here while I check her out you drink this apple juice
	let's see # Lucy? cough:
	[coughs, enacting Natalie's doll]

> [deep voice]: say ah mmm mm hmm [short pause]
> I think she's got a little bit of a cold
> she needs to rest and keep warm:
>
>> Adapted and reprinted under STM guidelines from Gordon, Cynthia, Framing and positioning, In: Deborah Tannen, Heidi E. Hamilton and Deborah Schiffrin (eds.), The Handbook of Discourse Analysis, Second edition 2015, pp. 329–330, Chichester: John Wiley & Sons.

Steve shifts to the play frame, enacting the role of a doctor, which he signals by lowering the tone of his voice; this contextualisation cue signals that he is not speaking as himself. Natalie does not change the quality of her voice. However, she refers to Lucy as *my daughter* and attributes feelings to her, contributing to the play frame that is being constructed. "Doctor" Steve examines Natalie's "daughter" and directs her, *cough*, diagnoses her and recommends treatment. He also **blends frames** (Gordon 2008, 2009), when he directs Natalie to drink some apple juice, while playing the doctor role. At this point he is constructing two simultaneous frames, or definitions of the situation.

Framing was introduced as a means of exploring everyday interaction, including how people make sense of what is going on, how contextualisation cues function, and how interaction is collaboratively created. Frames, like contextualisation cues, are culturally variable. When people use their own frames to interpret what others are trying to communicate, but they do not share the same frames, then communication can break down. People tend to assume their frames are the same as everyone else's because they are so unconscious. When things go wrong, therefore, they either blame the other person as somehow incompetent or as a member of a group that is somehow defective. They do not understand that they have different norms and expectations.

5.2.4 Norms and conversational style

Social and cultural **norms** are constructed through interaction, and we all have expectations based on our own interactional experience and history of what the cues and conventions are when we interact. If people do not share contextualisation conventions or recognise contextualisation cues or frames when they interact, this can lead to misunderstandings. Misunderstandings can then have damaging social consequences, particularly for those from minority groups, restricting their access to resources and services. The interviewers in (4) had differing norms and expectations about ways of interacting than the applicant. This meant that the applicant, Tahir, in not sharing or recognising these norms, did not interact in a way the others expected him to. The consequence of this was that he was unsuccessful in securing the job.

There are many aspects of communication where norms between social and cultural groups may differ. This may be style, as in (4), or as noted in reference to Gumperz (2015), norms around intonation and stress can differ. The norms and expectations around non-verbal aspects of communication can also vary. An example of this is the use and value placed on silence. In Samoan culture for instance silence is "overtly recognised as a form of communication and therefore of social practice" (Salanoa

2020: 89). Remaining silent does not have negative connotations as it may have for some cultural groups; it does not indicate a lack of engagement or that someone is not a team player. Salanoa found lengthy stretches of no talk among the Samoan seasonal workers who were the focus of her research, see (6).

(6)   Orchard fieldnotes

Context: Fieldnotes from observation of Samoan seasonal workers at work in New Zealand.

Length 1 hr 30 mins
Description
Lengthy period of silence here as Filipo and his partner are focused on getting their lines done before work finishes. Both carry on with work silently and the recorder picks up brief stops for toilet breaks, then the men resume work.

Length 49 minutes
Description
Work resumes for everyone – complete silence here. Everyone is focusing on the task. No interactions from Filipo or his partner. The music in the background has stopped, continuous sound of ladders being moved from one block to another.

Adapted from Salanoa (2020: 92–93).
Reprinted with permission of the author.

Filipo and his partner are occupied with their work and one hour and 30 minutes of silence is recorded. Salanoa notes that they were comfortable with this silence and happy to work this way as they focused on their tasks. For the groups of seasonal workers she researched with, operating in silence is not the absence of noise, nor is it withholding information, "rather, they are actually in 'companionable' silence. Arguably, being silent is being cooperative especially if the hierarchical differences require one to be silent" (Salanoa 2020: 89).

A tolerance of silence was also observed in the research of Murata (2011) who compared business meetings between Japan and New Zealand, where even short periods of silence in the Japanese data was considered uncomfortable and unpleasant to watch by New Zealanders. The New Zealand data was understood as involving too much talking by Japanese. Like the Samoans in Salanoa's research, for the Japanese in Murata's study a different cultural understanding of silence exists than found in many Western cultures. This of course has important implications when people from different groups with different norms and expectations interact.

Tannen used the term **conversational style** to help account for the types of differing norms that we each have when we interact. **Conversational style** refers to "the basic tools with which people communicate" (Tannen 2005a: 4), that is, the way someone says something. Features of conversational style include aspects such as how fast someone speaks, their tone of voice, how loudly they speak and when and how much they pause or overlap others. Often it is not what someone says but how they say it that affects how successfully they are able to communicate.

5.2.5 Indexicality and stance

A theoretical development often referred to in Interactional Sociolinguistics is the notion of **indexicality** (Ochs 1992, 1996; adapted from Peirce 1955 and Silverstein 1976). Elinor Ochs proposed the **Indexicality Principle** (Ochs 1996: 411) to account for the way that language becomes associated with different groups, such as women and men. Indexicality asserts that very few linguistic features **directly index** aspects of identity such as gender identity. More commonly, there is an **indirect indexing** through speech features and styles that are associated with a group through regular use. These expectations about speech patterns then determine people's language choices. Expectations also affect how people are assessed. An example would be a woman leader who is judged negatively because she does not use hedging, a feature which is stereotypically associated with a feminine speech style.

An important part of Ochs' model is the idea of **stance**. Through using a different linguistic feature a speaker can invoke different **stances**, or qualities. In Japanese, for instance, the sentence final particles *ze* and *wa* denote either a coarse or delicate intensity respectively (Ochs 1992: 342). Because women tend to more frequently use the particle that denotes a delicate intensity, this has become associated with women. Similarly, the tendency of men to use the particle which denotes coarse intensity means this has become associated with men. This aligns with the societal expectations of how women and men should talk. Women can still of course use the particle that denotes coarse intensity, just as men can use the one that denotes delicate intensity. Such choices however lead to more complex interpretations about the speaker's intentions and motivations and why they have made such a choice.

The data excerpt in (7) demonstrates the variable use of address terms in Chilean Spanish from a grandmother to her grandson (bolded in the Chilean Spanish and marked in the English translation with T, U and V). Fernández-Mallat (2020) discusses the use of address terms by the grandmother in terms of identity, but, related to this, we can see their use as corresponding with the indexing of different stances at different points of the interaction. When the excerpt begins, Gladys has just got her baby granddaughter Gabriela to stop crying.

(7) Family interaction between a grandmother and two grandchildren (Chilean Spanish)

Context: Gladys has been trying to get Gabriela to stop crying by offering her toys. Andrés, her grandson who is drinking juice from a box, is not happy because some of these toys are his. Gladys' strategy has paid off and Gabriela has stopped crying. Variant forms are in bold.

GLADYS:
[Gabriela stops crying and is looking at a ball]
[Andrés looks concerned]
espérate que vio la pelota ya?
[Andrés starts walking towards the ball]

GLADYS:
déjasela ahí nomás
para que la vaya a buscar Andrés
[Andrés keeps going towards the ball]

GLADYS:	**déjesela** ahí
	[Andrés stops and lets Gabriela grab the ball]
GLADYS:	**viste?**
	[Andrés attempts to grab the ball from Gabriela's hands]
GLADYS:	no
	tú **estái** tomando juguito
	déjala ahí tranquilita
	[Andrés leaves Gabriela alone and finishes drinking his juice quietly]
	[Gabriela drops the ball and grabs some papers]

Translation

	[Gabriela stops crying and is looking at a ball]
	[Andrés looks concerned]
GLADYS:	***wait**$_T$ she saw the ball alright?*
	[Andrés starts walking towards the ball]
GLADYS:	*just **leave**$_T$ it there*
	so that she goes for it Andrés
	[Andrés keeps going towards the ball]
GLADYS:	***leave**$_U$ it there*
	[Andrés stops and lets Gabriela grab the ball]
GLADYS:	***you**$_T$ see?*
	[Andrés attempts to grab the ball from Gabriela's hands]
GLADYS:	*no*
	***you're**$_V$ drinking juice*
	***leave**$_V$ her alone*
	[Andrés leaves Gabriela alone and finishes drinking his juice quietly]
	[Gabriela drops the ball and grabs some papers]

Adapted from Journal of Pragmatics 161, Fernández-Mallat, Víctor, Forms of address in interaction: Evidence from Chilean Spanish, p. 99, © 2020, with permission from Elsevier.

Fernández-Mallat (2020: 99) comments that Gladys uses the whole tripartite address system available to her as a speaker of Chilean Spanish in this excerpt. She starts by referring to Andrés with *tuteante* forms of address, the preferred address selection for a grandparent to grandchildren as they are commonly used to express the closeness typical of this type of relationship, but also strictness in family situations. Gladys may have chosen them to index a mildly disciplinary stance in order to calmly instruct Andrés to let Gabriela grab the ball. The calm non-confrontational nature of her utterance is further indexed through the use of a tag question, which further softens the directive.

This strategy does not work, however, and Andrés keeps threatening the recently restored peace by wanting his ball. In response, Gladys invokes a more clearly authoritative identity by shifting from the *tuteante* forms to an *ustedeante* one. The *ustedeante* form that she uses at this point allows her to index an authoritative stance. Andrés is very responsive to Gladys' address switch here and the stance it denotes. He immediately stops and lets Gabriela grab the ball. This is despite the fact that Gladys' utterance has "the exact same neutral tone as the previous ones" (Fernández-Mallat 2020: 100). Since Andrés responded positively to her command, Gladys instantly abandons her more authoritative stance in favour of the mildly corrective one initially indexed by shifting back to a *tuteante* address form. Andrés then tries to rip the ball from Gabriela's hands and Gladys immediately goes back to a more clearly authoritative stance, as she reminds Andrés that he is drinking juice and tells him, once again, to leave Gabriela alone. She accomplishes her goal of making sure that Andrés finally gets the message and respects her authoritative stance by shifting to two *voseante* address forms, indexing annoyance or mild anger. Andrés seems to understand the message this time.

Indexicality and stance are useful concepts in Interactional Sociolinguistics. They help focus on why someone might be using a particular feature of interaction, whether verbal or non-verbal, and what they might intend to convey through its use. As seen in (7), people can change stances throughout an interaction, as they negotiate with others and respond to their actions.

5.2.6 Summary

Key concepts in Interactional Sociolinguistics include **contextualisation cues** and **conversational inference**. Both involve understanding features of discourse which speakers and listeners use to construct and interpret meaning. **Framing** is another important concept which may be used by Interactional Sociolinguistics researchers. This refers to the goals or purposes and any interaction may have multiple **frames**, for example, a doctor appointment where a physician may switch between the frames social encounter, examination and consultation. **Norms** and **conversational style** are useful concepts because they highlight different expectations and ways of communicating. Finally, **indexicality** and **stance** foreground the way language features become associated with different groups and why people choose to use (and assess) features in certain ways.

5.3 SOME KEY TOPICS IN INTERACTIONAL SOCIOLINGUISTICS

Some key topics that have been explored by researchers using an Interactional Sociolinguistics approach and concepts include:

- how various discourse strategies are used
- how routine encounters are constructed
- how relationships are discursively created, and
- how identities are enacted and negotiated

5.3.1 The use of discourse strategies

A focus of Interactional Sociolinguistics research in different parts of the world has been the way participants in an interaction use particular discourse strategies and how these function. Example (8) is drawn from a study which explored the use of questioning in medical counselling sessions in Malawi.

(8) Medical counselling session (Chichewa)

Context: Women interacting with a counsellor in a session for pregnant women at a clinic. The session precedes testing for HIV. Recorded in Malawi.

HEALTH PROFESSIONAL:	mmm chabwino inuyo ngati amayi woyembekezera mukuwona kuti ndikofunikira kuti inuyo muyezetse magazi? +
WOMEN (ENA):	//eee\
WOMEN (ENA):	/mmm\\ ndikofunika
HEALTH PROFESSIONAL:	kufunika kwake ndikotani?
WOMAN 1:	udziwe mmene muliri mthupi mwako
HEALTH PROFESSIONAL:	mudziwe mmene muliri mthupi mwanu eti?
WOMEN:	mmm
HEALTH PROFESSIONAL:	ndeno mukadziwa?
WOMAN 2:	kutetezera mwana amene tikumuyembekezerayo
HEALTH PROFESSIONAL:	kumutetezera mwana amene tikumuyembekezerayo eti? makamaka ngati mwapezeka kuti muli ndi HIV tili limodzi?
WOMEN:	eee
HEALTH PROFESSIONAL:	ngati mulibe kachilombo? (2.5)
WOMAN 2:	kudzisamala
HEALTH PROFESSIONAL:	kudzisamala?
WOMAN 2:	eee

Translation

HEALTH PROFESSIONAL:	mmh alright as pregnant women do you think it is important for you to have a blood test? +
WOMEN (SOME):	//yes\
WOMEN (SOME):	/mhm\\ it is important
HEALTH PROFESSIONAL:	what is its importance?
WOMAN 1:	so that you should know how your body is
HEALTH PROFESSIONAL:	you should know how your body is right?
WOMEN:	mhm
HEALTH PROFESSIONAL:	and when you know?
WOMAN 2:	to protect the baby we are expecting
HEALTH PROFESSIONAL:	to protect the baby you are expecting right? especially if you are diagnosed with HIV are we together?
WOMEN:	yes
HEALTH PROFESSIONAL:	if you do not have the virus? (2.5)
WOMAN 2:	to take care of yourself.

HEALTH PROFESSIONAL:	to take care of yourself?
WOMAN 2:	yes

> Adapted from Chimbwete-Phiri, Rachel and Stephanie Schnurr, Improving HIV/AIDS consultations in Malawi: How interactional sociolinguistics can contribute, pp. 137–138, © Zsófia Demjén and Jonathon Tomlinson, 2020, "Applying Linguistics in Illness and Healthcare Contexts", Bloomsbury Academic, an imprint of Bloomsbury Publishing Plc.

After the first question, the healthcare provider asks further questions, which tend to be derived from the women's responses. This use of questions elicits the women's knowledge, resulting in active participation from the women as they share and negotiate knowledge. This contrasts with situations in which the healthcare provider delivers the information in the form of a monologue or lecture. The questions here are relatively informal (often mirroring what a woman has just said) and the use of this questioning strategy is successful as it involves the women in the interaction and gets them to participate by showing that they have the relevant and appropriate knowledge. In addition, this participation enhances shared ownership of knowledge by ensuring that relevant information is not only provided by the healthcare provider but also conjointly produced among all participants.

The use of this type of questioning strategy also constructs the role of the healthcare professional as a facilitator whose main aim is to make explicit the already existing knowledge of the women. Chimbwete-Phiri and Schnurr (2020: 142) note that one of the women referred in an interview to the counselling sessions as a dialogue where the women were given the opportunity "to remind one another and discussing in order to help each other. You say this, she also says that, that way knowledge is advanced, learning is on-going". This was seen as evidence that the questions engaged the clients in the promotion of health messages.

Other discourse strategies that have been explored with an Interactional Sociolinguistics approach include humour (e.g., Holmes and Marra 2006; Schnurr 2009) and narrative (e.g., Tannen 2008; Holmes, Marra and Vine 2011).

5.3.2 The construction of routine encounters

Routine encounters such as family interactions or meetings and the way these are constructed have been another focus for Interactional Sociolinguistics researchers. This includes interactions that are high stakes, that is, interactions where one or more of the participants have a lot to lose from the outcome. Example (4) came from a high stakes interaction, in that case a job interview. Example (9) is from a different type of high stakes interview. In the study from which this is drawn, Weston (2021) explores admission interviews for Cambridge University. He identifies a number of phases in the interviews and the types of talk that are found in each phase. Example (9) comes from a section where the candidate for admission is required to discuss two poems with the interviewer. The analysis indicated that the interviewer modified or reformulated questions in order to provide candidates with the quickest route to the answers he was looking for.

(9) University admission interview

Context: A candidate is being interviewed for admission to study English literature at Cambridge University. Recorded in the UK.

INTERVIEWER: where where does where in other kinds of sonnets do we find the turn?
CANDIDATE: oh is it [inhales] six and eight? + is that the volta?
INTERVIEWER: well how is a sonnet organised?
CANDIDATE: um
INTERVIEWER: how is this sonnet organised?
CANDIDATE: it's in + is it packs of four? + four lines which which with strong //[louder]: a b a b: lines?\
INTERVIEWER: /okay what do we call\\ units of four lines? (4) ( ) (2) quatrains you do know?
CANDIDATE: oh I //[laughs]\
INTERVIEWER: /yeah quatr- yeah\\ okay so okay so yeah four lines and then what=
CANDIDATE: =yeah and that so four line four lines four lines and then the two at the end
the rhyming couplets so twelve and two fourteen lines ++ is that right?
INTERVIEWER: yeah
CANDIDATE: I haven't actually counted the lines yet I'll do it ++ yeah
INTERVIEWER: so s- in summary yeah

Adapted from Journal of Pragmatics 176, Weston, Daniel, Gatekeeping and linguistic capital: A case study of the Cambridge university undergraduate admissions interview, p. 142, © 2021, with permission from Elsevier.

Weston (2021: 142) notes that the tightly linked Initiation-Response-Feedback sequences (Sinclair and Coulthard 1975) clearly show this to be a pedagogical mode of talk involving an instructor and a student. This is further indexed by how the interviewer reformulates his questions to scaffold the candidate's responses. After a dispreferred response in the candidate's first turn, for instance, the interviewer reformulates the question, making it more general, *how is a sonnet organised?* He then modifies it again, so that it concerns the poem at hand, *this sonnet?*, providing the candidate with a methodology to arrive at the correct answer (counting the lines). The candidate herself clearly understands this to be a pedagogical exchange, as she orients to a student role by framing many of her answers as questions designed to elicit the interviewer's help. Indeed, the interviewer does in fact provide an answer to his own question concerning the technical term *quatrain*, which helps the candidate to refine her answer.

5.3.3 The discursive creation of relationships

As noted in Chapter 1, relationships are always important when people communicate, whether they wish to develop, maintain, neglect or challenge rapport. The way that rapport can be managed in transactional talk through humour or the use of indirect strategies was briefly explored, and this is a topic that has been another key focus for Interactional Sociolinguistics researchers. How are relationships discursively created? Example (1) provided an excerpt from a dinner party involving a group of friends. In this, Urs created a fantasy scenario in order to entertain his friends, and this contributes to his ongoing friendly relationship with them. Relationships are constantly affirmed and constructed through interaction. In (10), a sister and brother are interacting. The sister initiates social talk, asking her brother how things are going with his girlfriend.

(10) Family interaction

Context: Interaction between a sister (a woman in her thirties) and her brother (a few years younger). Recorded in the US.

SISTER: so how's things with Kerry?
BROTHER: cool
SISTER: cool does that mean very good?
BROTHER: yeah
SISTER: true love?
BROTHER: pretty much
SISTER: <u>pretty</u> much? when you say pretty much what do you mean?
BROTHER: I mean it's all good

> Adapted and reprinted under STM guidelines from Tannen, Deborah, Gender and family interaction, In: Susan Ehrlich, Miriam Meyerhoff and Janet Holmes (eds.), The Handbook of Language, Gender and Sexuality, Second edition 2014, p. 498, Chichester: Wiley-Blackwell.

Social talk is one obvious way that people can maintain and develop rapport with others. The sister here seems more enthusiastic about the topic than her brother, and although her brother's responses do not give too much away, he does reply to her questions. His minimal responses though, lead her to ask more specific questions as she tries to get him to engage with her and provide more detailed information. Tannen notes that one way that women tend to create and maintain closeness is by sharing information about their lives "including (perhaps especially) romantic relationships" (2014: 498). This can cause problems when male and female family members interact because there are gender differences in the expectations around this type of talk.

Social talk, humour and narrative are all discourse strategies that can be used to build relationships, although at times they can also challenge them. This may be deliberate but can be unintentional if participants in an interaction have different norms and expectations (see Vine 2020: Chapter 4).

5.3.4 Identity

In Chapter 1, there was also a brief discussion of identity. Because of the central focus in Interactional Sociolinguistics on diversity, including social diversity, researchers have explored how identities are discursively constructed. How does the way people interact reflect the groups they belong to? The examples presented so far in this chapter have illustrated people enacting a range of identities. Family relationships and identities were evident in (5), (7) and (10). The grandmother in (7), for instance, oriented to her role and identity as a grandparent as she marked different stances to discipline her grandson and maintain the newly achieved peace. The father in (5) enacted his identity as a father as he simultaneously directed his daughter to drink her juice while also cooperating with her request to play with her and her doll.

In (1), Urs enacted an identity as a friend and in entertaining the others constructed himself as an amusing, social and convivial person. The children in (3), also interacted as peers and Emmanuel and Jorge, in their orientation to what Sonia was doing, enacted identities as good friends who show interest and support.

The other examples presented so far in this chapter come from different workplace or institutional interactions. Examples (4) and (9) were drawn from interviews. In order to enact the interviewer role, the interviewers use questions, and this immediately sets up a frame which the interviewee can respond to and in so doing enact their own identities. The questions from the interviewer in (9), also position him as an instructor and enable him to create this type of identity. The interviewee in this case quickly orients to the student role. The counsellor in (8), also used questions to enact an identity as a facilitator. The enactment of these identities by the participants was additionally achieved by the way that the people they were interacting with oriented to their questions and so there was joint identity construction; the identities of all participants were co-constructed.

The colleagues in (2) and (6), also enacted respect and collegiality in their interactions. The way this was evident through non-verbal interaction was highlighted in (2), while in (6) the use of silence was an important means of conveying collegiality. In addition, (6) demonstrated the enactment of identity by drawing on cultural norms and expectations, ones which in this case may be misinterpreted quite easily by others who do not share the same norms.

The next three examples illustrate how people may simultaneously index a range of identities when they interact. The first comes from work by Georgakopoulou (2007), who explores the way three adolescent girls index their identity as part of their friendship group. One way they do this is through the telling of **small stories** (brief narratives). This includes the topics of the small stories and how they tell them. Their interaction patterns show the specific roles they take on within the group. Example (11) presents an excerpt of the three friends talking.

(11)   Interaction between friends   (translated from Greek)

Context: Conversation between three young women, Tonia, Fontini, and Vivi. The conversation takes place in a public place, one of their hang-outs. They are talking about men and Fontini has mentioned a guy she is interested in. Vivi is not impressed by this person and tells her to focus on another guy they all think likes Fontini. They refer to this young man by the nickname Ekleraki. Recorded in Greece.

VIVI:	... *I'm saying it to save you the pain since Ekleraki is around*=
TONIA:	=*Ekleraki's s- [slowly]: so: much better*=
VIVI:	=*by far by far*
FONTINI:	*don't by far me Vivi*
	you tell me on account of [louder]: what?:
VIVI:	*[quickly]: on account of looks:*=
TONIA:	=*[quickly]: on account of character:*=
VIVI:	=*[quickly]: on account of personality:*

Adapted and reprinted with permission. From Georgakopoulou, Alexandra, Small Stories, Interaction and Identities, pp. 104–105, © 2007, John Benjamins Publishing.

Identifying as part of this friendship group includes the use of nicknames to refer to others. These have been developed by the girls through the course of their friendship and have developed layers of meaning for them. Here they refer to a man they have nicknamed *Ekleraki*, which is a type of pastry which he often buys from Fontini's father's patisserie. The girls suspect he does this because of his interest in Fontini. The closeness of the girls is apparent in their use of nicknames, along with the way Vivi and Tonia feel they can advise Fontini about her love life.

Vivi is constructed as the main participant here: her participation defines the sequence, with Tonia then using Vivi as a model for how she participates. Fontini also contributes to this by directly addressing Vivi, even though both Vivi and Tonia have given their opinions on Ekleraki. Georgakopoulou (2007: 106) notes that Vivi's right to give advice and the acceptance of this within the friendship group comes from her accepted social identity amongst the girls as someone who is "street-wise, assertive and, generally, experienced in the domain of male-female relationships".

People have complex identities relating to a range of social groups that they identify with. The young women in (11) are all young, Greek and heterosexual, and these aspects of their identity, as well as their close friendship, are all evident in their talk. In (12), a group of people interact at work. Again, the way they talk illustrates how people can enact a range of aspects of their identity when they interact.

(12)   Meeting opening   (Māori and English)

Context: Beginning of a management meeting in a government workplace. Seven people are present, three of whom identify as Māori (indigenous people of New Zealand) and four as Pākehā (New Zealanders of European origin). Recorded in New Zealand.

GREG:	um so if we start off with our whakataukī ["*proverb*"]
	I think the whakataukī that's in here is actually um
	last week's one it's been repeated again
	so I've actually got the one that was for this week
	um up on the pānui ["*bulletin board*"] so um you haven't got it in front you
	this is gonna be a test of how well you can listen

MARAMA:	yes
GREG:	//[laughs]\ a listening skills test
MARAMA:	/[laughs]\\
THEO:	how long is it?
GREG:	it's only quite short
MARAMA:	it's //it's very short\
THEO:	/[laughs]\\ //[laughs]\ [laughs]
GREG:	/yeah\\
MARAMA:	e iti noa ana nā te aroha
ALL:	e iti noa ana nā te aroha
MARAMA:	though my present is small //my love\ goes with it
KENDRA:	/[quietly]: it's given:\\
GREG:	yeah
MARAMA:	although it's small
GREG:	yeah
MARAMA:	it's given with love
GREG:	yeah
MARAMA:	that's //my\ interpretation
F?:	/mm\\
AROHA?:	( ) [laughs]
GREG:	and e- there are other variations of that though people often say //ahakoa e iti\ nā te aroha e whakanui even though it's small
MARAMA:	/ahakoa e iti\\
GREG:	my love will make it big sort of mm . . . okay [executive management group] discussion Kendra

Adapted from Vine, Holmes and Marra (forthcoming) (Source: LWP)

Example (12) comes from the beginning of a management meeting in a government organisation. The CEO of this organisation leads the meeting and always begins the meetings with a *whakataukī* "Māori proverb" (Holmes and Vine 2021; Vine, Holmes and Marra forthcoming). In Māori workplaces, meetings often begin with a *karakia*, that is, a prayer or recitation in Māori. This organisation identifies as bicultural, but they do not use karakia to open meetings. Greg instead uses whakataukī at the beginning of each meeting as a means to teach his team, some of whom do not know much Māori. The meeting opening here provides us with a number of insights regarding how he constructs a range of facets of his social identity, including his identity as the leader of the group, his ethnic identity and his identity as an expert in Māori language.

Greg opens the meeting by referring to the whakataukī which they typically recite and talk about at the beginning of each meeting. The whakataukī for this week has not been put in the papers for the meeting so the team cannot read it out as they usually do. Greg jokes that they will have a listening skills test. The organisation's business is related to the education sector and most who work there have been teachers, so such a test is something they may have administered themselves. Greg himself began his career as a teacher and so his joke indexes this aspect of his identity, which he shares with many of them.

The positioning of himself as the teacher highlights his role as the leader of the group. He also enacts his leadership role in being the one who brings the meeting to order, after pre-meeting social talk, and then after the whakataukī he introduces the first agenda item. Greg's practice of using whakataukī to open meetings illustrates some distinctive features of his leadership style: he is concerned to encourage learning among his team members, while simultaneously enacting his Māori identity. It also indexes the identity of the organisation as bicultural.

Greg always asks Marama to read the whakataukī first, acknowledging her status as the other senior Māori member of the team and thus contributing to the conjoint construction of her identity (Holmes and Vine 2021). This was a role she took on in each of the six meetings we recorded, where she first recited the whakataukī and then gave her understanding of its meaning in English. Greg would then clarify the meaning, or, as in this case, mention a common alternative wording. This clearly marked him as an expert in the language. Fluency in Māori is also a way of indexing his ethnic identity and he frequently used other Māori words and phrases in his speech when speaking English, for example *pānui*.

5.3.5 Summary

The focus in Interactional Sociolinguistics research may involve questions which revolve around different types of issues. This could be the discourse strategies people use and what is achieved through their use. It could be how routine encounters are constructed. The focus may be on how relationships between participants in an interaction are evident in their discourse. As interaction in Interactional Sociolinguistics is viewed as a way of developing, maintaining, neglecting or challenging rapport, the discursive creation of relationships has been a common focus. A final issue discussed in this chapter, which is an important focus in Interactional Sociolinguistics research, is identity. The way people interact reflects the groups they belong to and identify with, so an Interactional Sociolinguistics analysis can provide important insights concerning the enactment of identity.

CHAPTER SUMMARY

Interactional Sociolinguistics is an approach that was developed through the work of John Gumperz. It has been further developed and applied by other researchers working in different social and cultural contexts around the world.

Workplace discourse has been a focus of Interactional Sociolinguistics since the beginning, with an early focus on gatekeeping encounters, such as interviews. In these interactions speakers from ethnic and linguistic minority groups may face difficulties and experience restricted access to services and resources. Gumperz established Interactional Sociolinguistics as an approach to intercultural communication that exposes how social injustices are exacerbated when participants have different contextualisation conventions and cultural assumptions. Discourse in interaction between friends and family, including children and adolescents, has also been a focus for Interactional Sociolinguistics researchers, again with exploration of norms around communication and concerns with why at times communication breaks down.

With Interactional Sociolinguistics the focus is on close analysis of interactional data in order to explore what people do with language, how they do this and how they either succeed or fail in their communication goals. Two key concepts are contextualisation cues and conversational inference. Other concepts that have helped in exploring these aspects and that have been briefly considered and illustrated in this chapter, are framing, norms and conversational style, indexicality and stance.

Some key topics that have been explored by researchers using an Interactional Sociolinguistics approach have also been covered in this chapter. This includes how various discourse strategies are used, how routine encounters are constructed, how relationships are discursively created and how identities are enacted and negotiated.

FURTHER READING

For some introductions to Interactional Sociolinguistics that provide relatively brief but useful overviews see Tannen (2005b), Günthner (2008), Gordon (2011), Bailey (2015), and Gumperz (2015). In the area of workplace discourse see Gordon and Kraut (2018). For some book-length studies which take an Interactional Sociolinguistics approach, see Mullany (2007), Tannen (2007), and Holmes, Marra and Vine (2011).

The examples presented in this chapter are all from face-to-face interaction, but Tannen (2013) provides an interesting discussion of conversational style in new modes of interacting such as text messaging.

There are also a range of other concepts that some Interactional Sociolinguistics researchers use, which I have not explored here because of space constraints. These include footing and positioning (see e.g., Gordon 2015). Footing helps explore participants' ongoing negotiation of relationships and identities. The theory of positioning has been applied in understanding identity construction.

EXERCISES

These exercises present three short transcripts of authentic data for you to analyse. There are notes at the end for feedback and guidance. As you go through you could also think about whether any aspects you identify are consistent with your own communication practices or whether they demonstrate contrasting norms.

Discourse samples (A) and (B) both illustrate the same discourse strategy. Answer the questions about how it is operating in each case.

1. What discourse strategy is prominent in (A) and (B)?
2. Why do you think the speaker(s) use this strategy and what does it achieve?
3. What cues can you identify from what is shown in the transcripts about the way the utterances are intended and interpreted?
4. What observations can you make about the enactment of identity in (A) and (B)?

(A)   Workplace meeting   (Japanese)

Context: Hosoi, a computer system development manager, is demonstrating a new (software) product in a meeting and Manabe is checking it. Others are also present at the meeting. Manabe is in charge of checking and revising (if necessary) the software. Recorded in Japan.

HOSOI:	sooiu bubun de ano- sensei no sooitta jikan tanshuku ni wa
	a- yakudatsu to omou n desu yo ne
MANABE:	yakudatsu yakudatsu to omoimasu ne
TANIMOTO:	yakudachimasu ne ee
MANABE:	[slows down, humorous tone]: soshitara motto takusan-:
	[laughter]
	hatarake tte koto ka-
	[laughter]
ASHIZAWA:	ie
KOMEDA:	kooritsuteki ni hatarake masu yo

Translation

HOSOI:	*in this point well this [new software]*
	will be helpful for spending less time for work
	well it will be helpful
MANABE:	*I think it will be helpful too*
TANIMOTO:	*yeah it will be helpful*
MANABE:	*[slows down, humorous tone]: in such a case*
	you mean this software will make me:
	[laughter]
	work harder
	[laughter]
ASHIZAWA:	*no*
KOMEDA:	*you'll be able to work effectively*

> Adapted from Journal of Pragmatics 60, Murata, Kazuyo. An empirical cross-cultural study of humour in business meetings in New Zealand and Japan, p. 261, © 2014, with permission from Elsevier and the author.

(B)   Informal interaction

Context: AM1 and AM2 are non-native speakers of English, while EM is a native speaker. They meet for English conversation practice, along with some other non-native speakers. Recorded in the US.

AM1:	now my roommates didn't understand me I feel bad . . .
EM:	well do they still do you sti- do they still have trouble understanding you?
AM1:	[nods] some # not as much as at the beginning
EM:	mm
AM1:	but there are

AM2: your problem # just your roommate # go //get another one\
/[laughter]\\

> Adapted from Journal of Pragmatics 35, Davies, Catherine Evans, How English-Learners Joke with Native Speakers: An Interactional Sociolinguistic Perspective on Humor as Collaborative Discourse across Cultures, p. 1379, © 2003, with permission from Elsevier.

5. In (C), a CEO is reflecting on his leadership in response to questions from an interviewer. He uses the pragmatic marker *you know* three times. *You know* has been found to have a number of functions and to index different stances. What does its use index here and why do you think the CEO uses it?
6. What type of identity does the CEO enact in (C)?

(C) Research interview

Context: Interview with Greg, the CEO of a company, about his leadership. Recorded in New Zealand.

GREG: I think that's what's happened over time is
I'm a lot more confident in my leadership ability
because **you know** I did start off quite young as
in in management roles
and in **you know** chief executive role
and you think oh my god
this is the kind of imposter syndrome
I'm gonna get [laughs]: found out: any minute here . . .
but **you know** I don't have that feeling now
[laughs]: yeah:
INTERVIEWER: no with good reason
BOTH: [laugh]

(Source: LWP)

NOTES ON EXERCISES

These notes give some reflections on issues that might be considered in answering the questions. These are not meant to be definitive answers, and there may be other things that stand out for you in each sample.

The transcripts in (A) and (B) both include humour. In both cases, humour builds rapport within the group. In (B), the humour also builds rapport between AM1 and AM2. Instead of AM1 being seen as the one with a problem because of his English proficiency, AM2 suggests the problem is with AM1's (presumably) native speaker roommate.

In (A), Manabe slows down and it is noted that he uses a humorous tone to signal he is being funny. In (B), AM2 uses short phrases and the content of his turn, in proposing an unexpected solution, provides the humour. In both (A) and (B), there is laughter. Laughter is a common response to humour, although it may also be present for other reasons.

The use of humour can allow speakers to enact a positive friendly identity, and in responding positively to the humour others also construct themselves as good-natured. For (A), Murata (2014: 261) argues that Manabe's use of humour enables him to enact an expert identity because the topic of the humour is his area of responsibility. Typically, in this meeting it was the CEO (Komeda) who instigated humour and not less senior people such as Manabe. Humour is a strategy that is widely used also cultures and languages to achieve a range of goals (see Vine 2020, Chapter 4).

For (C), *you know* can index an informal stance, as well as indexing solidarity. It suggests Greg is trying to establish rapport with the interviewer and not be too formal. He also uses humour for these purposes when he jokes about *imposter syndrome*, and the interviewer responds positively by joining in and they laugh together. The impression we get of Greg and the type of identity he enacts is that he is humble but confident in his leadership and pays attention to the relational aspect of communication. We also saw him joking in (12), showing his attention to relational goals when interacting with his team.

6

Critical Discourse Studies

INTRODUCTION

Critical Discourse Studies (CDS) is an approach to analysing discourse which is theoretical rather than involving a set method. A range of tools may be used, but there is a fundamental feature which typifies CDS research: the primary focus is power and inequality and the way discourse constructs and reinforces power differences.

As with Interactional Sociolinguistics, taking a CDS approach involves a close analysis of authentic discourse, and this is informed by looking at wider contextual factors. However, for CDS analysts the beginning point is "a social problem that needs to be described, explained and solved, or at least suggestions made as to how it could be solved" (Koller 2018: 27). Researchers taking a CDS approach aim to raise awareness about the way that discourse is used in different contexts and to help bring about change where this use reflects inequality and discrimination (Fairclough 2015).

This chapter introduces CDS. The chapter begins with a brief overview of the origins and development of CDS, with Section 6.2 then exploring and illustrating some key concepts. Section 6.3 examines two key domains that have been researched using a CDS approach, whilst Section 6.4 briefly considers types of analysis and methodologies.

In this chapter I use the term CDS but originally this type of approach was known as Critical Discourse Analysis (CDA). Some researchers still use the term CDA, but CDS is now used more often as this term is felt to better capture the fact that such studies may use a range of tools and methods rather than just one analytical approach.

Another important aspect of modern CDS research is that the data analysed can include any form of communication. In this chapter there are examples which focus on a range of different types of data in order to illustrate some of the possibilities, from analysing interactional data to song lyrics, from television shows to statues. Because of the concerns of CDS, much of the data analysed is in the public domain, an aspect which contrasts with CA and Interactional Sociolinguistics.

6.1   THE ORIGINS AND DEVELOPMENT OF CRITICAL DISCOURSE STUDIES

CDS grew out of earlier approaches within British linguistics which had begun to explore issues of power and ideology. Five people are generally regarded as being the founders of CDS: Norman Fairclough, Teun van Dijk, Ruth Wodak, Theo van Leeuwen and Gunther Kress. Initially, these researchers were mainly working independently on similar issues and developing their own individual approaches. These approaches have developed over the years and are still all influential today. These researchers have at times collaborated, both as editors and as co-researchers; see for example, van Leeuwen and Kress (1996, 2006), van Leeuwen and Wodak (1999), Wodak and van Dijk (2000) and Wodak and Fairclough (2010).

Norman Fairclough is one of the founders of CDS within sociolinguistics. He was concerned with how social practices are discursively shaped and how power is exercised through language, as well as the subsequent effects. Along with other areas, Fairclough has scrutinised the language of the mass media as a site of power and of struggle (e.g., Fairclough 1995), as well as the discourse of politicians (Fairclough 2000, 2005; see example (7), this chapter). His approach is referred to as the dialectical-relational approach (see e.g., Fairclough 2016).

Teun van Dijk has taken a CDS approach since the 1980s, focusing especially on the study of the discursive reproduction of racism by what he terms the "symbolic elites" (journalists, scholars, writers and politicians), for example, see van Dijk (1998). He has studied press news, and developed theories of ideology, context and knowledge. His approach is known as the socio-cognitive approach (see e.g., van Dijk 2016).

Another key figure in this area is Ruth Wodak. Wodak's approach advocates an interdisciplinary, problem-oriented approach to analysing the change of discursive practices over time and in various genres. Along with her colleagues, she has explored data highlighting many issues from many countries, genres and using a range of methods. Some of this research is mentioned later. Her approach is called the discourse-historical approach (see e.g., Reisigl and Wodak 2016).

The work of Theo van Leeuwen and Gunther Kress is seen as important in CDS for their approach to analysing visual forms of communication. Their book *Reading Images: The Grammar of Visual Design*, originally published in 1996 and updated in 2006 and 2021, is one of the most influential books on this topic. Their approach to CDS is known as the social-semiotic approach (see e.g., van Leeuwen 2016).

6.2 WHAT ARE SOME KEY CONCEPTS IN CRITICAL DISCOURSE STUDIES?

Some key concepts in CDS are:

- power
- ideologies
- the *critical* aspect in CDS
- history

6.2.1 Power

Power is a central concept in CDS approaches with close analysis of the language used (or other aspects) in light of who holds power, how this is evident, and what this says about society. Power can be related to a range of factors, such as job role or status, gender, race or ethnicity. This may be individual or group power. At a basic level, a person in a powerful position can control and constrain the way less powerful participants communicate (Fairclough 2015: 76).

Consider (1):

(1)   Workplace interaction

Context: A policy analyst in a government department is asking her senior manager why she was not appointed acting manager when her immediate manager was away. Recorded in New Zealand.

CLAIRE:	yeah um yeah I want to talk to you about um
	oh it's a personal issue um +
	well I- the decision to make um Jared acting manager
	while //Joseph\ is away
TOM:	/mm\\
TOM:	mm
CLAIRE:	and I wanted to get some [phone rings]: well
	I've been overlooked quite a few times
	//but\ I wanted to find out specifically
TOM:	/(mm)\\
CLAIRE:	how what I could do to help myself be considered next time
TOM:	can I just grab th- just grab that phone? sorry about that
CLAIRE:	that's okay: [Tom answers the phone] . . .
CLAIRE:	(well) I just want to talk to you about it and and I suppose [swallows]
	[tut] I just want to get some ideas on what I could do to actually
	be considered favourably next time
TOM:	yeah I don't think it's a it's a question of er favourability
	I mean it was a question more practicalities more than anything else
	um I was urgent need of someone to fill in
	and Jared had done that in the past already

> Adapted and reprinted under STM guidelines from Discourse Studies 5, Stubbe, Maria, Chris Lane, Jo Hilder, Elaine Vine, Bernadette Vine, Meredith Marra, Janet Holmes and Ann Weatherall, 2003. Multiple discourse analyses of a workplace interaction, p. 381. (Source: LWP)

Even in this short extract we can see the way a more powerful participant in an interaction controls a number of aspects of the discourse. The contents of Claire's turns here are constrained by the fact that she is speaking to Tom, her senior manager, who has more power through his work role and institutional status. She therefore phrases her complaint as a request for advice. Tom's power is also evident as he answers the phone, making her wait, and then constrains her turns when he makes her repeat herself after this interruption.

Power, dominance and inequality can be evident in discourse due to factors such as gender, ethnicity, race, language, age, institutional power. Often more than one factor is relevant when examining discourse data. Resistance or challenges to power may also be observed. In (1), in coming to Tom and making the complaint, albeit indirectly, Claire is resisting and challenging the decision that Tom has made to appoint Jared instead of her as acting manager of her unit. Example (2) presents an example where the text is challenging dominant societal norms.

(2)   Song lyrics   (translated)

Context: Song sung by women at the Tij (Teej) women's festival in central Nepal in 1990. The annual festival which is celebrated across Nepal and in parts of northern India started over 300 years ago.

parents just keep the daughters to do work at home
but even a small piece of courtyard [i.e., land] is not given {to daughters}
{the parents say} the small piece of yard is needed to dry the paddy
go daughter to your husband's house to get your property
{the daughter says} we have to go empty-handed {to our husband's home}
the brothers fence in their property
brothers' clothes are so many that they rot away in a box
but when they have to give us a single cloth tears come to their eyes

Adapted from *American Ethnologist 22*, Holland, Dorothy C. and Debra G. Skinner, 1995. Contested ritual, contested femininities: (Re)forming self and society in a Nepali women's festival, p. 284. Used with permission of the American Anthropological Association.

The song criticises the privileged treatment that sons receive compared to daughters; sons get land and material goods while the daughters do all the housework. Such songs publicly express criticism at the unfair privileging of males and the place of women in this society. Holland and Skinner (1995) show that the festival and the singing of songs that comment on their lives have major significance for the women. The lyrics of the songs do not directly challenge specific fathers or husbands, but represent an important way the women understand themselves, their lives and each other. For a few days each year the women and girls can publicly acknowledge the frustrations about the realities of their day-to-day lives.

6.2.2   Ideologies

Another important concept in CDS is **ideologies**. **Ideologies** are systems of beliefs and values shared by a group of people in society. Reality is constructed and interpreted on the basis of people's beliefs and values, so ideologies may influence what is understood and accepted as true or false. This is relevant when considering aspects related to religious, political and social life.

Ideologies are produced and reflected in discourse. Unequal power relations between, for instance, social classes, women and men (as in (2)), and ethnic groups, can therefore be reproduced through the ways in which discourse represents and positions people. As Fairclough, Mulderrig and Wodak (2011: 358) note "discourse may, for example, be racist, or sexist, and try to pass off assumptions (often falsifying ones) about any aspect of social life as mere common sense". Ideological assumptions and underlying power relations may often not be clear to people. CDS provides ways to explore ideology and challenge the social, cultural and political ideologies and values often covertly encoded within texts. Analysts seek to uncover ideologies, whether explicit or implicit.

Gender ideologies

Gender ideologies have been a common focus of CDS research, with many different types of data examined from different countries and contexts. An example is research by Smith (2015), who explored children's literature, examining two different versions of the story of *Rapunzel* published by the same publisher for the same age group but at different times (Southgate 1968; Baxter 1993). *Rapunzel* is a fairy tale about a young woman who is rescued by a prince from a tower where she has been imprisoned by a witch. In undertaking a Critical Discourse Analysis of the two versions, Smith (2015) highlights evidence of shifts in gender politics and popular culture. In the 1968 version, Rapunzel is represented as passive, while the prince is active, he has *climbed* the tower and he *talked* to her. This positions the prince as having greater power. This contrasts with the 1993 version, where Rapunzel and the prince are depicted as both speaking, although of course he is still the one who is there to rescue her.

Overall, Smith's analysis of specific scenes in the two versions demonstrate how issues of gender and power have become more prominent over the time, "reflecting the different social contexts of production" (2015: 436). The characters in the 1968 version endorse clearly defined traditional gender roles, and although Rapunzel is less passive in the 1993 version, Smith asserts that there is an explicit rejection of female empowerment with the depiction of the witch serving as a warning of the consequences of allowing women such "unnatural" power (2015: 436). The 1993 version appears to reject second-wave feminism, perhaps alerting readers to the dangers of renouncing traditional gender roles. Smith's research provides insight into the ways in which Western society ideologically positions men and women, and how this is reproduced in literature aimed at children.

Gender ideologies are also the focus of Clifton, Schnurr and Van De Mieroop (2019), but they consider the way these intersect with traditional understandings of leadership. Example (3) presents an example analysed in their study.

(3)　　TED talk excerpt

Context: Personal anecdote told at the beginning of the TED talk *3 Lessons for Success from an Arab Business Woman*. The speaker Leila Hoteit is a partner and managing director at a Boston Consultancy Group in Dubai.

LEILA HOTEIT:　mom who are these people?
　　　　　　　　it was an innocent question from my young daughter Alia
　　　　　　　　around the time when she was three

we were walking along with my husband
in one of Abu Dhabi's big fancy malls
Alia was peering at a huge poster
standing tall in the middle of the mall
it featured the three rulers of the United Arab Emirates
as she tucked in my side I bent down and explained
that these were the rulers of the UAE
who had worked hard to develop their nations
and preserve its unity
she asked mom why is it that here where we live
and back in Lebanon where grandma and grandpa live
we never see the pictures of powerful women on the walls
is it because women are not important
this is probably the hardest question I've had to answer
in my years as a parent
and in my sixteen plus years of professional life for that matter

Republished with permission of Taylor & Francis Informa UK Ltd – Books, from The Language of Leadership Narratives: A Social Practice Perspective, Clifton, Jonathan, Stephanie Schnurr and Dorien Van De Mieroop, 2019, pp. 148–149; permission conveyed through Copyright Clearance Center, Inc.

As an example of narrative, (3) is relatively typical. After starting with a reconstructed dialogue which establishes the characters, action and location of the story, Leila Hoteit recounts how her daughter Alia asked her questions about leadership and gender. These were triggered by a poster displayed in the mall. This is followed by the evaluation of the narrative, with Leila commenting *this is probably the hardest question I've had to answer*. The resolution of the story is not explicitly stated and the audience is left to figure out what Leila might have said to her daughter in response. The incident may not have taken place as Leila recounts, but the message of the story is still clear: the under-representation of women in leadership positions.

The use of this anecdote at the beginning of her talk enables the speaker to highlight gender as an issue, in particular as it relates to leadership. She questions and challenges archetypal leadership stories. Clifton, Schnurr and Van De Mieroop (2019: 149) note that this is achieved with the help of various discursive strategies, such as repeatedly using her daughter's words to not only give a young and innocent girl a voice but also to provide "a simple yet powerful way to pinpoint an obvious issue of leadership, which many adults . . . tend to take for granted and do not recognise anymore as noteworthy or perhaps even problematic" (2019: 149–150). The highlighting of the issue is made in relation to the setting, Abu Dhabi, and elsewhere in the Middle East. Because the TED talk has both a local and a global audience this however reaches further. Gender inequality is an issue everywhere, "and if a young child can see it, why has everyone else stopped noticing it?" (2019: 150). The story foregrounds the pervasive "think leader think male" discourse, problematising and challenging its underlying assumptions and ideologies about what leaders look like and who can and cannot be a leader.

Cultural/racial ideologies

Issues of racism have also been a common focus for CDS research. In his 1998 book *Ideology: A Multidisciplinary Approach*, van Dijk explores racial ideologies. After the theoretical chapters, he provides an example of racism and racist ideologies by examining in detail the book *The End of Racism: Principles for a Multiracial Society* by Dinesh D'Souza. Van Dijk discusses how even in the name of this book there is an underlying ideology that implies the US is not a racist country, noting that this "denial of racism . . . constitutes one of the core attitudes of modern elite racism" (van Dijk 1998: 285). The book's subtitle advocates a *multiracial* society, but van Dijk demonstrates how the contents clearly show that "the supremacy of the dominant white 'race' should not be challenged" (1998: 285).

One of the most prominent devices used to legitimise racism that van Dijk (1998) identifies is the use of assertions of "naturalness" and the "universality" of dominant cultural values and norms. Underlying this ideological legitimation of inequality is a belief that Western culture is superior (1998: 287). Outgroups are constructed as enemies, criminals or deviants, and as coming from uncivilised and primitive cultures. Negative stereotypes are often drawn on to do this. Consider (4):

(4) Comments in an online news forum (Czech)

Context: Comments responding to a news article about Slovakian Roma migrants in Sheffield, UK, which has been reported in the Czech Press. The original news article reported statements by David Blunkett, an MP for the Sheffield area, about a need for re-education so that the migrants can integrate into British society. Writers are responding to this.

    a.   Ani při své velice bujné fantazii si nedokážu představit, čím v té převýchově začnou . . . ;-)

        Translation: *Not even given my very creative imagination can I envisage what they will start the re-education with . . . ;-)*

    b.   ty převychová jen chladná cela a rány bičem;-€

        Translation: *those can be re-educated only by a cold cell and whip lashes;-€*

Adapted and reprinted under STM guidelines from Discourse & Society 32(2), Chovanec, Jan. 2020. "Re-educating the Roma? You must be joking . . .": Racism and prejudice in online discussion forums, p. 161.

The people commenting adopt a superior position, asserting that they know that any re-education attempt would be futile. They situate themselves as members of an ingroup based on their alleged negative experience and knowledge of the ethnic outsiders. Chovanec (2020: 162) notes that this was a common, recurring theme in the reader comments. These types of comments reflect the common ingroup stereotype of the Roma as lacking education, being ignorant and stupid (see also Breazu and Machin 2019). Example (4b) takes this to the extreme, calling for incarceration and physical violence towards members of the outgroup as the only way to re-educate them, constructing the Roma as deviant and uncivilised.

Political ideologies

Political ideologies are a third common type explored in CDS research. Richardson and Colombo (2014), for instance, examine European far right political parties and the shift in the way migrants are represented, from being "alien" to "enemy", and how this is discursively realised. This draws on "the dominant-dominated dimension on which racist supremacist ideology is grounded" (2014: 521). The political ideology therefore also incorporates racist ideology. One example they examine is a poster produced by the nationalist Swiss People's Party in 2007, a party which took a strong anti-immigration stance. The poster depicts a cartoon white sheep kicking a black sheep. This was accompanied by the slogan *pour plus de sécurité*, "for more security". The poster was designed after the proposal of a new law which would authorise the deportation of foreign criminals. The white/black division plays on the expression *the black sheep*, though Richardson and Colombo (2014: 528) note that "this also communicates a clear (though inherently deniable) racialised agenda". The legitimisation of expulsion is justified by the linguistic content, this is *pour plus de sécurité*. No explicit reference to migrants is made, with the audience being left to determine who the excluded might be. The slogan "My home – Our Switzerland" is also used, positioning the Swiss People's Party as defending the homeland. The use of the first person possessive pronouns "my" and "our" establishes a strong link between the personal and the collective and encourages strong identification with the ingroup.

Abousnnouga and Machin (2010) explore political ideologies as expressed through a form of communication that does not necessarily use words at all, this time the discourse involves public statues. In a study of two World War I monuments erected in the UK in the 1920s, they begin by examining the context in which the monuments were produced. The statues represent a deliberate attempt to place artefacts in a public space in order to communicate political values. Much of the press of the time was filled with pro war propaganda, however many working class people in Britain did not view the war as having been a good thing; 90% of the estimated three million UK dead or wounded in World War I were working class men. The ruling classes were aware of the unease and worried about the consequences, particularly considering the communist uprisings in Europe and local labour movement activities (Hobsbawm 1983). Monuments were used to help "(re)contextualise the massive death toll into a discourse of common sacrifice for God and nation" (Abousnnouga and Machin 2010: 140). The figures they depict have calm expressions, for instance, and either look upwards, or forwards and upwards to the horizon. This means that they "do not engage with the viewer and therefore demand no response through gaze" (2010: 144). Instead, they seem to be part of a different world and do not confront the viewer. They look to the heavens, or a far-off place, and represent high ideals.

Discourse is used to create, reproduce and reinforce ideologies. Ideologies that have been explored in CDS include those that relate to a range of factors such as gender, race and politics as illustrated in this section. CDS aims to uncover inequalities, so identifying ideologies is an important aspect of this.

6.2.3 What about the *critical* aspect of Critical Discourse Studies?

The critical aspect of CDS is, as the name suggests, of central importance. To be **critical** can have different meanings, but in CDS research it relates to the fact that it is not enough to highlight and describe discourse practices which construct and reinforce power differences and ideologies, they must also be critiqued, and feedback (where possible) should be given. This is particularly important when there is an abuse of power, or a lack of awareness about an issue which causes inequalities and injustice. Researchers using a CDS approach explicitly position themselves on the side of those being dominated, typically examining the discourse of the more powerful participant or group involved. The statues analysed by Abousnnouga and Machin (2010) for example were commissioned and placed in location by the dominant ruling classes of the time who were trying to exert influence on the working classes, and the research highlights and reminds people of the intentions behind the works.

Example (5) provides an example where a more powerful group interact with a young woman. It is taken from a study investigating an incident which occurred on the Turkish version of the show *The Voice* in 2012. The show involves contestants singing while potential singing coaches have their backs to the stage, meaning they judge the contestant only on their singing and not on their appearance. If a coach likes a contestant's singing then they turn and the contestant can then choose from those who have turned which coach they would like to work with.

(5)   The Voice Turkey (2012)   (translated from Turkish)

Context: A contestant has been using the informal form *sen* "you" when talking to the judges, two of whom had turned. The host has reprimanded her for this, challenging her that she is being disrespectful in not using the formal version, *siz*. One of the coaches then challenges her.

COACH D:	*I think you are speaking in a very wrong style*
	there is a big disrespectfulness towards us really
CONTESTANT:	*but I didn't mean it*
COACH D:	*I feel that way though*
	as a coach this is the first time I am feeling this way
CONTESTANT:	*I don't know*
	I don't think that I spoke wrongfully jaa [informal hesitation marker]
	did I do something wrong?
	no I only asked who turned
	I asked who turned
HOST:	*no okay you*
COACH D:	*yes*

HOST:	let's not continue this anymore
	thank you for coming
	we send you off with applause
AUDIENCE:	[applause and cheering]
	[Contestant comes off the stage]
CONTESTANT:	this is nonsense
AUNT:	it is okay my dear no no no
	it is okay it is normal
	okay okay okay you will learn over time

Adapted from Er, Ibrahim, "The voiceless in The Voice: A multimodal critical discourse analysis"; in: Text & Talk 40/6, 2020, p. 718, lines 108–123. Used with permission of De Gruyter.

In (5), the end of the interaction between the contestant and the host and one of the coaches on the television programme is shown. The coach directly criticises the way the contestant is speaking, which has involved the informal form of "you", *sen*, rather than the more formal one, *siz*. Even though two judges had turned, the host then disqualifies her and she leaves the stage. Her aunt then tells her that she will learn these norms over time. Er (2020) notes that the contestant did learn from this experience and appeared on the same stage in the following season of the show. Her second performance attracted all four coaches, and all of them turned their chairs without knowing that it was her. This time, however, she was extremely cautious about her words and style of speech. Er (2020) also explores how the stylistic elements of the show create and contribute to "constructing and maintaining social power relationships and the hierarchical construction of difference" between the show's hosts, the coaches and the contestants (2020: 714). Er's study therefore does not just describe the incident, but highlights and provides a critique of the way the contestant was treated by the judges.

Critique may highlight positive aspects as well; being critical does not mean being only negative. Wodak (2009), for example, explores data from members of the European Parliament, demonstrating how much backstage work they do. One of the politicians in her research, Hans, even used lunch as a chance for a meeting to discuss work issues. Her assessment of the politicians communication practices is positive and she argues that the invisibility of this backstage work leads to widespread politicisation and misunderstanding.

Another study which highlights positive aspects is Romano and Porto (2018). They explore the use of the metaphor which conceptualises a mass of people as a tide, *marea*, and the way this shifted from negative or neutral meanings to a more positive meaning within a specific context, see (6).

(6) News headlines (Spanish)

Context: Reporting on public protest demonstrations in Spain.

    a. (ABC 09/10/2011): Una **marea verde** sale a las calles en defensa de la enseñanza pública.

Translation

A **green tide** comes out to the streets in defence of public education.

b. (El País 17/023/2012): La **marea blanca** contra la privitización y los recortes se extiende.

Translation

*The **white tide** against privatisation and cuts spreads.*

> Adapted and reprinted under STM guidelines from Discourse & Society 29(6), Romano, Manuela and M. Dolores Porto, 2018. "The tide, change, nobody can stop it": Metaphor for social action, pp. 662, 663.
> (Sources: ABC and El País)

Romano and Porto (2018) view the use of the *marea* "tide" metaphor as an important tool in the legitimation of social action in Spanish society. With the green tide, the whole educational community, including teachers, parents and students, joined the protests, (6a). This gave rise to a general feeling of sympathy towards the protesters. When the regional government in Madrid presented a plan in October 2011 for the privatisation of several hospitals in the public health system, health specialists started their own demonstrations. This time the protestors chose white coats as a symbol of the fight for a public health system. They recontextualised the green tide, with the protesters for public healthcare becoming a white tide, (6b). This metaphor produced the same feelings of support and sympathy that were already associated with the green tide. The *marea* metaphor soon extended to all social and professional groups fighting against austerity measures, privatisations and cuts, each choosing different colours. The metaphor was reused from one demonstration to another, from one group to another, becoming a powerful and positive tool for challenging government policies in Spain.

The critical aspect of CDS research means that discourse is examined with a view to highlighting features that may not be evident to people at first glance. This often explores negative aspects but may also highlight positive ones.

6.2.4 History

A fourth concept that Wodak and Meyer (2001: 3) highlight as important in CDS is the role of **history**. **History** is important because discourse is historically produced and interpreted; time and place shape discourse. Ideologies have developed over time, and the effects of power often become obscured and part of the status quo. Resistance requires raising awareness, breaking conventions and challenging accepted ways of doing things, as highlighted in (3), where Leila Hoteit questions leadership ideologies.

The importance of history, the time of production, was evident in Smith's (2015) research. The different ways the story of *Rapunzel* was told in 1968 and 1993 reflected a shift in gender politics. Understanding the historical context in Abousnnouga and Machin's (2010) research on World War I statues unveiled in the 1920s also helped make sense of the ideologies involved in the way the soldiers in the statues are depicted. Abousnnouga and Machin (2010) comment that the negative view of the war by working class people and the associated concern of the ruling classes about the possible consequences of this, is not well documented in British history books. This is an important factor, however, in interpreting the historical context in which the statues were produced.

6.2.5 Summary

Two key concepts in CDS are **power** and **ideologies**. Exploring these and the way they are evident in discourse is a primary concern in CDS research. The **critical** focus of CDS research is also central. To be **critical** can at times mean to simply examine something, but in CDS the focus is on uncovering inequalities, bias and prejudice, and critiques tend to highlight negative aspects, although do not exclude the possibility of analysing positive features. One last key idea briefly outlined earlier is the significance of **history** for CDS research. This acknowledges the fact that discourse is located in a specific time, place and context, and these factors shape discourse.

6.3 KEY DOMAINS IN CRITICAL DISCOURSE STUDIES

Because of an interest in power and ideologies there are some key domains that have been explored in CDS research:

- political discourse; and
- media discourse

There is overlap between these two domains: research on political discourse may include the way it is represented in the media and media discourse may of course also reflect underlying political ideologies. CDS research tends to focus on discourse in these types of public domains since this is where power and ideologies can be readily seen to be produced and reinforced.

6.3.1 Political discourse

Given the focus on power and ideologies, including political ideologies, it is unsurprising that political discourse has been a central focus in CDS. This is a domain where language "gains power by the use powerful people make of it" (Wodak and de Cillia 2006: 714), so it is an important context in which to explore power. This has involved the analysis of political speeches (e.g., Fairclough 2005; Sarfo and Krampa 2013), but also a range of other political genres, such as debates (e.g., van der Valk 2003; Boyd 2013) and blogs (e.g., Kopytowska 2013). Fairclough (2005), for instance, examines a move towards a new regime of international relations and security, focusing on speeches by the then Prime Minister of the UK, Tony Blair. He discusses how Blair contributed to the emergence of "a new hegemonic discourse of international relations and international security" in his speeches given between 2000 and 2003. The context is one where the use of military force is being justified, and at the time British forces were deployed in Kosovo, Afghanistan, and Iraq. Example (7) illustrates how Blair talks about values in these speeches.

(7) Political speech

Context: Speech by the UK Prime Minister Tony Blair in January 2003.

TONY BLAIR: in the end all these things come back to one basic theme
the values we stand for
freedom human rights the rule of law democracy
are all universal values
given a chance the world over people want them
but they have to be pursued alongside another value
justice the belief in opportunity for all
without justice the values I describe can be portrayed as western values
globalisation becomes a battering ram for western commerce and culture
the order we want is seen by much of the world as their order not ours
the consensus can only be achieved if pursued with a sense of fairness
of equality of partnership

> Adapted and reprinted with permission. From Fairclough, Norman. Blair's contribution to elaborating a new doctrine of "international community". Journal of Language and Politics 4(1), p. 52, © 2005, John Benjamins Publishing.

Blair asserts that the values of freedom, human rights, the rule of law, and democracy are universal values. This assertion, however, as Fairclough (2005: 52) points out, is immediately undermined when Blair says *given a chance... people want them*. Values which people *want* (*given a chance*) cannot therefore be truly *universal*. Blair then provides an implicit recognition that these values are in fact widely seen as western rather than being universal, *the values I demonstrate can be portrayed as western values*, but maintains that *consensus can... be achieved*. If these values are truly *universal* the implication is that there is already consensus. Close analysis of the speeches demonstrates many points where there are apparent contradictions like this (see also Fairclough 2000). Fairclough concludes that Blair's reference to values is one of the ways that he justifies the use of force in Iraq. Alongside other nations, he is saying that Great Britain is helping the Iraqi people, for example, because they, among other things, desire democracy.

Political discourse has been a major focus for Ruth Wodak as well. In *The Politics of Fear*, for instance, Wodak analyses the texts and images used by far-right groups, from speeches to cartoons to social media posts (2015, 2020). This research demonstrates a range of types of data that can be examined, and Wodak highlights the strategies, rhetoric and half-truths employed. She explores how far-right politics have moved from the margins to the centre of the political landscape in Europe. This normalisation of far-right political discourse is built around ideologies of nationalism, xenophobia, racism, sexism, antisemitism and Islamophobia.

6.3.2 Media discourse

Fairclough has also scrutinised the language of the mass media as a site of power and of struggle (e.g., Fairclough 1995), and media discourse has been another central focus in CDS research more generally. This includes a range of media types, from newspapers (e.g., Archakis and Tsakona 2010) to movies and television programmes (e.g., Machin and van Leeuwen 2007; van der Houwen 2015), and social media such as Twitter (e.g., Krzyżanowski 2018) and YouTube (e.g., Way 2015).

News reporting is an area where language is widely assumed to be transparent and reporting on newsworthy items is generally considered unbiased. Media institutions often maintain that they are neutral. CDS research demonstrates the inaccuracy of such assumptions (e.g., van Dijk 1987; Fairclough 1995), and illustrates the mediating and constructing role of the media. Examples (8) and (9) provide reporting on the same event, but with different perspectives. They also show the cross-over of focus between media and politics. These examples are drawn from a study by Archakis and Tsakona (2010) which provides a critical analysis of journalists' articles on parliamentary discourse. As well as comparing five articles from different newspapers, they also examine the parliamentary proceedings that the articles refer to, finding that the texts produced in the press are coherent "yet often fictional" (2010: 913). The reports also differ between newspapers. Compare (8) and (9):

(8)   Newspaper extract   (Greek)

Context: Extract from the newspaper *Ethnos*.

Φανατικά υπέρ του νόμου τάχθηκε ο Β. Πολύδωρας, ο οποίος μίλησε για "λυκανθρώπους" και παρομοίασε τους συμβασιούχους με τους "νεκρούς" που "αρνείται το ΠΑΣΟΚ την ταφή τους".

Translation

Viron Polidoras supported the bill fanatically, speaking of "werewolves" and comparing the short-term contract-employees to "dead people" whom "PASOK refuses to bury".

(9)   Newspaper extract   (Greek)

Context: Extract from the newspaper *Vradini*.

Κατά την παρέμβασή του, ο κοινοβουλευτικός εκπρόσωπς της ΝΔ Βύρων Πολύδωρας ανέφερε: "Έπρεπε να το ψηφίσετε το νομοσχέδιο. Εμείς τακτοποιούμε τις δικές σας εκκρεμότητες. Αυτά που εσείς αφήσατε πίσω σας. Που κάνατε στρατιές χιλιάδων ομήρων συμβασιούχων, που πους καταντήσατε νεκρούς. Και τώρα αρνείστε να ψηφίσετε".

Translation

During his intervention, the spokesperson of ND Viron Polidoras mentioned: "You should have voted for the bill. We are settling your unfinished business. What you've left behind. It's you who made hostages out of thousands of contract-employees; who have committed these people to the dead. And now you refuse to vote".

> Adapted from Journal of Pragmatics 42, Archakis, Argiris and Tsakona, Villy, "The wolf wakes up inside them, grows werewolf hair and reveals all their bullying": The representation of parliamentary discourse in Greek newspapers, p. 918, also Appendix pp. 3 and 4 © 2010, with permission from Elsevier.

The reporting by the two newspapers on the same political speech is very different, reflecting the different political orientations of the two papers. The wording in (8), with the politician Viron Polidoras being noted to "fanatically" support the bill contrasts sharply with (9), where the journalist uses much less emotive language, providing direct quotes "mentioned" by Polidoras. The journalist writing (9) also quotes a much longer section of direct speech, rather than just words and brief phrases.

In comparing the five newspaper reports to the parliamentary records, Archakis and Tsakona note that although at times the extracts from Polidoras' speech "appear to be reproduced verbatim", as in (9), many parts are omitted, others come from different passages in the proceedings, and the chronological order of the extracts presented is often violated. The news reports "are not 'impartial' reflections of reality, but rather value-laden representations of it" (2010: 920). The political and ideological orientation of the publication in which texts appear strongly influence the way the events are reported.

Forms of media, as public engagement, are obvious places where ideologies are created and reproduced, and power inequalities reinforced and maintained. In exploring media representations of crime fighting, Mayr and Machin (2012) show how both police and criminals can be personalised and individualised, and the effects of this. Consider (10):

(10) Newspaper article

Context: Article reporting on bike thefts in Coventry, UK in 2011.

Police warning after string of bike thefts

POLICE in Rugby are warning owners of motorbikes and mopeds to remain vigilant following an increase of thefts in the area.

On two days last week, three bikes were stolen from driveways in the town – two of which were secured by disc locks.

Rugby Inspector Paul Judson said: 'Motorbikes and mopeds are popular targets for thieves as they can be sold easily or broken up for parts, which are harder to trace. In addition to this, we believe low-powered motorbikes are also being stolen to be used as off-road vehicles. These are often discovered discarded nearby'.

Adapted from p. 144, © Andrea Mayr, and David Machin, 2012, "Language of Crime and Deviance: An Introduction to Critical Linguistic Analysis in Media and Popular Culture", Continuum UK, an imprint of Bloomsbury Publishing Plc. (Source: Coventry Evening Telegraph 8 February 2011)

This story is about a series of bike thefts which took place over two days. The police have not actually caught the thieves, but the report frames the story as a warning from the police to the public. The police are therefore performing their public role within the community, looking out for citizens. Inspector Paul Judson is directly quoted and this personalises and humanises the police. The mental process indicated with the verb *believe* adds to this since it gives access to the mental world of the police, suggesting they have information and knowledge about the thefts (Mayr and Machin 2012: 144).

Mayr and Machin (2012: 144) also note the importance of the phrase *in addition to this*. A device often found in political speeches, this phrase signposts a sense of quantity. The police, therefore, clearly have a good amount of information and knowledge. Here we get the sense of a confident police force. They appear, even when they are unsure about how to solve a case, to have information about their work and emphasise both "their officialdom and their human face" (2012: 145).

The police may be humanised, but issues of social context are suppressed (e.g., social reasons behind thefts such as this). Crime is portrayed as a battle of good against evil rather than about social contexts such as poverty and disadvantage.

A further category of media discourse that has been explored involves television shows, as illustrated in (5). Van der Houwen (2015) analyses another type of reality television, this time set in a courtroom where a judge in the US, Judge Judy Sheindlin, makes rulings on cases. The judge resolves disputes between, for example, neighbours, family members, friends, or employers and employees. The cases people bring to the show are about issues such as assault, breach of contract and property damage. Van der Houwen (2015) examines how the interactions between the litigants and the judge at times highlight side issues which become central and which may even form the basis for a ruling. In (11), the plaintiff is suing the defendant for medical costs incurred after an assault. The defence is self-defence, a version of events which the judge aligns with.

(11) Reality television courtroom transcript

Context: Rachel Manden, 17-years-old, and her mother, 33-year-old Vera Hammer, are suing 15-year-old Carol Bond, and her mother, 39-year-old Amanda East. Rachel says she was severely injured during a fistfight with Carol.

JUDGE: how old are you?
RACHEL: seventeen

JUDGE: you should be smarter at seventeen
I don't expect you to be fully cooked but you shouldn't be an idiot
you went there looking for trouble . . .
and you're a moron for being there
for that you don't get rewarded you got injured . . .
anyway you went there looking for trouble and you found it
pay your own medical bills # case is dismissed that's all

> Adapted from "If it doesn't make sense it's not true": How Judge Judy creates coherent stories through "common-sense" reasoning according to the neoliberal agenda, van der Houwen, Fleur, Social Semiotics, 2015, p. 261–262, reprinted by permission of the publisher (Taylor & Francis Ltd, www.tandfonline.com).

In (11), the judge invokes a judgement based on the assumption that one should not look for trouble and risk provoking someone. The reasoning in (11) is characteristic of the judge and complements her judgement based on the "facts". In order to understand (if not agree with) the decision in which Rachel is held responsible for her actions, van der Houwen comments that it is necessary to understand the moral common-sense reasoning brought into play; the judge holds Rachel responsible for the fight because had she possessed more intelligence (and moral strength), as she should have by the age of 17, she would not have gone to the park *looking for trouble* and there would not have been a fight (2015: 262). Directing Rachel to pay for her medical bills is a lesson which the judge, as an authority, imposes to help Rachel. The reasoning which assigns responsibility to Rachel for going to the park overshadows the legal judgement that the judge has found that the defendant acted out of self-defence.

6.3.3 Summary

This section has illustrated research from two key domains which have been the focus of CDS: political discourse and media discourse. Research on **political discourse** may involve examining speeches, but other possibilities include debates and blogs. Some different types of **media discourse** which have been explored in CDS research include newspapers and television shows. Other newer forms of media have been examined, such as social media (see e.g., Wodak 2020). Political and media sources provide rich and accessible data for exploring power and ideologies because of their public nature.

6.4 TYPES OF ANALYSIS AND METHODOLOGIES IN CRITICAL DISCOURSE STUDIES

Because CDS is a theoretical approach rather than an analytical one, researchers undertaking Critical Discourse Analysis may draw on a range of analysis techniques. The methodologies of CDS differ greatly: sometimes for example small qualitative case studies have been undertaken and at other times large corpora may be examined. Researchers may analyse the words and meanings in a text, for example, in Mayr and

Machin (2012) the language used to describe crime and policing frames it as a battle against evil individuals and the way the police are said to *believe* certain things in (10) humanises them. Smith's (2015) highlighting of the verbs used in relation to Rapunzel and the prince places the prince in a more powerful position. Metaphor is another common focus of CDS analysis. Researchers examine how metaphors present groups and actions in a particular way and draw attention to the persuasiveness and effectiveness of this in creating and reproducing different ideologies. Analysis may also focus on grammatical aspects. In examining the statement of the chairman of a UK defence firm, for instance, Merkl-Davies and Koller (2012), focus on the grammatical devices used to represent organisational activities and outcomes in ways which impersonalise and evaluate. These devices are used strategically to guide the readers' "interpretations of financial performance and to legitimise and normalise violence and destruction by depicting it in an abstract and sanitised manner" (2012: 178).

Analytical approaches adopted in CDS include those described in Chapters 3 to 5 of this book, along with a range of other approaches. Within the array of approaches used in undertaking Critical Discourse Analysis, there are a growing number of studies using corpus linguistics techniques, and this is now recognised as an important strand of CDS (see e.g., Catalano and Waugh 2020). Multi-modal analyses are also becoming more common as technology presents new forms of communication and new possibilities for analysis. I briefly explore these two strands of CDS research.

6.4.1 Corpus linguistics and Critical Discourse Studies

A common criticism of CDS approaches has been that researchers often "cherry-pick" data, that is, choose only sections of data that match a preconceived argument (Baker 2012). The integration of corpus techniques within CDS research can thus be seen as a response to such criticisms, as well as to a related criticism that CDS has traditionally lacked quantitative and comparative methods.

It has been proposed that using corpus linguistics techniques within CDS results in more vigorous and valid findings, improving the objectivity of such research. Nartey and Mwinlaaru (2019), for example, in reviewing 121 studies which combined CDS and corpus linguistic approaches concluded that corpus-based CDS presents both discourse analysts and corpus linguists with a robust methodology to tackle research questions involving discourse and social issues.

A good example of this approach is provided by Rheindorf and Wodak (2018), who explore the "refugee crisis" in Austrian politics as reported in the media in 2015 and 2016. At this time, the discourse was dominated by terminology related to building a *Grenzzaun* "border fence" and setting an *Obergrenze* "maximum limit" on refugees. Corpus techniques allowed them to explore all instances of the relevant terminology, and the quantitative and qualitative analysis highlighted the way that the issues were largely euphemised. This demonstrated how restrictive policies may be normalised.

Another example of a study which uses this approach is Don, Knowles and Fatt (2010). They explored the Malay speeches of Tun Dr Mahathir Mohamad as Malaysian Prime Minister, investigating key words associated with Malaysian identity. Example (12) illustrates key phrases which contain the word *kita* (addressee-inclusive "we").

Malay also has a form *kami* (addressee- exclusive "we"). As a function word, *kita* can collocate with a very wide range of words, but a significant finding of their study was that it collocated with other key words.

(12) Key phrases (clusters) containing the word *kita* in the political speeches of Tun Dr. Mahathir Mohamad (Malay)

Phrase	Translation	Frequency	Rank
di negara kita	*in our country*	360	1
kita tidak boleh	*we cannot*	204	2
kita tidak akan	*we will not*	161	3
jika kita tidak	*if we do not*	114	4
ekonomi negara kita	*our country's economy*	87	10
negara kita ini	*this nation of ours*	79	11

Adapted from Don, Zuraidah Mohd, Gerry Knowles and Choong Kwai Fatt, "Nationhood and Malaysian identity: A corpus-based approach"; in: Text & Talk 30/3, 2010, p. 277. Used with permission of De Gruyter.

Tun Dr Mahathir's explicitly stated objectives as Prime Minister were to emphasise economic development, national development and national unity and the analysis demonstrates that these themes do come through in his speeches. As the inclusive "we", *kita* refers to an ingroup, and by implication contrasts that group with outgroups. *Kita* unites the speaker and his audience into a single community bound by a common destiny and common economic interests; it constructs a common identity despite the diversity within the country's population. In critically assessing its use, Don, Knowles and Fatt (2010) conclude that the use of *kita* obscures the asymmetrical power relation between the Prime Minister and his audience because it claims common ground.

Corpus methods allow identification of patterns within a dataset. Combining this with a CDS approach enables researchers to explore these patterns qualitatively with a critical lens, through analysing key words and phrases, concordance lines or larger sections of text.

6.4.2 Multi-modal analysis in Critical Discourse Studies

One last type of approach utilised in CDS that is briefly considered here is a multimodal approach. This is a form of CDS research that includes analysis of visual representations. Some examples of research taking this approach are mentioned earlier, for example, Richardson and Colombo (2014) who explored the imagery of the black and white sheep on the political poster of the nationalist Swiss People's Party from 2007, as well as the language. Abousnnouga and Machin (2010) focused on the style and design of the statues in their study, as well as their poses, gaze, materials and form, while Er (2020) not only examined the interaction between the host, coaches

142 *Some key approaches to analysing discourse*

and the contestant on *The Voice Turkey*, but also stylistic elements of the show and how the show was edited. A range of types of data were analysed by Wodak (2020), including the texts and images used by far-right groups, from speeches to cartoons to social media posts.

Websites provide rich visual material for CDS analysis. Brookes and Harvey (2017) examine the website of a money-lending company in the UK, Wonga, who provided what are referred to as *payday loans*. Payday lending entails providing customers with high-interest, short-term credit. Wonga rebranded and relaunched itself in 2015 after being involved in a series of financial scandals and Brookes and Harvey analyse the, at the time, new Wonga website, "the gateway to its financial services" (2017: 167). They explore not just the linguistic representations of social actors and processes but also the visual representations. They identify for example the way the website constructs empowered and responsible borrowers. One way this is accomplished is through photos, for instance, the inclusion on the central homepage of a naturalistic photographic image of a young, seemingly contented woman in a kitchen (a clearly identifiable conventional domestic setting). The details and objects in the background of the photo "help convey the impression that this participant, evidently a Wonga borrower, is a responsible, hard-working and devoted mother" (2017: 172). The kitchen is clean and orderly and although she is pictured on her own, the family oriented nature of the scene is suggested by her wedding and engagement rings and a child's colourful pictures. This image conveys the impression of a happy, flourishing, and secure household, and encourages prospective borrowers to align themselves with this idealised setting and scenario.

The use of multi-modal analysis has been an important methodology from the early days of CDS. The work of van Leeuwen and Kress is significant here and their approach to analysing visual aspects of discourse and what these communicate about ideologies is still very influential (see Kress and van Leeuwen 2021).

CHAPTER SUMMARY

CDS research focuses on power and inequality. Discourse is viewed as part of major processes and activities, and as such the interest extends beyond the discourse, for example, the focus is on racism or sexism. Key concepts include **power** and **ideologies**. The **critical** nature of CDS is important, with the aim of highlighting inequalities, power and ideologies. **History** is another aspect that some CDS researchers foreground, since communication does not exist outside the historical and social contexts in which it is produced.

CDS studies have highlighted a range of issues, for example:

- the way discourse reinforces and maintains power differences
- how people may resist social and political inequality
- the way discourse reproduces and reflects people's biases and prejudices
- how people may manipulate discourse to reflect their own position on an issue or the way they want to be perceived

Critical Discourse Studies

Because of the concerns of CDS research, data that are in the public domain, for instance, political or media discourse, are commonly the focus of research. The analytical tools utilised in CDS research are many and varied. Two important strands of CDS research employ corpus linguistics techniques and multi-modal analysis.

FURTHER READING

Catalano and Waugh (2020) is an excellent resource, proving a comprehensive record of the history and development of CDS. It covers a broad array of critical approaches, including the corpus linguistic approach touched on earlier. Other useful texts include Wodak's edited four-volume *Critical Discourse Analysis* (2013), Wodak and Meyer's (2016) *Methods of Critical Discourse Studies* and Hart and Cap's (2014) *Contemporary Critical Discourse Studies*. If you wish to explore visual aspects more, see Kress and van Leeuwen (2021) and Ledin and Machin (2020).

There are also a number of recent handbooks which are excellent resources in this area, including *The Routledge Handbook of Critical Discourse Studies* (Flowerdew and Richardson 2017), *The Routledge Handbook of Language and Media* (Cotter and Perrin 2018) and *The Routledge Handbook of Language and Politics* (Wodak and Forchtner 2018). A number of journals publish CDS research so are great sources for exploring the types of studies undertaken. This includes *Discourse and Society* (edited by Teun van Dijk) and *Critical Discourse Studies* (edited by John Richardson).

EXERCISES

These exercises present a description of authentic data for you to analyse, (A), along with two images with background information, (B) and (C). There are notes at the end for feedback and guidance.

1. Consider (A), which describes a sports news broadcast. Compare and contrast the way the story about the woman's sporting success and the men's sport stories are reported.
2. What would your conclusions be about the differences when taking a critical perspective?

(A) Broadcast Sports News

Context: Description of a segment from a daily televised sports news programme called *SportsCenter* in the US. The segment is called *Top Ten Plays*.

The tenth best play of the day is awarded to an India vs. Pakistan men's cricket game, with a commentator saying India had a "wicked victory". The ninth best play goes to Missy Franklin, "who competed at the women's NCAA swimming and diving championship today". The commentator says, "Missy Franklin. In the NCAA women's swimming and diving championship. Way ahead of the pack in the 200-yard freestyle. Wins easily".

The commentators also note that she "sets the American, NCAA and U.S. Open record in the event". The seventh best play goes to a golfer at the Arnold Palmer golf invitational, who sunk a 116-foot shot. In a voice-over the ESPN commentator exclaims, "That's what I'm talking about!" Number six is from a spring training MLB game between the Cubs and the White Sox. The second baseman catches the ball and tags a player out, and a commentator gushes, "I think he's ready for the regular season! Let's get it going!" Number four is from the heat vs. Grizzlies basketball game, showing Ray Allen scoring. The voice-over from the in-studio commentator exclaims, "From fizzle to sizzle!"

> Reprinted under STM guidelines from Musto, Michela, Cheryl Cooky and Michael A. Messner. 2017. "From fizzle to sizzle!" Gender and Society 31(5), p. 585.

The photos and their descriptions in (B) and (C) are of two WWI memorial statues located in Wellington, New Zealand. Both were commissioned by branches of the Royal New Zealand Returned and Services' Association. Examine the photos and descriptions and then answer the questions.

1. How do these memorials differ?
2. What do you think were the intentions behind the memorials in each case?
3. What do any differences suggest about the political values and ideologies of the times in which they were made?

(B) World War I Memorial Statue unveiled in 1923 in the suburb of Brooklyn, Wellington, to honour the men of the district who served in WWI, see Photo 6.1. A lone figure made of white Italian marble stands on top of a tall plinth, which is on top of a hill. He is 2.4 metres (8 feet) tall. He gazes off into the distance. It is said he is looking over Gallipoli. The plaque under the front of the statue reads *the Motherland called and they went*. According to a local newspaper report from 1923, the memorial was unveiled by the Governor-General of New Zealand and the Acting Prime Minister of the time was present, along with several other Members of Parliament.

(C) World War I Memorial Statue unveiled in 1990 to honour the medics and stretcher bearers on the 75th anniversary of the Gallipoli landings, see Photo 6.2. It stands in what is now known as Pukeahu National War Memorial Park in Wellington. This bronze statue depicts two figures – one an injured soldier riding a donkey, the other a stretcher bearer escorting him. It is based on a photograph taken in 1915 of New Zealander Richard Alexander Henderson, his donkey and a soldier at Gallipoli. The figures are 75 centimetres (29 inches) tall and are on a short plinth. The sculptor was Paul Walshe. It was unveiled by Richard Henderson's son in the presence of one of the Gallipoli stretcher bearers. This information is noted on the plaque beneath the statue. The park it stands in has since been extended and includes various other memorials (see Macalister 2020).

Photo 6.1
(Image credit: Bernadette Vine)

146 Some key approaches to analysing discourse

Photo 6.2
(Image credit: Bernadette Vine)

NOTES ON EXERCISES

These notes give some reflections on issues that might be considered in answering the questions. These are not meant to be definitive answers, and there may be other things that stand out for you.

In (A), the woman's achievements are more significant than the men's, but they are reported in a very matter of fact way. This contrasts with the way the men's events are presented. In these strong adjectives and verbs are used, for example, *wicked* and *sizzle*, and the commentators report them with enthusiasm. Musto, Cooky and Messner (2017: 592) conclude that this "gender-bland sexism" renders women's sports accomplishments less impressive and interesting than men's. This is a shift from the overt forms of sexism in past televised sports news in the US in their research but makes the unequal status of women's and men's sport more difficult to see, and thus to challenge.

There are many aspects of the memorials that contrast – both in the way they are presented and the way they were unveiled – and these elements reflect the different times in which they were erected. For example, the statue in (B) is much larger than the one in (C) (larger than life) and is also on a very tall plinth so is not easy to see from the ground, although it can be seen from far away. (B) is similar in style to the statues mentioned in Abousnnouga and Machin (2010), with an anonymous soldier gazing off into the distance and representing high ideals. The inscription that refers to the *Motherland* below this statue shows the political attitude of New Zealand to Great Britain in the 1920s, which was no longer the case in 1990. (C) is a memorial to medics and stretcher bearers rather than soldiers and is based on a photograph of specific people (and donkey), capturing a moment in time. The honoured guests at the unveiling of (C) were the son of the stretcher bearer depicted and another stretcher bearer rather than political figures. War is not glorified and it tells a story with identifiable individuals, one of whom is injured, signifying at least a little of the realities of the war.

Part III

Conclusions and applications

7

Key approaches and applications

INTRODUCTION

This book has provided an introduction to discourse analysis and has outlined four influential approaches, each of which presents a different perspective on discourse. In Section 7.1, the approaches are compared and contrasted. There are many real-world applications which highlight the usefulness of discourse analysis and in Section 7.2 some applications of research are explored.

7.1 COMPARISON OF APPROACHES

I begin by comparing and contrasting the approaches from Chapters 3 to 6. I examine the types of data each approach explores, the analytical and practical aspects of each approach, and the issues and themes that each addresses.

7.1.1 Types of data explored

Studies using a Corpus Approach to Discourse Analysis can focus on spoken or written data. There is not a strong tendency for using one type of data over another, although earlier corpora tended to consist of written data for practical reasons; it was much easier and faster (and still is) to compile written genres or corpora, especially since corpus linguistics research often utilises large collections of texts. Any type of written data may be explored and some types examined in the research cited in Chapter 3 include popular science writing (Kim 2009) and web news (Butler and Simon-Vandenbergen 2021). Spoken data may include monologues but also genres which involve dialogues, such as calls to health phone help lines (Adolphs et al. 2004) and workplace interactions (Vine 2021b). Background information which might inform analysis does not tend to feature in research taking a Corpus Approach to Discourse Analysis, although this depends on any qualitative analysis the analyst undertakes and which approach is used for this.

Many of the examples in this book come from spoken sources. Spoken sources are especially favoured by CA and Interactional Sociolinguistics, approaches which are discussed in Chapters 4 and 5. CA began as a means for exploring spoken English data in depth, particularly face-to-face personal conversations and telephone calls, and this type of data was the main focus for CA researchers for many years. In Chapter 4, many of the illustrative examples were from studies of family and friends talking

DOI: 10.4324/9781003184058-10

(e.g., Zinken and Deppermann 2017; Drew and Walker 2009). The emphasis in CA has expanded to incorporate interactions from institutional domains. This includes data from medical settings, including doctor-patient consultations (Heritage and Robinson 2006), legal settings, such as courtroom discourse (Komter 2012) and media discourse, for instance, news interviews (Clayman 2013). Newer mediums of communication have been examined, such as WhatsApp chats (König 2019) and online discourse (Collister 2011). Research in these areas has analysed how features of conversation are adapted to specialised and new contexts. CA researchers concentrate on interactions without reference to background information; this is because CA asserts that nothing should be assumed that is not evident in the discourse itself.

Interactional Sociolinguistics also typically focuses on spoken discourse. This may be face-to-face personal interactions, as with CA, but also, since the beginning, institutional talk has been investigated. The examples in Chapter 5 demonstrate a range of types of talk that can be examined, including job interviews (Roberts 2011), research meetings (Kimura and Canagarajah 2020) and medical counselling sessions (Chimbwete-Phiri and Schnurr 2020), as well as private conversations (e.g., Tannen 2014; Gordon 2015). An Interactional Sociolinguistics analysis may also take account of relevant background information gathered separately from recordings, such as interviews conducted with participants, or observational and ethnographic notes.

CDS is an approach which may consider spoken discourse, but often explores written data. In contrast to CA and Interactional Sociolinguistics, the discourse examined is typically public; as illustrated in Chapter 6, two key domains in CDS are political discourse and media discourse. The focus is often on texts such as transcripts of speeches (e.g., Fairclough 2005) or newspaper articles (e.g., Archakis and Tsakona 2010), rather than data which involves two or more people interacting, although this type of data may be analysed at times (e.g., van der Houwen 2015; Er 2020). Other types of data focused on in CDS research include images and visual forms of communication. In Chapter 6, one study cited analysed statues (Abousnnouga and Machin 2010), while another explored both the language and visual presentation on a company website (Brookes and Harvey 2017). Visual aspects are not typically explored in the other approaches outlined, although there has been more consideration of these features of communication with advances in technology and the expansion to study online mediums of communication. Understanding the social and/or political context is essential to analysis in CDS and generally provides the starting point of the research. This involves looking beyond the primary data, so analysis is informed by reference to other sources or to the analyst's knowledge of social and political factors.

7.1.2 Analytic approaches and methods

The tools of corpus linguistics provide ways of describing what makes a genre or corpus distinctive and can identify items for analysis. Basic word searches, frequency lists and keyword analysis highlight words and phrases of interest. Collocations and concordances bring a small amount of the surrounding discourse into focus, placing words and phrases into their discourse context. The closer qualitative analysis that typifies more recent Corpus Approaches to Discourse Analysis can then widen the view, providing consideration of the way items are functioning within larger sections of discourse. This qualitative analysis may utilise one of the approaches outlined in Chapters 4 to 6, or may use other approaches.

CA, Interactional Sociolinguistics and CDS identify a range of discourse features that people utilise to achieve specific communicative goals, and these can be at a number of different levels. Each approach also recognises that meaning resides in the interplay between features and the social context in which they are used. Words and utterances in themselves do not convey particular meanings; they need to be considered in context.

CA provides a framework for analysing the micro detail of how participants jointly construct interaction, zooming in on the detail of texts. This includes exploring aspects of interaction such as adjacency pairs, sequence organisation, preference and repair. In Chapter 4, for instance, one of the examples illustrated how interaction unfolds across a sequence of talk as different participants contribute (Drew and Walker 2009), while another demonstrated how a speaker can self-repair during an ongoing turn during a conversation if they say something that they feel is inaccurate (Jackson and Jones 2013).

Interactional Sociolinguistics focuses explicitly on the social and linguistic meanings created during interaction, and like CA, views interaction primarily as joint activity. Participants are understood to make inferences about one another's intentions and goals based on a wide range of verbal and non-verbal contextualisation cues. These cues are interpreted as indexing intended meanings, assuming shared knowledge of sociolinguistic or cultural norms. The men in Salanoa's research, for example, shared norms around silence, and were happy to work together for long periods without speaking (Salanoa 2020).

CA and Interactional Sociolinguistics analyses are based on a turn-by-turn analysis of the interaction from the perspective of each participant. An Interactional Sociolinguistics analysis may not be as detailed as CA, and considers the wider social context to inform analysis, potentially drawing on other sources of information. This contrast is evident if we examine one piece of data from each perspective. A CA analysis of (1) would highlight aspects such as the adjacency pairs, for example, questions and answers, and the way the speakers align and express affiliation with each other, e.g., agreeing and laughing. An Interactional Sociolinguistics analysis could explore how shared norms and expectations are evident, and how knowing the background of the young women, who are both Māori (indigenous people of New Zealand), provides us with insight into their shared understandings about appropriate behaviour. The man they are talking about is Pākehā (New Zealanders of European origin) and does not share their norms.

(1) Informal workplace meeting

Context: Two young women are discussing a project they are working on. Recorded in New Zealand.

INGER: . . . cos wasn't Jack originally the one
who was //supposed\ to be?
MERIMERI: /yep\\

INGER:	and then I didn't see anything of him for a couple of months while I was //working on it\
MERIMERI:	/that's why\\ it cracks me up that he's like well you should know me I'm Jack Standish //it's like hello have you been to any meetings?\
INGER:	/yeah [laughs]\\ [laughs]
MERIMERI:	//don't think so\
INGER:	/I just thought\\ I thought it was was kind of rude just coming in not even saying hi- you know introducing himself or saying hello cos he'd never met me before + obviously ++

Adapted from Holmes, Vine and Marra (2020: 9). (Source: LWP)

CDS differs in a number of ways from CA and Interactional Sociolinguistics when we consider analytic aspects. Firstly, CDS is a theoretical approach and can adopt a range of analytic methods. The primary focus is on how power and ideologies are created and reproduced; language and other forms of communication are explored in order to illuminate this wider concern.

Secondly, analysis tends to be based on the analyst's interpretations of discourse, without reference to participants' interpretations. The writer of the news report on the bike thefts, which was presented in Chapter 6 (from Mayr and Machin 2012), for instance, may not have intended to humanise the police. The analysts interpret it in this way, but the writer may have been focusing on writing in a style appropriate/expected for news reporting of this type.

Thirdly, CDS also tends to investigate the speech, writing or visual aspects of communication of the powerful. Politicians are often the focus (e.g., Fairclough 2005; Don, Knowles and Fatt 2010) or others who hold powerful positions (e.g., the judge in van der Houwen 2015). At times challenges and resistance to power are explored so communication of individuals or groups who hold less powerful positions may be analysed. The protestors in the study reported in Romano and Porto (2018) were utilising a metaphor from one demonstration to another, from one group to another, and this was becoming a powerful and positive tool for challenging government policies. A CDS analysis of (1) may focus on the way the two young women are questioning the behaviour of a man who is from the dominant group in society and who is probably unaware of the Māori norms around introducing and greeting people which he has violated.

A fourth factor of CDS research which differentiates it from CA and Interactional Sociolinguistics is that analysis is often largely based on exploration of features of discourse isolated from the texts in which they occur, rather than examining them as part of sequences. This also means that there is not typically a focus on joint construction.

CDS focuses on linguistic aspects as a reflection of social and cultural processes and structures. Interactional Sociolinguistics considers the social context of discourse, but CDS takes this a step further, exploring the big picture to identify the societal constructs which underlie the use of specific discourse strategies. CDS may involve a much more fine-grained analysis of relevant excerpts as done in CA and Interactional Sociolinguistics, although researchers do not always do this.

7.1.3 Issues explored

Corpus linguistics was an approach developed by researchers interested in describing the lexicon and grammar of languages (Kennedy 1998). This included exploring the use of words and phrases, and the distinctiveness of genres or varieties of a language. A Corpus Approach to Discourse Analysis enables researchers to identify patterns from often large collections of texts, and then explore meaning-in-use more closely through applying qualitative discourse analytic techniques. Examples of broader and more specific issues explored by researchers whose work was highlighted in Chapter 3 include:

- what makes the language of a particular text or genre so distinctive?

    → why is Shakespeare's play *Macbeth* so unsettling? (Hope and Witmore 2014)

- do different languages use similar language features with a similar frequency and in the same way?

    → do Hungarian and English use *blood* metaphors as often and to refer to the same types of themes? (Simó 2011)

- what can we learn about the influence of one language on another when exploring a range of examples drawn from both languages?

    → what can a corpus analysis reveal about the pragmatics of lexical borrowing from German into English? (Schröter 2021)

- what does analysis of a large corpus tell us about resistant or changing discourses?

    → how have the frequency, meanings and collocations of some words changed due to the worldwide Covid-19 pandemic? (Butler and Simon-Vandenbergen 2021)

CA as a research approach was motivated by a desire to explore how social relationships are enacted in everyday conversation, with a focus on how actions are realised and recognised, and how participants jointly construct understanding as visible in sequences of talk. It allows investigation of communication at the micro-level. Examples of broader and more specific issues explored by CA researchers whose work was highlighted in Chapter 4 include:

- how do speakers take turns at talk and communicate coherently?

    → what rules seem to govern overlapping speech in English? (Sacks, Schegloff and Jefferson 1974)

- how does interaction unfold across a sequence of talk?

    → how do participants in an interaction express and respond to indirect complaints? (Drew and Walker 2009)

- how do people repair troubles that occur when interacting?

    → how do participants manage other-initiated repair when problems in understanding arise? (Hayashi and Kim 2015)

- how are features of conversation adapted to specialised contexts?

    → how does the form of physicians' initiating questions in consultations affect the way patients present problems? (Heritage and Robinson 2006)

Interactional Sociolinguistics developed with the aim of investigating linguistic and cultural diversity. It involves close analysis of texts while considering the social context of the discourse. Some broader and more specific issues that have been explored by researchers using an Interactional Sociolinguistics approach which were illustrated in Chapter 5 include:

- how is a particular discourse strategy used?

    → how is questioning utilised in medical counselling sessions in Malawi? (Chimbwete-Phiri and Schnurr 2020)

- how are routine encounters constructed?

    → what are the phases of university admission interviews and what types of talk are found in each phase? (Weston 2021)

- how are relationships discursively created?

    → how do family members maintain and attend to their relationships? (Tannen 2014)

- how are identities enacted and negotiated?

    → how does a leader enact aspects of his identity in team meetings? (Vine, Holmes and Marra forthcoming)

Interactional Sociolinguistics at times applies a critical lens to the analysis of discourse, exploring data from the perspective of power differences, especially in cross-cultural communication. This was an initial motivation for Gumperz in developing Interactional Sociolinguistics.

Critical discourse theory focuses explicitly on exploring how power and ideology are manifested in discourse, and the aim in CDS research is to reveal connections between language (and/or other forms of communication), power and ideology. Some broader and more specific issues explored in CDS research mentioned in Chapter 6 include:

- how are gender inequalities and ideologies reinforced in public discourse?

    → what can analysis of children's literature tell us about societal attitudes to women at different times? (Smith 2015)

- how is the socio-historical context relevant for understanding discourse?

    → what values were WWI statues erected in Britain in the 1920s aiming to communicate given the political concerns of the time? (Abousnnouga and Machin 2010)

- how do particular discourses become normalised?

  → how have far-right discourses in Europe moved to the centre of the political landscape? (Wodak 2020)

- how are powerful discourses resisted and challenged?

  → how do women in the Nepali women's festival challenge the ideologies and practices that dominate their lives? (Holland and Skinner 1995)

The issues focused on within research utilising these different approaches mean different fields make more or less use of them. Also of importance is that, as seen in Chapter 2, philosophers, anthropologists and sociologists as well as linguists were influential in the development of discourse analysis. Discourse analysis does not just provide theory and method within linguistics and nowadays is used in a wide range of fields.

7.1.4 Summary

Each of the approaches explored in this book provides a different lens with which to examine discourse, and each is capable of generating useful insights into what is going on within a sample or samples of discourse. The main types of data focused on differ between each, as do the analytic approaches typically utilised and the issues and questions explored. When considering which type of approach to adopt, an analyst needs to ensure there is a good match to each of these three aspects. What type of data do you want to examine, what techniques do you wish to employ, and what issues will be the focus?

7.2 APPLICATIONS OF DISCOURSE ANALYSIS

To take an *applied* approach within linguistics initially referred to contexts of language learning and second language acquisition. This has expanded and nowadays embraces a whole range of possible areas, from educational to institutional contexts and beyond. Applications can support professional practice and training but may also include publishing findings in outlets which have not traditionally disseminated academic research but which reach a wider audience. Some examples of applications are outlined in this section. Corpus Approaches to Discourse Analysis are not considered separately, but the potential integration of corpus techniques with CA, Interactional Sociolinguistics or within CDS means that applications in any area can be informed by discourse analysis research which integrates corpus tools.

7.2.1 Applied Conversation Analysis

CA is an approach which initially focused on describing and identifying patterns and rules within interaction, and a primary concern was not the possible applications of findings. With the expansion of CA methods to analyse data from a range of institutional settings, however, the implications for training and practice emerged (Drew 2005b). This has included areas such as speech and language therapy, medical and mental health contexts, and professional discourse, as well as language learning contexts.

The use of CA for speech and language therapy applications is a growing area. For instance, Bottema-Beutel et al. (2020) used Applied CA to investigate home interactions between a Spanish–English bilingual child with autism and his family members. Examination of the data highlighted two general ways parents performed other-repair within questioning sequences. They would either repeat their initial question (essentially restarting the sequence) or simply provide the correct answer. Both of these strategies are illustrated in (2).

(2) Family interaction (Spanish)

Context: Beatriz and her five-year-old son Herman are interacting in their family home. Recorded in the US.

BEATRIZ:	quién es tu hermano?
	cuántos hermanos tienes tú Herman?
ROCIO:	( )
HERMAN:	(5.0) cinco=
BEATRIZ:	=[slowly]: no: cuántos hermanos tienes?
	ah mm [gives spoonful of food to Sonia]
	cuántos hermanos tienes Herman?
HERMAN:	[slowly]: um: [hops off chair] (.) dos
	[turns around and puts two fingers up]
BEATRIZ:	solo [louder]: una: nada más tienes una hermana
	cómo se llama tu hermana? [faster]: cómo se llama tu hermana?:
HERMAN:	er (.) Rocio [chewing food] (2.0) Rocio
BEATRIZ:	[slowly]: Roc<u>ii</u>o:

Translation

BEATRIZ:	who is your brother?
	let's see how many siblings do you have Herman?
ROCIO:	( )
HERMAN:	(5.0) five =
BEATRIZ:	[slowly]: no: how many siblings do you have?
	ah mm [gives spoonful of food to Sonia]
	how many siblings do you have Herman?
HERMAN:	[slowly]: um: [hops off of chair] (.) two
	[turns around and puts two fingers up]
BEATRIZ:	just [louder]: one: you only have one sister
	what is your sister's name? [faster]: what is your sister's name?:
HERMAN:	er (.) Rocio [chewing food] (2.0) Rocio
BEATRIZ:	[slowly]: Roc<u>ii</u>o:

Adapted and reprinted under STM guidelines from Bottema-Beutel, Kristen, Gabrielle Oliveira, Shana R. Cohen and Jessica Miguel, Question – response – evaluation sequences in the home interactions of a bilingual child with autism spectrum disorder, in: International Journal of Language and Communication Disorders 55(2), p. 223, Royal College of Speech and Language Therapists.

Herman had claimed to have a brother, although he does not. Because of his claim, Beatriz has asked him his brother's name, before asking another question prompting Herman to tell her how many siblings he has. Bottema-Beutel et al. (2020: 223) note that Beatriz probably quickly revised her initial question because it is not answerable. After Herman provides an incorrect response to the question about the number of siblings he has, Beatriz repeats the question in order to initiate repair. When Herman provides another incorrect response, Beatriz supplies the correct response, completing the repair sequence. By providing the correct answer, Beatriz compromises. She could continue to encourage Herman to answer correctly, but wants to ensure that the interaction will move forward. This sequence comes in the middle of a larger sequence involving naming family members more generally; providing the correct answer allows Beatriz to continue with the wider activity of reciting names of family members.

The micro level CA analysis of the interactions in this study illustrates how a child and his caregivers collaborate to produce question-response sequences. This reveals "the caregiver's scaffolding techniques, the child's competencies in participating in such sequences, and the action trajectories they constitute" (Bottema-Beutel et al. 2020: 227). Intervention research in this field increasingly involves providing parents with strategies to interact more effectively with their children. CA analysis of the features of home interactions with a diverse range of participants can provide important input to the guidance provided, as well as aiding efforts to enable caregivers to develop their existing strengths to maximise children's engagement (2020: 227–228). Bottema-Beutel et al.'s article appears in a journal published by the *Royal College of Speech & Language Therapists* which provides "a forum for the exchange of information and discussion of issues of clinical or theoretical relevance" (https://onlinelibrary.wiley.com/page/journal/14606984/homepage/productinformation.html).

Exploring interaction between psychiatrists and patients is another area where research has utilised CA methods. Thompson, Howes and McCabe (2016), for example, focus on psychiatrists' questions, illustrating how certain types of questions are more or less effective for enabling psychiatrists to develop good relationships with patients, and therefore adherence with treatment plans. They provide recommendations to psychiatrists around how to communicate more efficiently and effectively. When interviewed about her research, Thompson commented that ideals of patient centeredness and shared decision-making within psychiatry are widely endorsed but it is difficult to translate these into specific practices. Using CA allowed her and her colleagues to examine in detail how interaction unfolds, for instance, the way psychiatrists ask questions and recommend treatment, and how these actions are designed and understood as part of sequences within interaction. "From this, it was possible to develop interactionally sensitive recommendations for clinicians that account for some of the contingencies of actual practice" (Thompson in interview, reported in Lester and O'Reilly 2019: Chapter 11).

One last context that I briefly explore here is applications of CA research which have analysed help line interactions. Research by Hepburn, Wilkinson and Butler (2014) highlights the way call takers manage problematic situations in help line calls in the UK and Australia. Their findings were fed back to help line providers through practice-based reports, consultancy exercises and training initiatives, including workshops with help line workers. These initiatives identify and facilitate good practice, with the training helping not only newcomers to the job, but also allowing existing workers to upskill.

7.2.2 Applications within Interactional Sociolinguistics

Considering applications of research was an important part of John Gumperz' approach from the beginning. As noted in Chapter 5, Gumperz developed Interactional Sociolinguistics with an aim of highlighting inequality and discrimination. He did not simply want to highlight it though; he had a concern for social justice and wanted to instigate change. A specific example of work by Gumperz and his colleagues which achieved this aim was their input into the 1979 BBC film *Crosstalk* (Twitchin 1979; see Gumperz, Jupp and Roberts 1979). *Crosstalk* focused on race discrimination in institutional encounters and encouraged people to think about their actions and the longer-term influences and effects of these. Watching reasonably familiar institutional interactions, viewers were able to bring their own first-hand experience to interpreting what was going on. At the same time, micro-analysis demonstrated how actions are jointly produced. It is much harder to blame individuals for any problems when the co-construction of talk and activity is made visible.

Deborah Tannen has used her research not only to write academic publications but also many general-audience books, enabling her to broaden the reach of her research findings and make them accessible to a large audience. Her focus on family relationships as well as workplace interaction and the insights her research has generated have captured the attention of the wider public in works such as *You Just Don't Understand: Men and Women in Conversation* (Tannen 1990), *Talking from 9 to 5: Women and Men at Work* (Tannen 1994a) and more recently *You're Wearing THAT?: Mothers and Daughters in Conversation* (Tannen 2006) and *You Were Always Mom's Favorite!: Sisters in Conversation Throughout Their Lives* (Tannen 2010). This extension of her research findings into non-academic writing is another way discourse analysis can be applied.

Applications within the area of workplace discourse research, which has been a strong strand within Interactional Sociolinguistics, include providing input to training and communication skills materials for both individuals and organisations. Janet Holmes and her colleagues in the LWP have developed applications of their research in a range of directions. Firstly, giving feedback to workplaces where data has been collected is an essential component of the LWP's research process (Vine 2016; Holmes and Vine 2021). Example (3) comes from a report to a workplace involved in data collection and draws on analysis of meetings collected in this workplace.

(3) Written report

Context: Report to a workplace from the LWP team

Humour is another of the ways groups manage their relationships. Our study shows that humour functions in complex ways in the workplace. Its power lies in its flexibility – it can function as a disguised weapon for those who want to complain, a cushion for criticism, and perhaps more importantly a source of fun and light relief among colleagues. . . . A successful attempt at humour indicates that the speaker shares a common view with others about what is amusing, thus creating rapport. Workplace humour is often jointly constructed by members of the group, thereby allowing all participants to contribute to the humour, and show their place within the in-group.

Example 1 (Capitals indicate emphasis. Pseudonyms are used throughout.)

1. JACOB:	oh is this THE FINAL	
2. BARRY:	this is THE FINAL final steering committee	
3.	oh Pete most probably enjoyed doing that	
4. DUDLEY:	he even sent me an e mail to reinforce it with you	
5.	[laughter]	
6. BARRY:	this is THE final	
7. DUDLEY:	THE final [laughs] I'm switching off the lights and I'm leaving now	
8. BARRY:	I'm switching off the lights and I'm leaving	

Each of the three, Jacob, Barry and Dudley, adds something to the humour, showing their place within the group and the shared background knowledge they have about the long awaited "final" steering committee meeting. Also, by echoing the comments of others (as in lines 7 and 8), Barry and Dudley are showing that they understand and approve of what is funny.

Adapted from Vine (2016: 328) (Source: LWP)

Feedback to workplaces working with the LWP researchers has drawn attention to issues such as the importance of humour and the role this plays in achieving transactional goals, along with aspects such as the way meetings are managed and the different leadership styles that people may enact. At times we have had organisations who were eager to work with us because they had questions they wanted to answer. The management at a factory for instance were interested to know why one of their teams was particularly productive, and whether the way the team communicated contributed to this. They hoped the insights gained would help other teams become more efficient. In another case an organisation approached us for help identifying why the meetings of a group were not running smoothly, while yet another contracted us to investigate bias and suggest ways to address this within the organisation's public documents.

A second level of applications for the LWP has involved reporting research findings more widely to foreground their importance for other organisations and contexts. This includes short articles in industry newsletters (e.g., Holmes and Major 2003), as well as working with government agencies supporting newcomers to New Zealand (see e.g., Immigration New Zealand 2021). A third level of applications of LWP research is its use in developing educational materials for migrants (see e.g., Riddiford and Newton 2010; Riddiford 2014; McCallum 2014), as well as a textbook for students studying workplace interaction (Vine 2020).

7.2.3 Applications and Critical Discourse Studies

CDS is based on the premise that discourse analysis can be a powerful tool in highlighting bias and the normalisation of harmful ideologies. This is the first step in addressing these types of issues and attempting to prompt a change in thinking. Raising awareness of the importance of language and other aspects of communication across a range of settings is a central concern of CDS; this approach therefore has potential applications at its heart. As with other approaches though, it is important to consider how research findings can be reported and applied beyond normal academic outputs.

One approach to addressing a particular issue within public discourse is to provide input to training. Teun van Dijk's research on racism in the print media is a prime example here. He has worked to persuade journalism courses to include modules on the role of media in (re)producing racism. In van Dijk (2011) he proposes an antiracist programme to be integrated into courses. This includes focusing on how to write news reports in multicultural societies, but goes beyond writing skills in providing, for example, guidelines for developing strategies that promote diversity in the newsroom and for raising awareness about the effects of ethnic coverage (2011: 29–30).

In conducting her research on far-right discourses, Ruth Wodak has, as Deborah Tannen did, reported her findings for a non-academic audience. In the preface to the first edition of her book *The Politics of Fear*, Wodak notes how she deliberately adopted a less academic and more accessible writing style in order to reach a wider audience (2015: xii). She did not just want academics to read it, but also journalists and other members of the public.

The final chapter of Catalano and Waugh's (2020) book on CDS, *Critical Discourse Analysis, Critical Discourse Studies and Beyond*, provides the responses of 21 researchers working within CDS to the question "How have you used your knowledge of CDS to do good in the world (besides publishing your academic work, which, unfortunately, tends to be read only by other academics and students)?" (2020: 326). The framing of their question highlights the concern that academic research, and the insights and recommendations that may result from it, do not reach a wide audience when published only through normal academic outlets.

The scholars that answered Catalano and Waugh's invitation to contribute responses to their question all work in different places around the world, and come from a range of academic disciplines; their responses demonstrate practical ways CDS theory and concepts are applied. As educators, many talked about how they drew on CDS to challenge their students to think critically, for example Leticia Yulita and Paul Chamness Iida. Yulita was frustrated by the rigid world-views of her students in East Anglia so implemented intervention which examined and challenged students' *common-sense* assumptions and social myths about Hispanics. Paul Chamness Iida used CDS with his students in Japan to model how to talk about and advocate for social justice.

Other scholars referenced work where they advocated for change with groups outside academia. Rebecca Rogers, for instance, was a founding member of the educator network in the US called *Educators for Social Justice*. One of the initiatives this group undertakes is to put positive pressure on school districts to take public stances on issues of racial equity and civil rights.

At the end of the chapter, Catalano and Waugh challenge academics working within CDS to think about applications of their research and how it can be used "to counter oppressive regimes, human rights abuses, policies or laws that discriminate against sexual orientation or gender, race, ethnicity, religion, nationality, or any other reason for 'Othering' people" (2020: 381).

7.2.4 Applying Discourse Analysis

Communication skills development across a range of situations can be improved by examining authentic interactional data. Often guidelines provided in training across a range of types of workplaces and roles do not adequately reflect the way people *actually* interact in these situations. Highlighting the use of different discourse strategies and the effects of these is important for understanding how to communicate effectively. Communication consultants may also refer to abstract concepts, for example, patient-centred care or shared decision-making within mental health and other medical contexts, but what does this mean in terms of practice? Discourse analysis can provide valuable insights on how people communicate in such situations and which strategies help achieve these more abstract goals.

Applications of discourse analysis research can support professional practice and training but may also include publishing findings in outlets not traditionally disseminating academic research. This enables researchers to reach a wider audience. Research can then help people understand the effect their communication choices have both for themselves and the people around them. It can prepare people for a range of new communication challenges, raising awareness of potentially differing norms and expectations that they might encounter, such as when they prepare for an interview or move to a new country to live and/or for work. Exploring good practice, as well as situations where there are potential difficulties, can help people understand the importance of interaction in achieving their transactional and relational goals. In identifying where there may be a mismatch between norms and expectations for a range of reasons, research can raise awareness of why problems occur, and thus of how to communicate more effectively.

Close analysis of discourse in public spheres can raise awareness of underlying ideologies and the ways power is created and reproduced. It can show how minorities and those with less power are discriminated against, and how harmful and unhelpful ways of talking about such groups are widely justified and normalised. Applying these findings in a range of contexts, such as training situations and within advocacy groups, can help facilitate change and, to quote Catalano and Waugh, "do good in the world" (2020: 326).

CHAPTER SUMMARY

This chapter has summarised common elements as well as differences between the approaches examined in Chapters 3 to 6 of this book. Differences and similarities in the type of data typically focused on, analytical techniques utilised and the issues explored are highlighted. Corpus techniques provide a broad picture view, highlighting how aspects that make up individual texts contribute to the overall distinctiveness of a genre or a variety of a language. The view zooms in to the micro detail of texts with a CA approach, while Interactional Sociolinguistics takes a step back out, with its exploration of the way communication reflects the social context in which it is produced. CDS takes a further step back, exploring the big picture to identify the societal constructs which underlie the use of specific discourse strategies.

Section 7.2 has discussed some applications of research which employs discourse analysis. This includes supporting training, and recommendations to practitioners and other educational applications, along with seeking outlets which reach the wider public. The possibilities for how to apply all four approaches, and the issues that can be focused on, are diverse and can encompass academic outputs, industry and professional training, as well as societal engagement.

FURTHER READING

The work cited in Section 7.2 provides a good starting point for exploring applications of discourse analysis research. Two useful edited books which contain chapters on Applied CA are Richards and Seedhouse (2005) and Antaki (2011). *Applied Conversation Analysis: Social Interaction in Institutional Settings* (Lester and O'Reilly 2019) is an excellent resource for newcomers to CA who want to explore applications. It covers the basics of CA, as well as providing guidance on how to plan and conduct an Applied CA study.

Some studies which engage with the implications and applications of workplace discourse research are outlined in the final chapter in Vine (2020). These draw on a range of discourse analysis approaches. The final section of Vine (2018) has four chapters explicitly exploring applied areas of workplace research: Vocational Education (Losa 2018), women in leadership (Baxter 2018) and issues of relevance for migrants (Kerekes 2018; Yates 2018). See also Mullany (2020).

As mentioned earlier, the final chapter of Catalano and Waugh's (2020) book on CDS, *Critical Discourse Analysis, Critical Discourse Studies and Beyond* focuses on ways CDS has been applied within a range of contexts and in different communities around the world.

References

Abousnnouga, Gill and David Machin. 2010. Analysing the language of war monuments. *Visual Communication* 9(2): 131–149.

Ädel, Annelie. 2014. Metonymy in the semantic field of verbal communication: A corpus-based analysis of WORD. *Journal of Pragmatics* 67: 72–88.

Adolphs, Svenja, Brian Brown, Ronald Carter, Paul Crawford and Opinder Sahota. 2004. Applying corpus linguistics in a health care context. *Journal of Applied Linguistics* 1(1): 9–28.

Antaki, Charles (ed.). 2011. *Applied Conversation Analysis: Intervention and Change in Institutional Talk*. Basingstoke: Palgrave Macmillan.

Archakis, Argiris and Villy Tsakona. 2010. "The wolf wakes up inside them, grows werewolf hair and reveals all their bullying": The representation of parliamentary discourse in Greek newspapers. *Journal of Pragmatics* 42: 912–923.

Atkinson, J. Maxwell and Paul Drew. 1979. *Order in Court: The Organisation of Verbal Interaction in Judicial Settings*. London: Macmillan.

Auer, Peter and Celia Roberts. 2011. Introduction: John Gumperz and the indexicality of language. Special issue of *Text & Talk* 31: 381–391.

Austin, John Langshaw. 1955/1962. *How to Do Things with Words: The William James Lectures Delivered at Harvard University in 1955, 1962*. James O. Urmson and Marina Sbisà (eds.). Oxford: Clarendon Press.

Austin, John Langshaw. 1975. *How to Do Things with Words*. Second edition. James O. Urmson and Marina Sbisà (eds.). Oxford: Oxford University Press.

Bailey, Benjamin. 2015. Interactional sociolinguistics. In Karen Tracy, Cornelia Ilie and Todd Sandel (eds.), *The International Encyclopedia of Language and Social Interaction*, 826–840. Chichester: John Wiley & Sons.

Baker, Paul. 2006. *Using Corpora in Discourse Analysis*. London: Continuum.

Baker, Paul. 2012. Acceptable bias? Using corpus linguistic methods with critical discourse analysis. *Critical Discourse Studies* 9(3): 247–256.

Barron, Anne. 2006. Understanding spam: A macro-textual analysis. *Journal of Pragmatics* 38: 880–904.

Barron, Anne. 2019. Using corpus-linguistic methods to track longitudinal development: Routine apologies in the study abroad context. *Journal of Pragmatics* 146: 87–105.

Barth, Danielle and Stefan Schnell. 2022. *Understanding Corpus Linguistics*. Abingdon: Routledge.

Bateson, Gregory. 1972. *Steps to an Ecology of Mind*. New York: Ballantine Books.

Baxter, Judith. 2018. Gender, language and leadership: Enabling women leaders. In Bernadette Vine (ed.), *The Routledge Handbook of Language in the Workplace*, 401–412. Abingdon: Routledge.

Baxter, Nicola. 1993. *Rapunzel: Favourite Tales*. London: Ladybird Books.

Berber Sardinha, Tony and Leila Barbara. 2009. Corpus linguistics. In Francesca Bargiela-Chiappini (ed.), *The Handbook of Business Discourse*, 105–118. Edinburgh: Edinburgh University Press.

Bottema-Beutel, Kristen, Gabrielle Oliveira, Shana R. Cohen and Jessica Miguel. 2020. Question – response – evaluation sequences in the home interactions of a bilingual child with autism spectrum disorder. *International Journal of Language and Communication Disorders* 55(2): 216–230.

Bousfield, Derek. 2005. *Impoliteness in Interaction*. Amsterdam: John Benjamins.
Boyd, Michael S. 2013. Reframing the American dream: The conceptual metaphor and personal pronouns in the 2008 US presidential debates. In Piotr Cap and Urzsula Ukulska (eds.), *Analyzing Genres in Political Communication*, 297–319. Amsterdam: Benjamins.
Breazu, Petre and David Machin. 2019. Racism toward the Roma through the affordances of Facebook: Bonding, laughter and spite. *Discourse & Society* 30(4): 376–394.
Brookes, Gavin and Kevin Harvey. 2017. Just plain Wronga?: A multimodal critical analysis of online payday loan discourse. *Critical Discourse Studies* 14(2): 167–187.
Brown, Penelope and Stephen C. Levinson. 1978/1987. *Politeness: Some Universals in Language Usage*. Cambridge: Cambridge University Press.
Burr, Vivien. 2015. *Social Constructionism*. London: Routledge.
Butler, Christopher and Anne-Marie Simon-Vandenbergen. 2021. Social and physical distance/distancing: A corpus-based analysis of recent changes in usage. *Corpus Pragmatics* 5: 427–462.
Catalano Theresa and Linda R. Waugh. 2020. *Critical Discourse Analysis, Critical Discourse Studies and Beyond*. Cham, Switzerland: Springer.
Cerović, Marijana. 2016. When suspects ask questions: Rhetorical questions as a challenging device. *Journal of Pragmatics* 105: 18–38.
Chałupnik, Małgorzata and Sarah Atkins. 2020. "Everyone happy with what their role is?": A pragma-linguistic evaluation of leadership practices in emergency medicine training. *Journal of Pragmatics* 160: 80–96.
Charnock, Ross. 2009. Overruling as a speech act: Performativity and normative discourse. *Journal of Pragmatics* 41: 401–426.
Cheng, Winnie, Chris Greaves and Martin Warren. 2008. *A Corpus-Driven Study of Discourse Intonation*. Amsterdam: John Benjamins.
Chimbwete-Phiri, Rachel and Stephanie Schnurr. 2020. Improving HIV/AIDS consultations in Malawi: How interactional sociolinguistics can contribute. In Zsófia Demjén and Jonathon Tomlinson (eds.), *Applying Linguistics in Illness and Healthcare Contexts*, 131–158. London: Bloomsbury.
Chovanec, Jan. 2020. "Re-educating the Roma? You must be joking . . .": Racism and prejudice in online discussion forums. *Discourse & Society* 32(2): 156–174.
Clayman, Steven E. 1988. Displaying neutrality in television news interviews. *Social Problems* 35(4): 474–492.
Clayman, Steven E. 2013. Conversation analysis in the news interview. In Jack Sidnell and Tanya Stivers (eds.), *The Handbook of Conversation Analysis*, 630–656. Chichester: John Wiley & Sons.
Clift, Rebecca. 2016. *Conversation Analysis*. Cambridge: Cambridge University Press.
Clifton, Jonathan. 2017. Taking the (heroic) leader out of leadership: The in situ practice of distributed leadership in decision-making talk. In Cornelia Ilie and Stephanie Schnurr (eds.), *Challenging Leadership Stereotypes through Discourse: Power, Management and Gender*, 45–68. Singapore: Springer.
Clifton, Jonathan, Stephanie Schnurr and Dorien Van De Mieroop. 2019. *The Language of Leadership Narratives: A Social Practice Perspective*. Abingdon: Routledge.
Clyne, Michael. 1994. *Intercultural Communication at Work: Cultural Values in Discourse*. Cambridge & New York: Cambridge University Press.
Collister, Lauren Brittany. 2011. *-repair in online discourse. *Journal of Pragmatics* 43: 918–921.
Cotter, Colleen and Daniel Perrin (eds.). 2018. *The Routledge Handbook of Language and Media*. Abingdon: Routledge.
Couper-Kuhlen, Elizabeth and Marja Etelämäki. 2014. On divisions of labor in request and offer environments. In Paul Drew and Elizabeth Couper-Kuhlen (eds.), *Requesting in Social Interaction*, 115–144. Amsterdam: John Benjamins.

Couper-Kuhlen, Elizabeth and Sandra A. Thompson. 2005. A linguistic practice for retracting overstatements: "Concessive repair". In Auli Hakulinen and Margret Selting (eds.), *Syntax and Lexis in Conversation: Studies on the Use of Linguistic Resources in Talk-in-Interaction*, 257–288. Amsterdam: John Benjamins.

Davies, Bethan L. 2007. Grice's cooperative principle: Meaning and rationality. *Journal of Pragmatics* 39: 2308–2331.

Davies, Catherine Evans. 2003. How English-learners joke with native speakers: An interactional sociolinguistic perspective on humor as collaborative discourse across cultures. *Journal of Pragmatics* 35(9): 1361–1385.

Declercq, Jana, Stéphan Tulkens and Geert Jacobs. 2021. The multidimensionality of eating in contemporary information society: A corpus-based discourse analysis of online audience reactions to a TV show about food. In Alla Tovares and Cynthia Gordon (eds.), *Identity and Ideology in Digital Food Discourse: Social Media Interactions across Cultural Contexts*, 33–57. London & New York: Bloomsbury Academic.

Dendenne, Boudjemaa. 2021. Complimenting on-the-go: Features from colloquial Algerian Arabic. *Journal of Pragmatics* 172: 270–287.

Depraetere, Ilse, Sofie Decock and Nicolas Ruytenbeek. 2021. Linguistic (in)directness in twitter complaints: A contrastive analysis of railway complaint interactions. *Journal of Pragmatics* 171: 215–233.

Don, Zuraidah Mohd, Gerry Knowles and Choong Kwai Fatt. 2010. Nationhood and Malaysian identity: A corpus-based approach. *Text and Talk* 30(3): 267–287.

Drew, Paul. 2005a. Conversation analysis. In Kristine L. Fitch and Robert E. Sanders (eds.), *Handbook of Language and Social Interaction*, 71–102. Mahwah, NJ: Lawrence Erlbaum.

Drew, Paul. 2005b. Foreword: Applied linguistics and conversation analysis. In Keith Richards and Paul Seedhouse (eds.), *Applying Conversation Analysis*, xiv–xx. London: Palgrave Macmillan.

Drew, Paul and John Heritage. 1992. Analyzing talk at work: An introduction. In Paul Drew and John Heritage (eds.), *Talk at Work*, 3–65. Cambridge: Cambridge University Press.

Drew, Paul and John Heritage. 2006. *Conversation Analysis*. 4 Volumes. London: Sage.

Drew, Paul and Traci Walker. 2009. Going too far: Complaining, escalating and disaffiliation. *Journal of Pragmatics* 41: 2400–2414.

D'Souza, Dinesh. 1995. *The End of Racism: Principles for a Multiracial Society*. New York: Free Press.

Duranti, Alessandro. 1997. Universal and culture-specific properties of greetings. *Journal of Linguistic Anthropology* 7(1): 63–97.

Eilittä, Tiina, Pentti Haddington and Anna Vatanen. 2021. Children seeking the driver's attention in cars: Position and composition of children's summons turns and children's rights to engage. *Journal of Pragmatics* 178: 175–191.

Er, Ibrahim. 2020. The voiceless in *The Voice*: A multimodal critical discourse analysis. *Text & Talk* 40(6): 705–732.

Fairclough, Norman. 1995. *Media Discourse*. London & New York: Edward Arnold.

Fairclough, Norman. 2000. *New Labour, New Language?* London: Routledge.

Fairclough, Norman. 2005. Blair's contribution to elaborating a new doctrine of "international community". *Journal of Language and Politics* 4(1): 41–63.

Fairclough, Norman. 2015. *Language and Power*. Third edition. Abingdon: Routledge.

Fairclough, Norman. 2016. A dialectical-relational approach to critical discourse analysis in social research. In Ruth Wodak and Michael Meyer (eds.), *Methods of Critical Discourse Studies*, 86–108. London: Sage.

Fairclough, Norman, Jane Mulderrig and Ruth Wodak. 2011. Critical discourse analysis. In Teun A. van Dijk (ed.), *Discourse Studies: A Multidisciplinary Introduction*. Second edition, 357–377. London: Sage.

Fernández-Mallat, Víctor. 2020. Forms of address in interaction: Evidence from Chilean Spanish. *Journal of Pragmatics* 161: 95–106.
Flowerdew, John and John E. Richardson (eds.). 2017. *The Routledge Handbook of Critical Discourse Studies*. Abingdon: Routledge.
Flowerdew, Lynne. 2012. Corpus-based discourse analysis. In James Paul Gee and Michael Handford (eds.), *The Routledge Handbook of Discourse Analysis*, 174–187. Abingdon: Routledge.
Foster, Elissa and Arthur Bochner. 2008. Social constructionist perspectives in communication research. In James Holstein and Jaber Gubrium (eds.), *Handbook of Constructionist Research*, 85–106. New York: Guilford Press.
Foucault, Michel. 1969. *The Archaeology of Knowledge*, translated by Alan M. Sheridan Smith [1972]. New York: Pantheon.
Friedland, Joanna and Merle Mahon. 2018. Sister talk: Investigating an older sibling's responses to verbal challenges. *Discourse Studies* 20(3): 340–360.
Friginal, Eric and Jack A. Hardy (eds.). 2021. *The Routledge Handbook of Corpus Approaches to Discourse Analysis*. Abingdon: Routledge.
Garcés-Conejos Blitvich, Pilar. 2018. Globalization, transnational identities, and conflict talk: The superdiversity and complexity of the Latino identity. *Journal of Pragmatics* 134: 120–133.
García, Carmen. 2010. "Cuente conmigo": The expression of sympathy by Peruvian Spanish speakers. *Journal of Pragmatics* 42: 408–425.
Garfinkel, Harold. 1967. *Studies in Ethnomethodology*. Englewood Cliffs, NJ: Prentice Hall.
Gee, James Paul. 2014. *An Introduction to Discourse Analysis: Theory and Method*. Fourth edition. London: Routledge.
Gee, James Paul and Michael Handford (eds.). 2012. *The Routledge Handbook of Discourse Analysis*. Abingdon: Routledge.
Georgakopoulou, Alexandra. 2007. *Small Stories, Interaction and Identities*. Amsterdam: John Benjamins.
Glenn, Phillip. 2003. *Laughter in Interaction*. Cambridge: Cambridge University Press.
Goffman, Erving. 1956. Embarrassment and social organization. *American Journal of Sociology* 62(3): 264–271.
Goffman, Erving. 1974. *Frame Analysis: An Essay on the Organization of Experience*. Cambridge, MA: Harvard University Press.
Gordon, Cynthia. 2008. A(p)parent play: Blending frames and reframing in family talk. *Language in Society* 37: 319–349.
Gordon, Cynthia. 2009. *Making Meanings, Creating Family: Intertextuality and Framing in Family Interaction*. New York: Oxford University Press.
Gordon, Cynthia. 2011. Gumperz and interactional sociolinguistics. In Ruth Wodak, Barbara Johnstone and Paul Kerswill (eds.), *Sage Handbook of Sociolinguistics*, 67–84. London: Sage.
Gordon, Cynthia. 2015. Framing and positioning. In Deborah Tannen, Heidi E. Hamilton and Deborah Schiffrin (eds.), *The Handbook of Discourse Analysis*. Second edition, 324–345. Chichester: John Wiley & Sons.
Gordon, Cynthia and Joshua Kraut. 2018. Interactional sociolinguistics. In Bernadette Vine (ed.), *The Routledge Handbook of Language in the Workplace*, 3–14. Abingdon: Routledge.
Grice, H. Paul. 1975. Logic and conversation. In Peter Cole and Jerry L. Morgan (eds.), *Syntax and Semantics: Vol. 3: Speech Acts*, 41–58. New York: Academic Press.
Grieve, Averil. 2010. "Aber ganz ehrlich": Differences in episodic structure, apologies and truth-orientation in German and Australian workplace telephone discourse. *Journal of Pragmatics* 42: 190–219.
Gumperz, John J. 1982. *Discourse Strategies*. Cambridge: Cambridge University Press.
Gumperz, John J. 1987. Foreword. In Penelope Brown and Stephen C. Levinson, *Politeness: Some Universals in Language Usage*, xiii–xiv. Cambridge: Cambridge University Press.

Gumperz, John J. 2015. Interactional sociolinguistics: A personal perspective. In Deborah Tannen, Heidi E. Hamilton and Deborah Schiffrin (eds.), *The Handbook of Discourse Analysis*. Second edition, 309–323. Chichester: John Wiley & Sons.

Gumperz, John J. and Jenny Cook-Gumperz. 2005. Making space for bilingual communicative practice. *Intercultural Pragmatics* 2(1): 1–23.

Gumperz, John J., Tom C. Jupp and Celia Roberts. 1979. *Crosstalk: A Study of Cross-Cultural Communication: Background Material and Notes to Accompany the B.B.C. Film*. Southall, Middx, UK: BBC/National Centre for Industrial Language Training.

Günthner, Susanne. 2008. Interactional sociolinguistics. In Gerd Antos, Eija Ventola and Tilo Weber (eds.), *Handbook of Interpersonal Communication*, 53–76. Berlin: De Gruyter.

Harris, Zellig S. 1952. Discourse analysis. *Language* 28(1): 1–30.

Harris, Zellig S. 1963. *Discourse Analysis Reprints*. The Hague: Mouton.

Hart, Christopher and Piotr Cap. 2014. *Contemporary Critical Discourse Studies*. London: Bloomsbury.

Hayashi, Makoto and Stephanie Hyeri Kim. 2015. Turn formats for other-initiated repair and their relation to trouble sources: Some observations from Japanese and Korean conversations. *Journal of Pragmatics* 87: 198–217.

Hepburn, Alexa, Sue Wilkinson and Carly W. Butler. 2014. Intervening with conversation analysis in telephone helpline services: Strategies to improve effectiveness. *Research on Language and Social Interaction* 47: 239–254.

Heritage, John. 1985. Analyzing news interviews: Aspects of the production of talk for an overhearing audience. In Teun A. van Dijk (ed.), *Handbook of Discourse Analysis*. Volume 3, 95–117. London: Academic Press.

Heritage, John. 2008. Conversation analysis as social theory. In Bryan S. Turner (ed.), *The New Blackwell Companion to Social Theory*, 300–320. Oxford: Blackwell.

Heritage, John and Jeffrey D. Robinson. 2006. The structure of patients' presenting concerns: Physicians' opening questions. *Health Communication* 19(2): 89–102.

Hobsbawm, Eric. 1983. Mass producing traditions: Europe 1817–1914. In Eric Hobsbawm and Terence Ranger (eds.), *Inventing Tradition*, 263–308. Cambridge: Cambridge University Press.

Hoey, Michael. 2002. Foreword. In Steven Jones, *Antonymy: A Corpus-Based Perspective*, xi–xvi. London/New York: Routledge.

Holland, Dorothy C. and Debra G. Skinner. 1995. Contested ritual, contested femininities: (Re)forming self and society in a Nepali women's festival. *American Ethnologist* 22(2): 279–305.

Holmes, Janet. 2006. *Gendered Talk at Work*. Malden: Blackwell.

Holmes, Janet and George Major. 2003. Nurses communicating on the ward: The human face of hospitals. *Kai Tiaki: Nursing New Zealand* 8: 14–16.

Holmes, Janet and Meredith Marra. 2002. Having a laugh at work: How humour contributes to workplace culture. *Journal of Pragmatics* 34: 1683–1710.

Holmes, Janet and Meredith Marra. 2006. Humor and leadership style. *Humor* 19(2): 119–138.

Holmes, Janet, Meredith Marra and Bernadette Vine. 2011. *Leadership, Discourse and Ethnicity*. Oxford: Oxford University Press.

Holmes, Janet and Maria Stubbe. 2015. *Power and Politeness in the Workplace: A Sociolinguistic Analysis of Talk at Work*. Second edition. London: Longman.

Holmes, Janet and Bernadette Vine. 2021. Workplace research and applications in real world contexts: The case of the Wellington Language in the Workplace Project. In Sofie De Cock and Geert Jacobs (eds.), *What Counts as Data in Business and Professional Discourse Research and Training?*, 25–54. Basingstoke: Palgrave Macmillan.

Holmes, Janet, Bernadette Vine and Meredith Marra 2020. Contesting the culture order: Contrastive pragmatics in action. *Contrastive Pragmatics* 1(1): 1–27.

Holt, Elizabeth. 2013. Conversation analysis and laughter. In Carol A. Chapelle (ed.), *The Encyclopaedia of Applied Linguistics*, 1033–1038. Chichester: Blackwell.

Hope, Jonathan and Michael Witmore. 2014. The language of *Macbeth*. In Ann Thompson (ed.), *Macbeth: The State of Play*, 183–208. London: Bloomsbury.

Hymes, Dell. 1972. Models of the interaction of language and social life. In John J. Gumperz and Dell Hymes (eds.), *Directions in Sociolinguistics: The Ethnography of Communication*, 35–71. Oxford: Blackwell.

Hymes, Dell. 1974. *Foundations in Sociolinguistics: An Ethnographic Approach*. Philadelphia: University of Pennsylvania Press.

Immigration New Zealand. 2021. *Worktalk*. Retrieved 14 May 2022 from https://worktalk.immigration.govt.nz/

Jackson, Clare and Danielle Jones. 2013. "Well they had a couple of bats to be truthful": Well-prefaced, self-initiated repairs in managing relevant accuracy in interaction. *Journal of Pragmatics* 47: 28–40.

Jefferson, Gail. 1972. Side sequences. In David Sudnow (ed.), *Studies in Social Interaction*, 294–338. New York: Free Press.

Jefferson, Gail. 1987. On exposed and embedded correction in conversation. In Graham Button and John R. E. Lee (eds.), *Talk and Social Organisation*, 86–100. Clevedon, England: Multilingual Matters.

Jefferson, Gail. 2004. Glossary of transcript symbols with an introduction. In Gene H. Lerner (ed.), *Conversation Analysis: Studies from the First Generation*, 13–23. Philadelphia: John Benjamins.

Johnstone, Barbara. 2018. *Discourse Analysis*. Third edition. Hoboken, NJ: John Wiley & Sons.

Jones, Rodney H. 2019. *Discourse Analysis: A Resource Book for Students*. Second edition. Abingdon: Routledge.

Jones, Steven. 2007. "Opposites" in discourse: A comparison of antonym use across four domains. *Journal of Pragmatics* 39: 1105–1119.

Kennedy, Graeme. 1998. *An Introduction to Corpus Linguistics*. London: Routledge.

Kerekes, Julie. 2018. Language preparation for internationally educated professionals. In Bernadette Vine (ed.), *The Routledge Handbook of Language in the Workplace*, 413–424. Abingdon: Routledge.

Kim, Chul-Kyu. 2009. Personal pronouns in English and Korean texts: A corpus-based study in terms of textual interaction. *Journal of Pragmatics* 41: 2086–2099.

Kimmel, Michael. 2010. Why we mix metaphors (and mix them well): Discourse coherence, conceptual metaphor, and beyond. *Journal of Pragmatics* 42: 97–115.

Kimura, Daisuke and Suresh Canagarajah. 2020. Embodied semiotic resources in research group meetings: How language competence is framed. *Journal of Sociolinguistics* 24(5): 634–655.

Kitzinger, Celia. 2013. Repair. In Jack Sidnell and Tanya Stivers (eds.), *The Handbook of Conversation Analysis*, 229–256. Chichester: Wiley-Blackwell.

Koller, Veronika. 2018. Critical discourse studies. In Bernadette Vine (ed.), *The Routledge Handbook of Language in the Workplace*, 27–39. Abingdon: Routledge.

Komter, Martha. 1998. *Dilemmas in the Courtroom: A Study of Trials of Violent Crime in the Netherlands*. Hillsdale, NJ: Lawrence Erlbaum Associates.

Komter, Martha. 2012. The career of a suspect's statement: Talk, text, context. *Discourse Studies* 14(6): 731–752.

König, Katharina. 2019. Stance taking with laugh particles and emojis: Sequential and functional patterns of "laughter" in a corpus of German WhatsApp chats. *Journal of Pragmatics* 142: 156–170.

Kopytowska, Monika. 2013. Blogging as the mediatization of politics and a new form of social interaction: A case study of "proximization dynamics" in Polish and British political blogs. In Piotr Cap and Urszula Ukulska (eds.), *Analyzing Genres in Political Communication*, 379–421. Amsterdam: John Benjamins.

Kress, Gunther and Theo van Leeuwen. 2021. *Reading Images: The Grammar of Visual Design*. Third edition. Routledge.

Krzyżanowski, Michał. 2018. Social media in/and the politics of the European Union: Political communication, organizational cultures, and self-inflicted elitism. *Journal of Language and Politics* 17(2): 281–304.

Lazzaro-Salazar, Mariana. 2018. Social constructionism. In Bernadette Vine (ed.), *The Routledge Handbook of Language in the Workplace*, 89–100. Abingdon: Routledge.
Ledin, Per and David Machin. 2020. *Introduction to Multimodal Analysis*. Second edition. Routledge.
Leech, Geoffrey. 1983. *Principles of Pragmatics*. London: Longman.
Leech, Geoffrey. 2014. *The Pragmatics of Politeness*. Oxford: Oxford University Press.
Lerner, Gene. 2004. *Conversation Analysis: Studies from the First Generation*. Philadelphia: John Benjamins.
Lester, Jessica N. and Michelle O'Reilly. 2019. *Applied Conversation Analysis: Social Interaction in Institutional Settings*. London: Sage.
Losa, Stefano A. 2018. Vocational education. In Bernadette Vine (ed.), *The Routledge Handbook of Language in the Workplace*, 389–400. Abingdon: Routledge.
Macalister, John. 2020. Forging a nation: Commemorating the great war. In Robert Blackwood and John Macalister (eds.), *Multilingual Memories: Monuments, Museums and the Linguistic Landscape*, 13–33. London & New York: Bloomsbury Academic.
Machin, David and Theo van Leeuwen. 2007. *Global Media Discourse*. London: Routledge.
Marra, Meredith. 2015. Workplace-meeting discourse. In Karen Tracy, Cornelia Ilie and Todd L. Sandel (eds.), *International Encyclopedia of Language and Social Interaction*, 1556–1566. Chichester: John Wiley & Sons.
Marra, Meredith, Janet Holmes and Bernadette Vine. 2019. Explicit or implicit? Facilitating interactional competence through mentoring discourse at work. *Langage & Société* 168: 69–91.
Marra, Meredith, Janet Holmes and Bernadette Vine. 2022. What we share: The impact of norms on successful interaction. In Janus Mortensen and Kamilla Kraft (eds.), *Norms and the Study of Language in Social Life*, 185–209. Berlin: De Gruyter.
Maynard, Douglas W. 2013. Everyone and no one to turn to: Intellectual roots and contexts for conversation analysis. In Jack Sidnell and Tanya Stivers (eds.), *The Handbook of Conversation Analysis*, 11–31. Chichester: Wiley-Blackwell.
Mayr, Andrea and David Machin. 2012. *Language of Crime and Deviance: An Introduction to Critical Linguistic Analysis in Media and Popular Culture*. London: Bloomsbury.
McCallum, Judi. 2014. *Working in an Eldercare Facility: An ESOL Resource: Unit 2: Daily Routines in an Eldercare Facility*. Wellington, New Zealand: Language in the Workplace Project, School of Linguistics and Applied Language Studies, Victoria University of Wellington. www.wgtn.ac.nz/lals/centres-and-institutes/language-in-the-workplace/docs/teaching/eldercare_unit_2.pdf
Mehan, Hugh. 1979. *Learning Lessons: Social Organization in the Classroom*. Cambridge, MA: Harvard University Press.
Merkl-Davies, Doris and Veronika Koller. 2012. "Metaphoring" people out of this world: A critical discourse analysis of a chairman's statement of a UK defence firm. *Accounting Forum* 36(3): 178–193.
Mullany, Louise. 2007. *Gendered Discourse in the Professional Workplace*. Basingstoke: Palgrave Macmillan.
Mullany, Louise. 2020. *Professional Communication: Consultancy, Advocacy, Activism*. Basingstoke: Palgrave.
Murata, Kazuyo. 2011. *Relational Practice in Meeting Discourse in New Zealand and Japan: A Cross-Cultural Study*. PhD dissertation. Victoria University of Wellington, New Zealand.
Murata, Kazuyo. 2014. An empirical cross-cultural study of humour in business meetings in New Zealand and Japan. *Journal of Pragmatics* 60: 251–265.
Musto, Michela, Cheryl Cooky and Michael A. Messner. 2017. From fizzle to sizzle! *Gender and Society* 31(5): 573–596.
Nartey, Mark and Isaac N. Mwinlaaru. 2019. Towards a decade of synergising corpus linguistics and critical discourse analysis: A meta-analysis. *Corpora* 14(2): 203–223.
Norrie, Cheryl. 2020. Fragile but beautiful: Otago academic's COVID-19 bubble concept. *Otago Bulletin Board*. Retrieved 20 June 2021 from www.otago.ac.nz/otagobulletin/news/otago739375.html

Obeng, Samuel Gyasi. 1999. Apologies in Akan discourse. *Journal of Pragmatics* 31: 709–734.
Ochs, Elinor. 1992. Indexing gender. In Alessandro Duranti, Charles Goodwin and Stephen C. Levinson (eds.), *Rethinking Context: Language as an Interactive Phenomenon*, 335–358. Cambridge: Cambridge University Press.
Ochs, Elinor. 1996. Linguistic resources for socializing humanity. In John J. Gumperz and Stephen C. Levinson (eds.), *Rethinking Linguistic Relativity*, 407–437. Cambridge: Cambridge University Press.
O'Keeffe, Anne and Michael J. McCarthy (eds.). 2022. *The Routledge Handbook of Corpus Linguistics*. Second edition. Abingdon: Routledge.
Paltridge, Brian. 2012. *Discourse Analysis: An Introduction*. Second edition. London: Bloomsbury.
Partington, Alan. 2004. Corpora and discourse, a most congruous beast. In Alan Partington, John Morley and Louann Haarman (eds.), *Corpora and Discourse*, 11–20. Bern: Peter Lang.
Peirce, Charles Sanders. 1955. *Philosophical Writings of Peirce*. Justus Buchler (ed.). New York: Dover Publications.
Peterson, Elizabeth and Kristy Beers Fägersten. 2018. Introduction to the special issue: Linguistic and pragmatic outcomes of contact with English. *Journal of Pragmatics* 133: 105–108.
Piazza, Roberta and Louann Haarman. 2011. Toward a definition and classification of human interest narratives in television war reporting. *Journal of Pragmatics* 43: 1540–1549.
Pietikäinen, Kaisa S. 2018. Silence that speaks: The local inferences of withholding a response in intercultural couples' conflicts. *Journal of Pragmatics* 129: 76–89.
Plappert, Garry. 2019. Not hedging but implying: Identifying epistemic implicature through a corpus-driven approach to scientific discourse. *Journal of Pragmatics* 139: 163–174.
Pomerantz, Anita. 1986. Extreme case formulations: A way of legitimizing claims. *Human Studies* 9: 219–230.
Rääbis, Andriela, Tiit Hennoste, Andra Rumm and Kirsi Laanesoo. 2019. "They are so stupid, so stupid": Emotional affect in Estonian school-related complaints. *Journal of Pragmatics* 153: 20–33.
Reisigl, Martin and Ruth Wodak. 2016. The discourse-historical approach. In Ruth Wodak and Michael Meyer (eds.), *Methods of Critical Discourse Studies*, 23–61. London: Sage.
Ren, Wei and Yaping Guo. 2020. Self-praise on Chinese social networking sites. *Journal of Pragmatics* 169: 179–189.
Rhee, Seongha and Hyun Jung Koo. 2017. Audience-blind sentence-enders in Korean: A discourse-pragmatic perspective. *Journal of Pragmatics* 120: 101–121.
Rheindorf, Markus and Ruth Wodak. 2018. Borders, fences, and limits: Protecting Austria from refugees: Metadiscursive negotiation of meaning in the current refugee crisis. *Journal of Immigrant and Refugee Studies* 16: 15–38.
Richards, Keith and Paul Seedhouse (eds.). 2005. *Applying Conversation Analysis*. London: Palgrave.
Richardson, John E. and Monica Colombo. 2014. Race and immigration in far- and extreme-right European political leaflets. In Christopher Hart and Piotr Cap (eds.), *Contemporary Critical Discourse Studies*, 521–542. London: Bloomsbury.
Riddiford, Nicky. 2014. *Working on a Building Site: An ESOL Resource: Unit 5: Understanding and Following Instructions on a Building Site*. Wellington, New Zealand: Language in the Workplace Project, School of Linguistics and Applied Language Studies, Victoria University of Wellington. Retrieved from www.wgtn.ac.nz/lals/centres-and-institutes/language-in-the-workplace/docs/teaching/building_site_unit_5.pdf
Riddiford, Nicky and Jonathan Newton. 2010. *Workplace Talk in Action: An ESOL Resource*. Wellington, New Zealand: School of Linguistics and Applied Language Studies, Victoria University of Wellington.

Roberts, Celia. 2011. Gatekeeping discourse in employment interviews. In Christopher N. Candlin and Srikant Sarangi (eds.), *Handbook of Communication in Organisations and Professions*, 407–432. Berlin: De Gruyter.

Roberts, Celia. 2013. The gatekeeping of Babel: Job interviews and the linguistic penalty. In Alexandre Duchene, Melissa Moyer and Celia Roberts (eds.), *Language, Migration and Social Inequalities*, 81–94. Bristol: Multilingual Matters.

Roberts, Celia and Srikant Sarangi. 2005. Theme-oriented discourse analysis of medical encounters. *Medical Education* 39: 632–640.

Romano, Manuela and M. Dolores Porto. 2018. "The tide, change, nobody can stop it": Metaphor for social action. *Discourse & Society* 29(6): 655–673.

Sacks, Harvey, Emanuel A. Schegloff and Gail Jefferson. 1974. A simplest systematics for the organization of turn-taking for conversation. *Language* 50: 696–735.

Salanoa, Honiara. 2020. *The Communicative Competence of Samoan Seasonal Workers under the Recognised Seasonal Employer (RSE) Scheme*. PhD dissertation. Victoria University of Wellington, New Zealand.

Sarfo, Emmanuel and Ewuresi Agyeiwaa Krampa. 2013. Language at war: A critical discourse analysis of speeches of Bush and Obama on terrorism. *International Journal of Social Sciences and Education* 3(2): 378–390.

Schegloff, Emanuel A. 1987. Recycled turn beginnings: A precise repair mechanism in conversation's turn-taking organisation. In Graham Button and John R. E. Lee (eds.), *Talk and Social Organisation*, 70–85. Clevedon, England: Multilingual Matters.

Schegloff, Emanuel A. 2007. *Sequence Organization in Interaction: A Primer in Conversation Analysis*. Cambridge: Cambridge University Press.

Schegloff, Emanuel A., Gail Jefferson and Harvey Sacks. 1977. The preference for self-correction in the organization of repair in conversation. *Language* 53: 361–382.

Schnurr, Stephanie. 2009. *Leadership Discourse at Work*. Basingstoke: Palgrave Macmillan.

Schröter, Melani. 2021. The "wanderlust" of German words and their pragmatic adaptation in English. *Journal of Pragmatics* 182: 63–75.

Searle, John R. 1969. *Speech Acts: An Essay in the Philosophy of Language*. Cambridge: Cambridge University Press.

Searle, John R. 1975. *A Taxonomy of Illocutionary Acts*. Minneapolis: University of Minnesota Press.

Searle, John R. 1976. A classification of illocutionary acts. *Language in Society* 5: 1–23.

Searle, John R. 1979. *Expression and Meaning: Studies in the Theory of Speech Acts*. Cambridge: Cambridge University Press.

Seedhouse, Paul. 2004. *The Interactional Architecture of the Language Classroom: A Conversation Analysis Perspective*. Oxford: Blackwell.

Shei, Chris (ed.). 2019. *The Routledge Handbook of Chinese Discourse Analysis*. Abingdon: Routledge.

Shi, Heidi Hui, Sophia Xiaoyu Liu and Zhuo Jing-Schmidt. 2020. Manual action metaphors in Chinese. In Bianca Basciano, Franco Gatti and Anna Morbiato (eds.), *Corpus-Based Research on Chinese Language and Linguistics*, 122–141. Venezia: Edizioni Ca' Foscari Digital Publishing.

Sidnell, Jack and Tanya Stivers (eds.). 2013. *The Handbook of Conversation Analysis*. Oxford: Wiley Blackwell.

Silverstein, Michael. 1976. Shifters, linguistics categories, and cultural description. In Keith H. Basso and Henry A. Selby (eds.), *Meaning in Anthropology*, 11–55. Albuquerque: University of New Mexico Press.

Simó, Judit. 2008. It's not all about the brain: A cross-linguistic exploration of body-part metaphors in chess. Paper presented at the Ninth Conference on Conceptual Structure, Discourse, and Language (CSDL 9), October, Cleveland, OH.

Simó, Judit. 2011. Metaphors of "blood" in American English and Hungarian: A cross-linguistic corpus investigation. *Journal of Pragmatics* 43: 2897–2910.

Sinclair, John and Malcolm Coulthard. 1975. *Towards an Analysis of Discourse*. Oxford: Oxford University Press.

Sliedrecht, Keun Young, Fleur van der Houwen and Marca Schasfoort. 2016. Challenging formulations in police interrogations and job interviews: A comparative study. *Journal of Pragmatics* 105: 114–129.

Smith, Angela. 2015. Letting down Rapunzel: Feminism's effects on fairy tales. *Children's Literature in Education* 46: 424–437.

Southgate, Vera. 1968. *Rapunzel: A Ladybird "Easy-Reading" Book*. Loughborough: Wills & Hepworth.

Stivers, Tanya, N. J. Enfield, Penelope Brown, Christina Englert, Makoto Hayashi, Trine Heinemann, Gertie Hoymann, Federico Rossano, Jan Peter de Ruiter, Kyung-Eun Yoon and Stephen C. Levinson. 2009. Universals and cultural variation in turn-taking in conversation. *PNAS* 106(26): 10587–10592.

Stokoe, Elizabeth and Derek Edwards. 2008. "Did you have permission to smash your neighbour's door?": Silly questions and their answers in police-suspect interrogations. *Discourse Studies* 10: 89–111.

Stubbe, Maria, Chris Lane, Jo Hilder, Elaine Vine, Bernadette Vine, Meredith Marra, Janet Holmes and Ann Weatherall. 2003. Multiple discourse analyses of a workplace interaction. *Discourse Studies* 5: 351–388.

Sugawara, Kazuyoshi. 2012. Interactive significance of simultaneous discourse or overlap in everyday conversations among |Gui former foragers. *Journal of Pragmatics* 44: 577–618.

Svennevig, Jan and Olga Djordjilovic. 2015. Accounting for the right to assign a task in meeting interaction. *Journal of Pragmatics* 78: 98–111.

Taboada, Maite, Radoslava Trnavac and Cliff Goddard. 2017. On being negative. *Corpus Pragmatics* 1: 57–76.

Takita, Fuyuko. 2012. Reconsidering the concept of negative politeness "enryo" in Japan. *Hiroshima University Foreign Language Research* 15: 189–196.

Tanaka, Hiroko. 2006. Turn projection in Japanese talk-in-interaction. In Paul Drew and John Heritage (eds.), *Conversation Analysis, Vol. III: Turn Design and Action Formulation*, 151–187. London: Sage.

Tannen, Deborah. 1990. *You Just Don't Understand: Women and Men in Conversation*. New York: William Morrow.

Tannen, Deborah. 1994a. *Talking from 9 to 5: Women and Men at Work*. New York: Harper Collins.

Tannen, Deborah. 1994b. *Gender and Discourse*. New York: Oxford University Press.

Tannen, Deborah. 2000. Indirectness at work. In Joy Peyton, Peg Griffin, Walt Wolfram and Ralph Fasold (eds.), *Language in Action: New Studies of Language in Society, Festschrift for Roger Shuy*, 189–212. Cresskill, NJ: Hampton Press.

Tannen, Deborah. 2005a. *Conversational Style: Analysing Talk among Friends*. New edition. New York & Oxford: Oxford University Press.

Tannen, Deborah. 2005b. Interactional sociolinguistics as a resource for intercultural pragmatics. *Intercultural Pragmatics* 2(2): 205–208.

Tannen, Deborah. 2006. *You're Wearing THAT?: Mothers and Daughters in Conversation*. New York: Ballantine Books.

Tannen, Deborah. 2007. *Talking Voices: Repetition, Dialogue, and Imagery in Conversational Discourse*. Cambridge: Cambridge University Press.

Tannen, Deborah. 2008. "We've never been close, we're very different": Three types in sister discourse. *Narrative Inquiry* 18(2): 206–229.

Tannen, Deborah. 2010. *You Were Always Mom's Favorite!: Sisters in Conversation Throughout Their Lives*. New York: Ballantine Books.

Tannen, Deborah. 2013. The medium is the metamessage: Conversational style in new media interaction. In Deborah Tannen and Anna Marie Trester (eds.), *Discourse 2.0: Language and New Media*, 99–117. Washington, DC: Georgetown University Press.
Tannen, Deborah. 2014. Gender and family interaction. In Susan Ehrlich, Miriam Meyerhoff and Janet Holmes (eds.), *The Handbook of Language, Gender and Sexuality*. Second edition, 491–508. Chichester: Wiley-Blackwell.
Tannen, Deborah, Heidi Hamilton and Deborah Schiffrin (eds.). 2015. *The Handbook of Discourse Analysis*. Second edition. Chichester: John Wiley & Sons.
Tannen, Deborah, Shari Kendall and Cynthia Gordon (eds.). 2007. *Family Talk: Discourse and Identity in Four American Families*. New York: Oxford University Press.
Tannen, Deborah and Cynthia Wallat. 1993. Interactive frames and knowledge schemas in interaction: Examples from a medical examination/interview. In Deborah Tannen (ed.), *Framing in Discourse*, 57–76. New York: Oxford University Press.
Tanskanen, Sanna-Kaisa and Johanna Karhukorpi. 2008. Concessive repair and the negotiation of affiliation in e-mail discourse. *Journal of Pragmatics* 40: 1587–1600.
Tchizmarova, Ivelina K. 2005. Hedging functions of the Bulgarian discourse marker "xajde". *Journal of Pragmatics* 37: 1143–1163.
ten Have, Paul. 2007. *Doing Conversation Analysis: A Practical Guide*. Second edition. London: Sage.
Thompson, Laura, Christine Howes and Rose McCabe. 2016. The effect of questions used by psychiatrists on therapeutic alliance and adherence. *British Journal of Psychiatry* 209(1): 40–47.
Tognini-Bonelli, Elena. 2001. *Corpus Linguistics at Work*. Amsterdam: John Benjamins.
Traverso, Véronique, Anna Claudia Ticca and Biagio Ursi. 2018. Invitations in French: A complex and apparently delicate action. *Journal of Pragmatics* 125: 164–179.
Twitchin, John (Director). 1979. *Crosstalk* [video]. London, UK: BBC.
Unuabonah, Foluke Olayinka and Florence Oluwaseyi Daniel. 2020. Haba! Bilingual interjections in Nigerian English: A corpus-based study. *Journal of Pragmatics* 163: 66–77.
Urbanik, Paweł and Jan Svennevig. 2019. Managing contingencies in requests: The role of negation in Norwegian interrogative directives. *Journal of Pragmatics* 139: 109–135.
van der Houwen, Fleur. 2015. "If it doesn't make sense it's not true": How Judge Judy creates coherent stories through "common-sense" reasoning according to the neoliberal agenda. *Social Semiotics* 25(3): 255–273.
van der Valk, Ineke. 2003. Right-wing parliamentary discourse on immigration in France. *Discourse & Society* 14(3): 309–348.
van Dijk, Teun A. 1987. *News Analysis: Case Studies of International and National News in the Press*. New York: Routledge.
van Dijk, Teun A. 1998. *Ideology: A Multidisciplinary Approach*. London: Sage.
van Dijk, Teun A. 2011. Teaching ethnic diversity in journalism school. *GRITIM Working Papers Series* 7: 1–35.
van Dijk, Teun A. 2016. Critical discourse studies: A sociocognitive approach. In Ruth Wodak and Michael Meyer (eds.), *Methods of Critical Discourse Studies*. Third edition, 62–85. London: Sage.
van Leeuwen, Theo. 2016. Discourse as the recontextualization of social practice – a guide. In Ruth Wodak and Michael Meyer (eds.), *Methods of Critical Discourse Studies*. Third edition, 137–153. London: Sage.
van Leeuwen, Theo and Gunther Kress. 1996/2006. *Reading Images: The Grammar of Visual Design*. Abingdon: Routledge.
van Leeuwen, Theo and Ruth Wodak. 1999. Legitimizing immigration control: A discourse-historical analysis. *Discourse & Society* 1(1): 83–118.
Vine, Bernadette. 2009. Directives at work: Exploring the contextual complexity of workplace directives. *Journal of Pragmatics* 41: 1395–1405.

Vine, Bernadette. 2014. Getting Things Done on a New Zealand Construction Site: Directives in a Workplace Learning Environment. Unpublished manuscript.

Vine, Bernadette. 2016. The Wellington Language in the Workplace Project: Engaging with the research and wider communities. In Karen P. Corrigan and Adam Mearns (eds.), *Creating and Digitizing Language Corpora, Volume 3: Databases for Public Engagement*, 321–346. Basingstoke: Palgrave.

Vine, Bernadette (ed.). 2018. *The Routledge Handbook of Language in the Workplace*. Abingdon: Routledge.

Vine, Bernadette. 2020. *Introducing Language in the Workplace*. Cambridge: Cambridge University Press.

Vine, Bernadette. 2021a. "Be strong, be kind": A portrait of a leader during times of crisis. Paper presented at the 17th International Pragmatics Conference (IPrA), June 27–July 2, 2021, Winterthur, Switzerland.

Vine, Bernadette. 2021b. Spoken workplace discourse. In Eric Friginal and Jack A. Hardy (eds.), *The Routledge Handbook of Corpus Approaches to Discourse Analysis*, 5–21. Abingdon: Routledge.

Vine, Bernadette and Janet Holmes. Forthcoming. Doing leadership in style: Pragmatic markers in New Zealand workplace interaction. To appear in *Intercultural Pragmatics*.

Vine, Bernadette, Janet Holmes and Meredith Marra. Forthcoming. "Climbing the same mountain": Meeting openings as bicultural practice in Aotearoa New Zealand. To appear in *Contrastive Pragmatics*.

Waring, Hansun Zhang. 2018. *Discourse Analysis: The Questions Discourse Analysts Ask and How They Answer Them*. New York: Routledge.

Way, Lyndon C. S. 2015. YouTube as a site of debate through populist politics: The case of a Turkish protest pop video. *Journal of Multicultural Discourses* 10(2): 180–196.

Wei, Li and Lesley Milroy. 1995. Conversational code-switching in a Chinese community in Britain: A sequential analysis. *Journal of Pragmatics* 23: 281–299.

Weston, Daniel. 2021. Gatekeeping and linguistic capital: A case study of the Cambridge University undergraduate admissions interview. *Journal of Pragmatics* 176: 137–149.

Wichmann, Anne. 2004. The intonation of *please*-requests: A corpus-based study. *Journal of Pragmatics* 36: 1521–1549.

Wodak, Ruth. 2009. *The Discourse of Politics in Action: Politics as Usual*. London: Palgrave Macmillan.

Wodak, Ruth (ed.). 2013. *Critical Discourse Analysis*. Volumes 1–4. London: Sage.

Wodak, Ruth. 2015. *The Politics of Fear: What Right-Wing Populist Discourses Mean*. London: Sage.

Wodak, Ruth. 2020. *The Politics of Fear: The Shameless Normalization of Far-Right Discourse*. Second revised and extended edition. London: Sage.

Wodak, Ruth and Rudolf de Cillia. 2006. Politics and language: Overview. In Keith Brown (ed.), *Encyclopedia of Language and Linguistics*, 706–719. Oxford: Elsevier.

Wodak, Ruth and Norman Fairclough. 2010. Recontextualizing European higher education policies: The cases of Austria and Romania. *Critical Discourse Studies* 7(1): 19–40.

Wodak, Ruth and Bernhard Forchtner (eds.). 2018. *The Routledge Handbook of Language and Politics*. Abingdon: Routledge.

Wodak, Ruth and Michael Meyer. 2001. *Methods of Critical Discourse Analysis*. London: Sage.

Wodak, Ruth and Michael Meyer. 2016. *Methods of Critical Discourse Studies*. Third edition. London: Sage.

Wodak, Ruth and Teun A. van Dijk (eds.). 2000. *Racism at the Top: Parliamentary Discourses on Ethnic Issues in Six European States*. Klagenfurt, Austria: Drava Verlag.

Yamada, Haru. 1992. *American and Japanese Business Discourse: A Comparison of Interactional Styles*. Norwood, NJ: Ablex.

Yates, Lynda. 2018. Language learning on-the-job. In Bernadette Vine (ed.), *The Routledge Handbook of Language in the Workplace*, 425–435. Abingdon: Routledge.

Yu, Guodong and Yaxin Wu. 2021. Managing expert/novice identity with actions in conversation: Identity construction and negotiation. *Journal of Pragmatics* 178: 273–286.

Zinken, Jörg and Arnulf Deppermann. 2017. A cline of visible commitment in the situated design of imperative turns: Evidence from German and Polish. In Marja-Leena Sorjonen, Liisa Raevaara and Elizabeth Couper-Kuhlen (eds.), *Imperative Turns at Talk: The Design of Directives in Action*, 27–63. Amsterdam: John Benjamins.

Index

adjacency pairs 80–81, 97, 153
advice 16, 41, 60–61, 116, 125
agreement 80, 82, 153; Leech's maxim 35, 37–38, 47; seeking 42, 90
Akan 25, 27, 37
alignment: choosing not to 84; encouraging 142; with expectations or stances 17, 108; with people 68, 82, 90, 153; with a viewpoint 138
anecdotes 127–128; *see also* narrative
apologies 12–13, 25, 27, 37; as a politeness strategy 42; by second language speakers 54, 61
Arabic, colloquial Algerian 36–37
assertives 23, 47; and the Ethnography of Communication 32–33, 34; and Leech's politeness theory 35, 38
asymmetry 60, 87, 141; *see also* leadership; power
Atkinson, J. Maxwell 75
Austin, John L. 23, 26, 76
authority 16, 139; *see also* leadership; power
awareness: of audience 34; lack of 103–104, 131, 154; of problems 130; raising 123, 133, 162–163; of rules 77

Baker 69, 140
boast 23, 27
Brown, Penelope 39
Bulgarian 24–25, 36

chair/chairing 16
challenging: another speaker 90–91, 97, 126, 131–132; of government policies 133, 154; rapport/relationships 12–13, 114; societal norms/ideologies 126, 127, 128, 157
Chichewa 111–112, 115
child language: antonyms 64–65; code-switching 102–103, 115; in family interactions 9–10, 105–106, 115, 158–159
Chinese 23, 63–64, 83; *see also* Mandarin
Clayman, Steven 75, 91
code-switching 98, 102–103
collegiality 115
collocations 62–65, 69, 71, 73, 141
commissives 24–25, 35

complaints/complaining: avoidance 43; customer 28–29; features of 6; indirect 6–7, 82; mitigating 160; workplace 125–126; *see also* challenging; criticism
compliments/complimenting 36–37, 84
concordances 65–67, 72–73, 152
control 125; *see also* power
conventions, cultural 11, 102, 103–105
conversation, family: Chilean Spanish 108–110; English 79, 96, 105–106, 114; Estonian 6; Finnish 9–10; Polish 81; Spanish 158–159
conversation, friends: Arabic, colloquial Algerian 36–37; English 120–121; German 100–101; Greek 115–116 (translated); |Gui 77–78; Japanese 40–41; South Indian Tamil 42; *see also* telephone calls, personal
corpus-based 53, 58, 69, 140
corpus-driven 53
courtroom discourse 26, 88–89, 138–139; *see also* legal discourse
Covid-19 7, 63, 69, 155
criticism: constructive 20–21; as face threatening 41; mitigating 160–161; personal 41, 42, 132; through song 126; *see also* challenging; complaints/complaining
Czech 129–130

decision-making 14, 16, 38, 159, 163
declarations 26
directives 23–24, 35, 42; family 108–110; friends 24; personal 47; questioning 32–33, 34; workplace 11, 12–13, 42, 43
disagreement 13, 37–38, 41, 47
doctor-patient interaction *see* health care communication
Drew, Paul 75, 82
Dutch: Belgium 58–59; the Netherlands 30, 88–89 (translated), 95–96

email 4, 11, 96; *see also* online data
Estonian 6–7
expert identity/knowledge 5, 15–16, 117–118, 122
expressives 25, 32, 34, 35, 37

Fairclough, Norman 123–124, 127, 134–136
fieldnotes 107
Finnish 9–10, 76–77
Foucault, Michel 22
French: Belgium 28–29; France 24; Switzerland 130

Garfinkel, Harold 75
gatekeeping *see* interviews, job/employment interviews
gender: and identity 14, 15; and Interactional Sociolinguistics 99, 108, 114; and power 125; and pragmatic markers 70; *see also* ideologies, gender; leadership; sexism
genre 34, 52–53, 57, 58, 155; Hymes' definition 33
German 63; Austria 140; borrowing in English 65–66, 69–70; Germany 12, 93, 100–101; as a second language 61
gestures *see* non-verbal communication
Goffman, Erving 39–40, 75, 105
Greek 115–116 (translated), 136–137
Grice, Paul 26–31, 35, 39, 43
group membership *see* ingroups; outgroups
|Gui 77–78
Gumperz, John: applications 160; code-switching 103; differing norms 105, 106; framing 105; Interactional Sociolinguistics 98–99; power 156

Harris, Zellig 22
health care communication: doctor-patient interaction 87–88, 94, 105; medical counselling 111–112; medical helpline 60–61, 72–73; medical training simulation 35–36; mental health 157, 159; patient-centred care 163
hedging 13, 20–21, 42, 97, 108
Heritage, John 75, 88
high stakes encounter/contexts *see* interviews
Holmes, Janet 73, 99, 160–161; *see also* Wellington Language in the Workplace Project (LWP)
humour: data 13–14, 19–20, 46, 120–122, 160–161; flouting of maxims 46, 47; to foster relationships 13–14, 114, 122; and identity 16, 122; to mitigate power 14, 16; to show group membership 160–161
Hungarian 57–58, 69, 155
Hymes, Dell 31–35, 52, 98

identity 14–17; within Interactional Sociolinguistics 108–110, 115–118, 122; in political speeches 140–141; professional 16; *see also* gender; ingroups; leadership; outgroups
ideologies 126–131, 133–134, 137, 156; applied discourse analysis 162, 163; cultural/racial 129–130; gender 127–129; leadership 127–129; political 130–131, 137; *see also* racism; sexism
imposition 8, 36, 42
ingroups 15, 42, 129–130, 141; *see also* outgroups
interviews: admission 112–113; and identity 115; job/employment interviews 95–97, 103–105, 106; news 33–34, 91–92; police 8–9, 30, 89–91; research 112, 121–122, 159

Japanese: data 13–14, 40–41, 120; language 80, 107, 108
Jefferson, Gail 75, 78–79, 81, 84, 85
journalism 124, 136–138, 154, 162; *see also* news

knowledge, shared 16, 112, 153, 161
Korean: data 8, 56–57, 85–86; language 63
Kress, Gunther 124, 142

Language in the Workplace Project *see* Wellington Language in the Workplace Project (LWP)
leadership: and gender 108, 127–129, 133; identity 16, 21, 117–118, 121–122, 156
Leech, Geoffrey 35–39, 47
legal discourse 88–91; *see also* courtroom discourse; interviews, police
Levinson, Stephen 39
log-likelihood 58, 59
LWP *see* Wellington Language in the Workplace Project (LWP)

Malay 71, 73, 140–141
Mandarin 15–16
Māori 116–118
media discourse 91–92, 124, 136–139; and politics 7, 91–92, 140, 152; and racism 162; and social media 58–59; *see also* journalism; news; online data; social media; TV data
medical contexts *see* health care communication
meetings, formal: hedging 20–21; humour 14, 46, 47, 120, 122; keywords 72–73; opening 116–118; pronouns 61; research report on 160–161
meetings, informal: complaining 125–126, 153–154; directives 7–8, 43; discussions 28, 37–38; humour 13–14; pragmatic markers 66–67, 68
metaphor 140; Chinese 63–64; English 7, 57–58, 69, 70; Hungarian 57–58, 69; Spanish 132–133, 154
minority groups 99, 106, 163
multi-modality 140, 141–142; *see also* non-verbal communication; statues

narrative: interviews 104; leader 127–128; in news report 31–32, 34; as rapport/relationship building 114, 115–116

Nepal 126
news 31–34, 63, 70, 132–133, 162; comments 129; sports 142–143, 147; *see also* interviews, news; journalism; media discourse; online data; social media
Nigerian English 55–56, 69
non-verbal communication: as contextualisation cues 101–102, 115, 153; and Hymes' Ethnography of Communication 31, 34; and turn-taking 80, 81; *see also* multi-modality; silence
Norwegian 45

Ochs, Elinor 108
online data: comments 15, 129; corpora 52, 62, 63, 65–66; website 142; *see also* social media
outgroups 129, 130, 141; *see also* ingroups

Polish 81
political discourse 134–136, 138, 152; data 7, 71, 130, 134–136, 141; *see also* ideologies, political
Portuguese, Brazilian 61
power 98, chapter 6 *passim*, 154, 156–157, 163; *see also* authority; control; ideologies; leadership
practices, shared 69, 105, 153
pragmatic markers 66, 67–68, 70, 73, 121
problem-solving 38
pronouns 56–57, 60, 61, 66, 130

questioning, as a discourse strategy 111–112, 156
questions, yes-no 90, 92

racism 26, 124, 127, 129–130, 136; and education 163; and the media 162; and political ideologies 130, 136
rapport 60, 68, 114, 121–122, 161
requests: for advice 60, 125; for agreement 90; between family/friends 40–41, 42, 80, 81, 103, 115; mitigating/softening 36; refusing 30, 40–41; use of *please* 54–55; workplace 7–8, 20
Roberts, Celia 99, 104, 160
role play 12, 38–39
roles: in family interaction 106, 115; gender 127; institutional 8, 43, 87, 112, 125; in interviews 33–34, 113, 115; leadership 16, 118, 121

Sacks, Harvey 75, 78–79, 84
Samoan 19–20, 80, 106–107
Schegloff, Emanuel 75, 78–79, 81, 84
scientific writing 56–57, 60, 61–62, 151
Searle, John 23–26, 39, 47
Serbo-Croatian 89–90
service encounters 4, 43
sexism 126, 147
Shakespeare, William 59–60
silence 14, 84, 115, 153; cultural value 106–107; and turn-taking 77–78
social constructionism 14–17, 39
social justice 160, 162–163
social media 23, 28–29, 58–59, 93
social order 39, 75, 76, 99
social talk 13, 114
solidarity 42, 68, 122
song lyrics 126
Spanish: Chile 108–110; Peru 38–39; Spain 132–133; US 102–103, 158–159
statues 130, 131, 133–134, 141, 144–147
stereotypes 15, 92, 108, 129–130
stories/storytelling *see* narrative

Tamil, South Indian 42
Tannen, Deborah 99, 105, 107, 114, 160
telephone calls 74, 75, 151; data, medical helpline 60, 72–73; personal 15–16, 24–25, 76–77, 82, 84–85; role play 12
transcription conventions xii, 74–75
Turkish 131–132 (translated)
TV data: broadcast news 31–34, 143–144, 147; comments on 15, 58–59; reality shows 131–132, 138–139

van Dijk, Teun 123–124, 129, 162
van Leeuwen, Theo 123–124, 142

Wellington Language in the Workplace Project (LWP) xii, 66, 70, 99, 160–161
Wodak, Ruth 123–124, 127, 133, 134, 140; data sources 142; political discourse 132, 135–136, 162
workplace interaction: blue-collar 11, 19–20, 106–107; role play 12; *see also* meetings, formal; meetings, informal

For Product Safety Concerns and Information please contact our EU representative GPSR@taylorandfrancis.com
Taylor & Francis Verlag GmbH, Kaufingerstraße 24, 80331 München, Germany

www.ingramcontent.com/pod-product-compliance
Lightning Source LLC
Chambersburg PA
CBHW071358290426
44108CB00014B/1592